Harville Hendrix, Ph. D., in partnership with his wife, Helen LaKelly Hunt, Ph.D., originated Imago Relationship Therapy, a unique healing process for couples, prospective couples, and parents. Harville is a pastoral counsellor with more than thirty years' experience as an educator and therapist. He works with couples in private practice, conducts couples workshops, teaches marital therapists, and give public lectures around the world. He is the author of *Keeping the Love You Find: A Single Person's Guide to Achieving Lasting Love*, and has co-authored, with Helen, *Receiving Love: Letting Yourself Be Loved Will Transform Your Relationship*; *Getting the Love You Want Workbook: The New Couples' Study Guide*; *Giving the Love that Heals: A Guide for Parents*; *The Personal Companion: Meditations and Exercises for Keeping the Love You Find*; *The Couples Companion: Meditations and Exercises for Getting the Love You Want*.

GETTING THE LOVE YOU WANT

a guide for couples

Harville Hendrix, Ph.D.

POCKET
BOOKS

LONDON • SYDNEY • NEW YORK • TORONTO

First published in Great Britain by Pocket Books, 1993
This edition published by Pocket Books, 2005
An imprint of Simon & Schuster UK Ltd
A CBS Company

7 9 10 8 6

Simon & Schuster UK Ltd
Africa House
64–78 Kingsway
London WC2B 6AH

www.simonsays.co.uk

Simon & Schuster Australia
Sydney

A CIP catalogue record for this book is available from the British Library

ISBN-10: 0-7434-9592-6
ISBN-13: 978-0-7434-9592-9

Printed and bound in Great Britain by Cox & Wyman Ltd, Reading

Contents

In Appreciation for Jo Robinson

TWO YEARS AGO, after I agreed to direct the ideas in this book to the general rather than the professional audience, my editor at Holt suggested that the assistance of a professional writer might be useful. Since this was my first attempt at a popular book, I readily agreed. After interviewing five writers, I was introduced to Jo Robinson, a professional writer and the author of *Unplug the Christmas Machine*, who lives in Portland, Oregon. She understood immediately what I was attempting to do. I was so impressed with her that I waited three months, until she completed her second book, *Full House*.

When she became available, I presented her with a lengthy rough manuscript and piles of transcriptions of lectures and workshops. To supplement all that I had written, she attended my workshops and seminars, interviewed me extensively, and read reams of clinical material. She has worked tirelessly to transform a badly organized and somewhat opaque manuscript and much supplementary material into a well-organized and finely polished product.

Acknowledgments

IN THE PROCESS of writing this book, I have become acutely aware of a truth so aptly stated by the poet John Donne, that "no man is an island," and by Walt Whitman, who said, "I contain multitudes." The pulling together of the ideas and clinical material presented here has deepened my awareness of my dependence upon many resources, persons, and experiences. The new vistas would not have been possible were it not for the intellectual giants upon whose shoulders I stand, and the contributions of many able teachers, stimulating students, trusting couples, supportive friends, and family. To all of them, I want to express my appreciation and ask forgiveness for any unwise liberties I may have taken.

Many special friends gave me much encouragement—some I want to mention by name. Dr. Robert Elliott read early versions of the manuscript and provided loving confrontation when my ideas needed more clarity and accuracy. Dr. Pat Love first introduced my ideas into a graduate school program on marriage and family and provided valuable feedback. Reed and Carolyn Whittle read later drafts of the manuscript and gave valuable advice along the way. Judy McCall graciously consented to read and comment on the final manuscript and helped with the endorsements. Drs. Joan and Robert Thorne opened doors for me to the professional community when I moved to New York and provided emotional support for the whole project.

I also want to express my appreciation for the enthusiasm,

support, and stimulation of the many therapists in Dallas and New York who studied at the Institute for Relationship Therapy and helped me test these ideas in their practice of marital therapy.

I am deeply indebted to the many couples who trusted me with their relationship and allowed me to use their stories for research and for the enrichment of this book. I learned most of what I know about couples from them.

I want also to thank Henry Holt and Company for their excitement about the ideas even before they saw a manuscript, and for waiting patiently for its completion long after it should have been due. I especially appreciate the patience and support of my editor at Holt, Channa Taub, who gently but firmly kept my feet to the fire, and my agent, Julian Bach, who shepherded me through the contract process and gave me valuable guidance in the world of publishing. Tamera Allred read several of the last drafts, and made many helpful suggestions. Sharon Morris provided excellent editing assistance. Finally, my thanks to Yvonne Singleton, my secretary, for her typing skills and patience when I wanted sections of the manuscript ready "yesterday."

In this revised edition I want to include appreciation for my new agent, Barney Karpfinger, whose support for this republication and for all the other books has been invaluable. He has been supportive as well for the development of my career as a writer. Our friendship has deeply enriched my life. I also want to thank all the new people at Henry Holt: John Sterling, publisher; Jennifer Barth, editor in chief; Deborah Brody, my editor; and Jenny Chikes, my publicist.

Thanks must also go to Norris Chumley for his excellent direction of the video series for public television, and to Jo Robinson, my writer, who has helped once again with the lyrical crafting of the introduction and revision. My thanks to Sanam Hoon, my assistant, for many years of excellent service in various capacities, and to Nancy Jones, the first executive director of the Institute who helped stabilize Imago organizationally. I am also indebted to Rick Brown, current executive director of the Institute, for his excellent shepherding of its growth and expansion of services.

I cannot express adequately my indebtedness to Oprah Winfrey for her support and for exposing Imago therapy to millions of people worldwide through her show.

Finally, I am deeply indebted to all the couples who have read this book and passed it on to others, to other professionals and friends who have recommended the book, and to all the Imago therapists, especially the Master Trainers and Faculty of the Institute who have helped to develop and deepen Imago Relationship Therapy and make it available in this country and around the world.

Most important, my deepest appreciation goes to my wife, Helen LaKelly Hunt, who has been my partner in this enterprise. Without her support and intellectual contribution, this book and others would not have come into being and Imago Relationship Therapy would not have been born. I also want to thank my six children for their support and patience while the book was written and revised. I also appreciate the lessons I have learned from them over the years. They and Helen have helped me to live the ideas and become a more whole person. They, and I, are excited for a second time that it is done!

Introduction to the Revised Edition

by Harville Hendrix and Helen LaKelly Hunt

IN THE INTRODUCTION to the first edition of this book written in 1988, I reported that *Getting the Love You Want* was born out of the dissolution of my first marriage, a break-up that compelled me to explore the mysteries of love relationships. In this introduction, written thirteen years later, I am happy to report a very different reality. Helen LaKelly Hunt and I have been married for nineteen years, and relying on the ideas described in this book, we have achieved its promise of "passionate friendship." As we have been pleased to discover, being in a close and loving relationship is far easier than being in a strained or distant one. These days, our life together is surprisingly peaceful. But, paradoxically, it also resonates with a new energy, an energy fueled by our close connection. Even our middle-aged bodies feel more alive!

In addition to having a passionate friendship, Helen and I also have what we call a "passionate partnership" because we are allies in our professional lives as well. Indeed, Helen has influenced my work from our very first date. We began to court each other in 1977, two years after my divorce. Helen was completing her master's degree in counseling, and I was a professor at the Perkins School of Theology. On our first night out together, I remember telling her that I wanted to leave Perkins and move on to something else, but I wasn't sure what I wanted to do. I talked about some options I was considering, which included an in-depth exploration of the psychology of the couple.

I wanted to know why couples were having such a difficult time staying together and why they were so devastated when their relationship fell apart. Nothing that I had read in the professional literature seemed to give an adequate explanation. Helen was drawn to this possibility above all the others I mentioned and encouraged me to share my half-formed ideas with her. Fifteen minutes into our conversation she said, "The way you're talking about the centrality of relationships brings to my mind the 'I-thou' of Martin Buber." Then she quoted a passage from Fyodor Dostoyevsky that she had committed to memory as a young woman: "The man who desires to see the living God face-to-face does not seek God in the empty firmament of his mind, but in human love." "No, no," I said, failing to see the obvious connection between my thinking and Buber's philosophy of relationship or Dostoyevsky's spirituality, "I don't think my thoughts have much to do with either one of them."

Then, as now, Helen had sensed where I was headed, even when I did not.

In the years that followed, Helen developed her own passions, but she continued to be actively involved in my work. To some degree, she played the traditional supporting role—caring for the family, offering financial help, and being a sympathetic ear. But there were many times when she stepped outside those bounds and strategically intervened in ways that would prove to be pivotal. When others would accept my ideas at face value, she would question my thinking or, more often, challenge me to deepen my understanding. What I valued most, however, is that she always cared enough about me and my work to be willing to enlarge my view with her own truth. I can honestly say that every idea in this book was forged within the crucible of our relationship. So when I was asked to write a new introduction to this revised edition of *Getting the Love You Want,* it was only natural that I ask Helen to write it with me. It was time to make her role as co-creator more visible.

As Helen and I began to reflect on what to write, we found

ourselves overcome with a wave of nostalgia. We recalled the long years of research, thinking, and talking that had gone into the first edition. In the beginning, we had debated whether to start with a book for couples or write a more academic book for therapists. Once we had decided to write a book for the general public, we discussed whether or not to include exercises in the book. If so, which ones? The writing itself took several years. We remembered with admiration our writer, Jo Robinson, who helped give order to our thoughts and wrote with a lyricism and simplicity that remains one of the keys to the book's success. We recalled our euphoria when the book was finally published in 1988 and then, to our great surprise, was featured on the Oprah Winfrey Show. Oprah's enthusiastic support propelled the book to the *New York Times* bestseller list, far exceeding our expectations. The readership for the book continued to grow over the years, until by now the book has sold over a million and a half copies and has been translated into more than thirty languages.

Helen and I also reflected on the groundswell of interest in Imago Therapy, the name for the couple's therapy that is described in this book. Starting in the late 1980s, a growing number of therapists began expressing an interest in being trained in this new way of working with couples. Today, there is a thriving international Imago community of about 1,500 therapists practicing in thirteen countries. More than 150 presenters conduct approximately 400 Imago workshops each year. Twenty faculty members of the Institute for Imago Relationship Therapy train a steady stream of new therapists in a dozen cities. The combination of all this talent and energy has transformed Imago into a movement that should become a significant force for social transformation.

As Helen and I replayed these wondrous events, we realized that, at times, we feel more like onlookers than creators. We set the process in motion, but we do not feel wholly responsible for its continued success. We feel like parents who helped a child learn to ride a bike by giving a push and running alongside, but now watch in awe as that adult child finishes first in a race. We were there at the beginning; we gave the initial push. But the child has attained a degree of proficiency for which we are only partly responsible.

To what, then, do we credit the success of *Getting the Love You Want* and the burgeoning growth of the Imago community? The simplest way to put it is that we have managed to further a dynamic that was already in place. In the second half of the twentieth century, the old notion of marriage was no longer working for many couples. In unprecedented numbers, people were deciding they would rather go through the pain and stigma of divorce than put up with an unhappy or stultifying relationship. In the 1960s and 1970s, marriage itself came into question as couples began experimenting with "open marriages" and cohabitation, hoping that they could create something more meaningful by transcending the restrictions of traditional relationships.

But many of the people in conventional marriages were also searching for a relationship that was larger, deeper, and more meaningful than what their parents and grandparents had. Thousands of couples sought that "something more" in couple's therapy. But the type of therapy that was offered at the time focused on the psyche of the individual, not on relationship dynamics. The underlying theory was that working on each person's issues would create two healthy, self-actualized people. These two people could then come together and—with little additional effort or insight—create a satisfying love relationship.

This traditional form of therapy had a limited success rate—if one defines success simply as keeping couples from getting divorced. About two-thirds of the couples would fail to reconcile their differences and decide to go their separate ways. But even some of those who managed to stay together would express a need for more support and insight than they'd been given. Counseling had given them a better understanding of their own issues and had improved their communication skills, but their relationship itself remained a bit of a mystery. Despite all the knowledge they'd gained, they continued to act in self-defeating ways. What's more, they sensed that their relationship held out a promise of healing and wholeness that they could not define, much less realize.

One of the reasons that *Getting the Love You Want* and Imago Therapy had something to offer these couples is that I, too, had experienced the frustration of being in a relationship that had not lived up to its potential. As I began to construct my own theory and practice of couple's therapy, it was critical to me that I answer the questions that had arisen from my own failed marriage. One of my main realizations was that the two individuals in a relationship need to let go of the illusion that they are the center of the universe and learn to see each other as equal partners. (I think of that old saying, "You and I are one, and I am the one.") There are indeed *two* people in the relationship. When two individuals surrender their centrality, something unexpected occurs—the relationship *itself* becomes the center. Once that fundamental shift occurs, they can begin to work *with* the unconscious purpose of their relationship, not against it. They can begin to accept the fact that being in an intimate love relationship calls forth all the unresolved issues of their childhood, and that they can learn how to work together to resolve them. We are born in relationship, we are wounded in relationship, and we can be healed in relationship. Indeed, we cannot be fully healed *outside* of a relationship. This is the idea that resonated with so many couples.

DETHRONING THE MARITAL THERAPIST

WITH HINDSIGHT, Helen and I can see another reason for the success of *Getting the Love You Want*. It challenges another fundamental tenet of couple's therapy, which is that the therapist is the source of the healing. In Imago Therapy, the therapist is transformed into a facilitator of the healing process. This does not make the therapist unimportant; in fact, the need for a competent therapist is increased. It's somewhat like requiring an obstetrician to take on the additional role of a midwife. The obstetrician becomes a highly skilled aide to a natural process rather than a remote authority figure with all of the answers.

Interestingly, even though transferring authority from the therapist to the couple was a monumental change, we were not fully aware that this is what was happening until after *Getting the Love You Want* was written. Once again, it was Helen who first had the insight: "You're dethroning the therapist," she said to me one day. "You're shifting the emphasis to the relationship between the couple, not the relationship between client and therapist." I immediately saw she was right. Once the idea had been verbalized, we began to understand the significance of the shift. In traditional therapy, one of the primary healing mechanisms involves "transference." Transference is when you assign to someone else either characteristics that belong to you (which is called "projective" transference), or characteristics that belong to somebody else: "You're like my mother." Once transference occurs between client and therapist, the therapist can use that misidentification in a positive way to help the client resolve issues from the past. Thus transference is a fundamental part of the therapy. The therapy is successful when the client "works through" the transference and begins to see the therapist as a distinct individual once again.

As you will see as you read this book, transference also occurs between couples in a love relationship. In fact, there's no way to avoid it. During the romantic love stage, this is a positive transference. You imagine that your partner has many of your own good qualities and also the positive traits of the people who influenced you most deeply in childhood. Later on, as conflict emerges, you begin to project *negative* traits onto your partner. This is typically when marriages fall apart. "You've changed. You're not the person I married," you say to each other. In reality, what has changed is not your partner, but the nature of the information you're projecting onto your partner. Imago Therapy helps you use this transference as a source of healing. This is very similar to the psychodynamics of traditional therapy, only in this context, the transference is between you and your partner, not between you and a therapist.

Some couples are able to resolve the transference without outside help. But like most people, you may need to work with a structured set of exercises or a competent therapist. The exercises or the therapist help create a zone of safety and provide the step-by-step instructions to guide you through the process. Like the millions of people who have read this book before you, you will find that reading the text and practicing the exercises will do this for you. If you require additional help, we are glad to say there are now many more trained therapists available to give you a hand.

CHANGES IN THE REVISED EDITION

WHEN WE REALIZED that this revised edition of *Getting the Love You Want* gave us the opportunity to make changes in the body of the text as well as write a new introduction, we read the book carefully, looking for flaws in the theory or changes that needed to be made in the therapy process. We were surprised to discover that most of what we've learned in the intervening thirteen years has been an extension, rather than a correction, of what we stated in the first edition. One of the gratifying extensions is that the partnership dynamics we described in heterosexual couples applies to all intimate partnerships, regardless of their sexual preference. We are excited about our new insights, of course, and will be elaborating on them in a forthcoming book. But we want to reassure you that the center still holds.

The only changes we felt obliged to make in this edition was to clarify some points about closing exits in chapter 7 and to enlarge upon an exercise in chapter 9 that was originally referred to as the "Mirroring Exercise." Regarding exits, we have learned how important it is to understand "closing an exit" as a process that takes time, rather than a particular action. The "Mirroring Exercise" is now called "The Couples Dialogue," and it has been expanded to include two additional steps—validation and empathy—which we had not discovered when the original edition was published. As will be explained in more detail in chapter 9, "mirroring" or paraphrasing your partner is an essential first step in exploring your partner's reality. But by itself, it may not be sufficient to establish a profound sense of connection. If you can go on to confirm the validity of your partner's view ("You make sense to me. You're not crazy.") and then empathize with his or her feelings ("I can see why you feel angry.") you deepen the bond between you. Or, as I say to couples, you go beyond mere contact to connection and then, ultimately, to communion.

In our own relationship, Helen and I have been privileged to experience this transcendent state. We have also seen it manifested in the lives of couples who have been through Imago Therapy. We'd like to close this introduction by sharing some of their comments with you. A man who read *Getting the Love You Want* expressed his new understanding this way: "I've learned that my view of the world is no more true than my wife's point of view. In fact, when we combine our views, we create something more valid than either one of us can create alone. We both give something up, only to gain a great deal more. It's been a profound change in our marriage." A couple that attended a weekend seminar wrote to us to say that "issues that have baffled us for years make perfect sense to us now, and we can truly empathize with each other. Perhaps for the first time in our relationship of almost 28 years, we feel safe. This is what we have always dreamed for our relationship, and we can hardly believe it is coming true!" Echoing their thoughts, another couple wrote, "what we have learned in your workshops and your books has been nothing short of transformational. We are in love again and marveling that this is so."

As so many other couples have discovered, if you take this book to heart and embrace the seemingly mundane exercises described herein, you, too, will attain a more loving, supportive, and deeply satisfying relationship. Imago Therapy is not just a theory of wishful thinking, it is a tried and true way to create the passionate friendship you've always wanted. As you will see, marriage *is* therapy—provided you honor its unconscious intent.

New Jersey, April 2001

Introduction

IN TODAY'S SOCIETY, you are encouraged to view marriage as a box. First you choose a mate. Then you climb into a box. Once you've had a chance to settle in, you take your first close look at your boxmate. If you like what you see, you stay put. If you don't, you climb out of the box and scout around for another mate. In other words, marriage is viewed as an unchanging state, and whether or not it works depends upon your ability to attract a good partner. The common solution to an unhappy marriage, the one chosen by nearly fifty percent of all couples, is to divorce and start all over again with a new and, it is hoped, better mate.

The problem with this solution is that there is a lot of pain involved in switching boxes. There is the agony of dividing up children and possessions and putting aside treasured dreams. There is the reluctance to risk intimacy again, fearing that the next relationship, too, might fail. And there is the emotional damage to the other inhabitants of the box—the children—who grow up feeling responsible for the divorce and wonder if they will ever experience lasting love.

Unfortunately, the only alternative many people see to divorce is to stay in the box, tighten the lid, and put up with a disappointing relationship for the rest of their lives. They learn to cope with an empty marriage by filling themselves up with food, alcohol, drugs, activities, work, television, and romantic fantasies, resigned to the belief that their longing for an intimate love will never be realized.

In this book I propose a more hopeful and, I believe, more accurate view of love relationships. Marriage is not a static state between two unchanging people. Marriage is a psychological and spiritual journey that begins in the ecstasy of attraction, meanders through a rocky stretch of self-discovery, and culminates in the creation of an intimate, joyful, lifelong union. Whether or not you realize the full potential of this vision depends not on your ability to attract the perfect mate, but on your willingness to acquire knowledge about hidden parts of yourself.

PERSONAL HISTORY

WHEN I BEGAN my career as a therapist, I counseled both individuals and couples. My preference was to work with one person at a time. My training was geared toward individuals, and when I saw clients singly, I felt competent and effective. Not so when a couple walked into my office. A marriage relationship introduced a complex set of variables that I was not trained to deal with. I ended up doing what most therapists did—problem-oriented, contractual marriage counseling. When this approach didn't work, I'd split up the couple and assign them to separate groups or counsel them individually.

In 1967 my confusion about the psychology of love relationships was compounded when I began to have problems with my own marriage. My wife and I were deeply committed to our relationship and had two young children, so we gave our marriage eight years of intensive examination, working with numerous therapists. Nothing seemed to help, and in 1975 we decided to divorce.

As I sat in the divorce court waiting my turn to see the judge, I felt like a double failure, a failure as a husband and as a therapist. That very afternoon I was scheduled to teach a course on marriage and the family, and the next day, as usual, I had several couples to counsel. Despite my professional training, I felt just as confused and defeated as the other men and women who were sitting beside me, waiting for their names to be called.

In the year following my divorce, I woke up each morning with an acute sense of loss. When I went to bed at night, I stared at the ceiling, trying to find some explanation for our failed marriage. Sure, both my wife and I had our ten reasons for divorcing, just as everyone else did. I didn't like this about her; she didn't like that about me; we had different interests; we had different goals. But beneath our litany of complaints, I could sense that there was a central disappointment, an underlying cause of our unhappiness, that had eluded eight years of probing.

Time passed, and my despair turned into a compelling desire to make sense out of my dilemma; I was not going to walk away from the ruins of my marriage without gaining some insight. I began to focus my efforts exclusively on learning what I could about relationship therapy. As I researched the professional books and journals, I was surprised to find few meaningful discussions of marriage, and the material that I did find was invariably slanted toward the psychology of the individual and the family. There seemed to be no comprehensive theory to explain the intricacies of the male-female relationship. No satisfactory explanation of the powerful emotions that can destroy a marriage. And there was nothing that explained what I found so painfully missing in my first marriage.

To fill in the gaps, I worked with hundreds of couples in private practice and thousands more in workshops and seminars. Out of my research and clinical observations, I gradually developed a theory of marital therapy called Imago (ih-MAH-go) Relationship Therapy. My approach was eclectic. I brought together depth psychology, the behavioral sciences, the Western spiritual tradition, and added some elements of Transactional Analysis, Gestalt psychology, systems theory, and cognitive therapy. In my view, each of these schools of thought made a unique and important contribution to the understanding of the psychology of the individual, but it was only when they were all brought together in a new synthesis that they illuminated the mystery of love relationships.

When I began implementing my ideas, my work with couples became immensely rewarding. The divorce rate in my practice sharply declined, and the couples who stayed together reported a much deeper satisfaction in their marriages. As my work became more visible, I began to lecture to both singles and couples. Eventually I developed an introductory workshop for couples, called Staying Together. In 1981 I began a training course for professionals. To date, more than thirty thousand people have been exposed to my ideas through counseling, workshops, and seminars.

ABOUT THIS BOOK

MY PURPOSE IN WRITING this book is twofold: to share with you what I have learned about the psychology of love relationships, and to help you transform your relationship into a lasting source of love and companionship. In short, it's a book about the theory and practice of becoming passionate friends.

The book is divided into three parts. In Part I, I chronicle the fate of most relationships: attraction, romantic love, and the power struggle. As I describe the familiar details of married life, I invite you to see them as an emerging psychological drama. I call this drama "The Unconscious Marriage," and by that I mean a marriage that includes all the hidden desires and automatic behaviors that are left over from childhood and that inexorably lead couples into conflict.

In Part II, I explore a radically different kind of marriage, "The Conscious Marriage,"[1] a marriage that helps you satisfy your unmet childhood needs in positive ways. First, I will explain a proven technique for rekindling romantic love. This process restores a spirit of cooperation and gives you the motivation to work on your underlying problems. Next I will show you how to replace confrontation and criticism, tactics learned in childhood, with a healing process of mutual growth and support. Finally, I will describe how to convert your pent-up frustration into empathy and understanding.

Part III takes all these ideas and packages them into a unique, ten-week course in relationship therapy. Through a series of proven, step-by-step exercises that you can do in the privacy of your home, you will not only gain insight into your marital problems, you will be able to resolve them—perhaps without the expense of a marital therapist.

This book can help you create a more loving and supportive relationship, and it is within this revitalized marriage that you will find peace and joy.

part I

THE UNCONSCIOUS MARRIAGE

THE MYSTERY OF ATTRACTION

The type of human being we prefer
reveals the contours of our heart.

—ORTEGA Y GASSET

WHEN COUPLES COME to me for marital therapy, I usually ask them how they met. Maggie and Victor, a couple in their mid-fifties who were contemplating divorce after twenty-nine years of marriage, told me this story:

"We met in graduate school," Maggie recalled. "We were renting rooms in a big house with a shared kitchen. I was cooking breakfast when I looked up and saw this man—Victor— walk into the room. I had the strangest reaction. My legs wanted to carry me to him, but my head was telling me to stay away. The feelings were so strong that I felt faint and had to sit down."

Once Maggie recovered from shock, she introduced herself to Victor, and the two of them spent half the morning talking. "That was it," said Victor. "We were together every possible moment for the next two months, and then we eloped."

"If those had been more sexually liberated times," added Maggie, "I'm sure we would have been lovers from that very first week. I've never felt so intensely about anyone in my entire life."

Not all first encounters produce seismic shock waves. Rayna and Mark, a couple ten years younger, had a more tepid and prolonged courtship. They met through a mutual friend. Rayna asked a friend if she knew any single men, and her friend said she knew an interesting man named Mark who had recently separated from his wife. She hesitated to introduce him to Rayna, however, because she didn't think that they would be a good match. "He's very tall and you're short," the friend explained; "he's Protestant and you're Jewish; he's very quiet and you talk all the time." But Rayna said none of that mattered. "Besides," she said, "how bad could it be for one date?"

Against her better judgment, the friend invited Rayna and Mark to an election-night party in 1972. "I liked Mark right away," Rayna recalled. "He was interesting in a quiet sort of way. We spent the whole evening talking in the kitchen." Rayna laughed and then added, "I suspect that I did most of the talking."

Rayna was certain that Mark was equally attracted to her, and she expected to hear from him the next day. But three weeks went by, and she didn't hear a word. Eventually she prompted her friend to find out if Mark was interested in her. With the friend's urging, Mark invited Rayna to the movies. That was the beginning of their courtship, but it was never a torrid romance. "We dated for a while, then we stopped for a while," said Mark. "Then we started dating again. Finally, in 1975, we got married."

"By the way," added Rayna, "Mark and I are still married, and the friend who didn't want to introduce us is now divorced."

Those contrasting stories raise some interesting questions.

Why do some people fall in love with such intensity, seemingly at first glance? Why do some couples ease into marriage with a levelheaded friendship? And why, as in the case of Rayna and Mark, do so many couples seem to have opposite personality traits? When we have the answers to these questions, we will also have our first clues to the hidden psychological desires that underlie marriage.

UNRAVELING THE MYSTERY OF ROMANTIC ATTRACTION

IN RECENT YEARS, scientists from various disciplines have labored to deepen our understanding of romantic love, and valuable insights have come from each area of research. Some biologists contend that there is a certain "bio-logic" to courtship behavior. According to this broad, evolutionary view of love, we instinctively select mates who will enhance the survival of the species. Men are drawn to classically beautiful women— ones with clear skin, bright eyes, shiny hair, good bone structure, red lips, and rosy cheeks—not because of fad or fashion but because these qualities indicate youth and robust health, signs that a woman is in the peak of her childbearing years.

Women select mates for slightly different biological reasons. Because youth and physical health aren't essential to the male reproductive role, women instinctively favor mates with pronounced "alpha" qualities, the ability to dominate other males and bring home more than their share of the kill. The assumption is that male dominance ensures the survival of the family group more than youth or beauty. Thus a fifty-year-old chairman of the board—the human equivalent of the silver-backed male gorilla—is as attractive to women as a young, handsome, virile, but less successful male.

If we can put aside, for a moment, our indignity at having our attractiveness to the opposite sex reduced to our breeding and food/money-gathering potential, there is some validity to this theory. Whether we like it or not, a woman's youth and physical appearance and a man's power and social status *do* play a role in mate selection, as a quick scan of the personal messages in the classified ads will attest: "Successful forty-five-year-old S.W.M. with private jet desires attractive, slim, twenty-year-old S.W.F.," and so on. But even though biological factors play a key role in our amorous advances, there's got to be more to love than this.

Let's move on to another field of study, social psychology, and explore what is known as the "exchange" theory of mate selection.[1] The basic idea of the exchange theory is that we select mates who are more or less our equals. When we are on a search-and-find mission for a partner, we size each other up as coolly as business executives contemplating a merger, noting each other's physical appeal, financial status, and social rank, as well as various personality traits such as kindness, creativity, and a sense of humor. With computer-like speed, we tally up each other's scores, and if the numbers are roughly equivalent, the trading bell rings and the bidding begins.

The exchange theory gives us a more comprehensive view of mate selection than the simple biological model. It's not just youth, beauty, and social rank that interests us, say the social psychologists, but the whole person. For example, the fact that a woman is past her prime or that a man has a low-status job can be offset by the fact that he or she is a charming, intelligent, compassionate person.

A third idea, the "persona" theory, adds yet another dimension to the phenomenon of romantic attraction.[2] The persona theory maintains that an important factor in mate selection is the way a potential suitor enhances our self-esteem. Each of us has a mask, a persona, which is the face that we show to other people. The persona theory suggests that we select a mate who will enhance this self-image. The operative question here is:

"What will it do to my sense of self if I am seen with this person?" There appears to be some validity to this theory. We have all experienced some pride and perhaps some embarrassment because of the way we believe our mates are perceived by others; it does indeed matter to us what others think.

Although these three theories help explain some aspects of romantic love, we are still left with our original questions. What accounts for the intensity of romantic love—as in the case of Maggie and Victor—those feelings of ecstasy that can be so overpowering? And why—as in the case of Rayna and Mark—do so many couples have complementary traits?

In fact, the more deeply we look at the phenomenon of romantic attraction, the more incomplete these theories appear to be. For example, what accounts for the emotional devastation that frequently accompanies the breakup of a relationship, that deadly undertow of feelings that can drown us in anxiety and self-pity? One client said to me as his girlfriend was leaving him: "I can't sleep or eat. My chest feels like it's going to explode. I cry all the time, and I don't know what to do." The theories of attraction we've looked at so far suggest that a more appropriate response to a failed romance would be simply to plunge into another round of mate selection.

There is another puzzling aspect of romantic attraction: we seem to have much more discriminating tastes than any of these theories would indicate. To see what I mean, take a moment to reflect on your own dating history. In your lifetime you have met thousands of people; as a conservative estimate, let's suppose that several hundred of them were physically attractive enough or successful enough to catch your eye. When we narrow this field by applying the social-exchange theory, we might come up with fifty or a hundred people out of this select group who would have a combined "point value" equal to or greater than yours. Logically, you should have fallen in love with scores of people. Yet most people have been deeply attracted to only a few individuals. In fact, when I counsel single people, I hear again and again that "there just aren't any good men (or women) out there!" The world is littered with their rejects.

Furthermore—and this is a curious fact—those few individuals that people are attracted to tend to resemble one another quite closely. Take a moment and think about the personality traits of the people that you have seriously considered as mates. If you were to make a list of their predominate personality traits, you would discover a lot of similarities, including, surprisingly, their negative traits.

From my vantage point as a marriage therapist, I see the unmistakable pattern in my clients' choice of marriage partners. One night, in a group-therapy session, I was listening to a man who was three months into his second marriage. When his first marriage broke up, he had vowed to the group that he would never be involved with a woman like his first wife. He thought she was mean, grasping, and selfish. Yet he confessed during the session that the day before he had "heard" the voice of his ex-wife coming from the lips of his new partner. With a sense of panic he realized that the two women had nearly identical personalities. *It appears that each one of us is compulsively searching for a mate with a very particular set of positive and negative personality traits.*

PLUMBING THE DEPTHS
OF THE UNCONSCIOUS MIND

FOR THIS HIGH DEGREE of selectivity to make any sense, we need to understand the role that the unconscious mind plays in mate selection. In the post-Freudian era, most people have become quite adept at rummaging around in the unconscious for explanations of daily events. We talk knowledgeably about "Freudian slips," analyze our dreams, and look for ways in which the unconscious might be influencing our daily behavior. Even so, most of us vastly underestimate the scope of the unconscious mind. There is an analogy that might give a better appreciation for its pervasive influence. In the daytime, we can't see the stars. We talk as if they "come out" at night, even though they are there all the time. We also underestimate the sheer number of stars. We look up at the sky, see a smattering of dim stars, and assume that's all there is. When we travel far away from city lights, we see a sky strewn with stars and are overwhelmed by the brilliance of the heavens. But it is only when we study astronomy that we learn the whole truth: the hundreds of thousands of stars that we see on a clear, moonless night in the country are only a fraction of the stars in the universe, and many of the points of light that we assume to be stars are in fact entire galaxies. So it is with the unconscious mind: the orderly, logical thoughts of our conscious mind are but a thin veil over the unconscious, which is active and functioning at all times.

Let's take a brief look at the structure of the brain, that mysterious and complex organ with many different subdivisions. For simplicity's sake, I like to use neuroscientist Paul McLean's model and divide the brain into three concentric layers.[3]

The brain stem, which is the inner and most primitive layer, is that part of the brain that oversees reproduction, self-preservation, and vital functions such as the circulation of blood, breathing, sleeping, and the contraction of muscles in response to external stimulation. Located at the base of the skull, this portion of the brain is sometimes referred to as the "reptilian brain," because all vertebrates from reptiles to mammals share this portion of the anatomy. For the purpose of this discussion, let's think of the brain stem as the source of physical action.

Flaring like a wishbone around the top of the brain stem is the portion of the brain called the limbic system, whose function seems to be the generation of vivid emotions. Scientists can surgically stimulate the limbic system of laboratory animals and create spontaneous outbursts of fear and aggression. In this book I use the term "old brain" to refer to the portion of the brain that includes both the brain stem and the limbic system. Think of the old brain as being hard-wired and determining most of your automatic reactions.

The final area of the brain is the cerebral cortex, a large, convoluted mass of brain tissue that surrounds the two inner sections and is itself divided into four regions or lobes. This portion of the brain, which is most highly developed in *Homo sapiens,* is the site of most of our cognitive functions. I refer to the cerebral cortex as the "new brain" because it appeared most recently in evolutionary history. Your new brain is the part of you that is conscious, alert, and in contact with your daily surroundings. It's the part of you that makes decisions, thinks, observes, plans, anticipates, responds, organizes information, and creates ideas. The new brain is inherently logical and tries to find a cause for every effect and an effect for every cause. To a degree, it can moderate some of the instinctual reactions of your old brain.[4] By and large, this analytical, probing, questioning part of your mind is the part that you think of as being "you."

OLD-BRAIN LOGIC

IN SHARP CONTRAST to the new brain, you are unaware of most of the functions of your old brain. Trying to comprehend this part of your being is a maddening task, because you have to turn your conscious mind around to examine its own underbelly. Scientists who have subjected the old brain to this kind of scrutiny tell us that its main concern is self-preservation. Ever on the alert, the old brain constantly asks the primeval question: "Is it safe?"

As it goes about its job of ensuring your safety, your old brain operates in a fundamentally different manner from your new brain. One of the crucial differences is that the old brain appears to have only a hazy awareness of the external world. Unlike the new brain, which relies on direct perception of outside phenomena, the old brain derives its incoming data from the images, symbols, and thoughts produced by the new brain. This reduces its data to very broad categories. For example, while your new brain easily distinguishes John from Suzy from Margaret, your old brain summarily lumps these people into six basic categories. The only thing your old brain seems to care about is whether a particular person is someone to: (1) nurture, (2) be nurtured by, (3) have sex with, (4) run away from, (5) submit to, or (6) attack.[5] Subtleties such as "this is my neighbor," "my cousin," "my mother," or "my wife" slide right on by.

The old brain and the new brain, different in so many ways, are constantly exchanging and interpreting information. Here is how this takes place. Let's suppose that you are alone in your house, and all of a sudden, person A walks through the door. Your new brain automatically creates an image of this creature and sends it to your old brain for scrutiny. The old brain receives the image and compares it with other, stored images. Instantly there is a first observation: "This humanoid is not a stranger." Apparently encounters with this creature have been recorded before. A millisecond later there is a second observation: "There are no dangerous episodes associated with this image." Out of all the interactions you have had with this mystery guest, none of them has been life-threatening. Then, rapidly, a third observation: "There have been numerous *pleasurable* episodes associated with this image." In fact, the records seem to suggest that A is someone who is nurturing. Having reached this conclusion, the limbic system sends an all-clear signal to the reptilian brain, and you find yourself walking toward the intruder with open arms. Operating out of your new brain, you say, "Aunt Mary! What a pleasure to see you!"

All of this has taken place outside your awareness in only a fraction of a second. To your conscious mind, all that has happened is that your beloved Aunt Mary has walked in the door.

Meanwhile, as you visit with your aunt, the data-gathering process continues. This latest encounter produces more thoughts, emotions, and images, which are sent to the limbic system to be stored in the part of the brain reserved for Aunt Mary. These new data will be a part of the information scanned by the old brain the next time she comes to visit.

Let's look at a slightly different situation. Let's suppose that the person who walked in the door was not Aunt Mary but her sister, Aunt Carol, and instead of greeting her with open arms, you found yourself resenting the interruption. Why such a different reaction to these two sisters? Let's pretend that when you were eighteen months old you spent a week with Aunt Carol while your mother was in the hospital having another baby. Your parents, trying to prepare you in advance for this visit, explained to you that "Mommy is going bye-bye to the hospital to bring home a little brother or sister." The words "hospital," "brother," and "sister" had no meaning to you, but "Mommy" and "bye-bye" certainly did. Whenever they mentioned those two words together, you felt anxious and sucked your thumb. Weeks later, when your mother went into labor, you were lifted out of your crib in a sound sleep and transported to Aunt Carol's house. You woke up alone in a strange room, and the person who came to you when you cried was not your mother or father but Aunt Carol.

You dwelled in anxiety for the next few days. Even though Aunt Carol was loving and kind to you, you felt abandoned. This primal fear became associated with your aunt, and for years the sight of her or the smell of her perfume sent you running from the room. In later years you had many pleasurable or neutral experiences with Aunt Carol; nonetheless, thirty years later, when she walks into the room, you feel the urge to run away. It is only with great discipline that you rise to greet her.

No Time Like the Present

THIS STORY ILLUSTRATES an important principle about the old brain: it has no sense of linear time. Today, tomorrow, and yesterday do not exist; everything that was, still is. Understanding this basic fact about the nature of your unconscious may help explain why you sometimes have feelings within your marriage that seem alarmingly out of proportion to the events that triggered them. For example, imagine that you are a thirty-five-year-old woman, a lawyer in a prestigious firm. One day you are sitting in your office thinking warm, loving thoughts about your husband and decide to call him. You dial his number, and his secretary informs you that he is out of the office and can't be reached. Suddenly your loving thoughts vanish, and you feel a surge of anxiety: where is he? Your rational mind knows that he's probably calling on a client or enjoying a late lunch, but another part of you feels—let's be honest—abandoned. There you are, a sophisticated, capable woman, and just because your husband isn't available you feel as vulnerable as you did when your mother left you all day with an unfamiliar baby-sitter. Your old brain is locked in an archaic perspective.

Or let's suppose that you are a middle-aged man, a middle manager in a large company. After a hectic day at work, where you manage to placate important clients and put the finishing touches on a multimillion-dollar budget, you drive home, eager to share your successes with your wife. When you walk in the door, you see a note from your wife saying that she will be late coming home from work. You stop dead in your tracks. You had counted on her being there! Do you recover from the disappointment and relish the time to yourself? Do you use the time to do a final check on the budget? Yes. But not before you head straight for the freezer and consume two bowlfuls of bland, sweet vanilla ice cream, as close a substitute for mother's milk as you can possibly find. The past and the present live side by side within your mind.

Now that we've spent some time pondering the nature of the unconscious mind, let's return to our original discussion of mate selection. How does this information about the old brain add to our understanding of romantic attraction? The curious phenomenon I noted earlier in this exploration was that we seem to be *highly selective* in our choice of mates. In fact, we appear to be searching for a "one and only" with a very specific set of positive and negative traits.

What we are doing, I have discovered from years of theoretical research and clinical observation, is looking for someone who has the predominant character traits of the people who raised us. Our old brain, trapped in the eternal now and having only a dim awareness of the outside world, is trying to re-create the environment of childhood. And the reason the old brain is trying to resurrect the past is not a matter of habit or blind compulsion but of a compelling need to heal old childhood wounds.

The ultimate reason you fell in love with your mate, I am suggesting, is not that your mate was young and beautiful, had an impressive job, had a "point value" equal to yours, or had a kind disposition. You fell in love because your old brain had your partner confused with your parents! Your old brain believed that it had finally found the ideal candidate to make up for the psychological and emotional damage you experienced in childhood.

2

CHILDHOOD WOUNDS

Age is no better, hardly so well,
qualified for an instructor as youth,
for it has not profited so much as it has lost.
— HENRY DAVID THOREAU

WHEN YOU HEAR the words "psychological and emotional damage of childhood," you may immediately think about serious childhood traumas such as sexual or physical abuse or the suffering that comes from having parents who divorced or died or were alcoholics. And for many people this is the tragic reality of childhood. However, even if you were fortunate enough to grow up in a safe, nurturing environment, you still bear invisible scars from childhood, because from the very moment you were born you were a complex, dependent creature with a never-ending cycle of needs. Freud correctly labeled us "insatiable beings." And no parents, no matter how devoted, are able to respond perfectly to all of these changing needs.

Before we explore some of the subtler ways in which you may have been wounded and how this affects your marriage, let's take a look at what you were like when you first came into the world, because this state of "original wholeness" contains an important clue to the hidden expectations you bring to marriage.

ORIGINAL WHOLENESS

THERE HAVE BEEN no miracle babies born with the ability to reveal to us the dark mysteries of life before birth, but we do know something about the physical life of the fetus. We know that its biological needs are taken care of instantly and automatically by an exchange of fluids between it and its mother. We know that a fetus has no need to eat, breathe, or protect itself from danger, and that it is constantly soothed by the rhythmical beat of its mother's heart. From these simple biological facts and from observations of newborns, we can surmise that the fetus lives a tranquil, floating, effortless existence. It has no awareness of boundaries, no sense of itself, and no recognition that it is encased in a sac inside its mother. There is a widely held belief that when a baby is inside its mother's womb, it experiences a sense of oneness, an Edenic experience free from desire. Martin Buber, a Jewish theologian, put it this way: "in fetal existence, we were in communion with the universe."[1]

This idyllic existence comes to an abrupt end as the mother's contractions forcibly expel the baby from the womb. But for the first few months, a developmental stage called the "autistic period," the baby still makes no distinction between itself and the rest of the world.[2] I have recently become a father again, and I have clear memories of when my daughter Leah was in this stage. When all her physical needs were taken care of, she would nestle in our arms and look around her with the contentment of Buddha. Like all babies, she had no awareness of herself as a separate being and no internal divisions between thoughts, feelings, and actions. To my eyes, she was experiencing a primitive spirituality, a universe without boundaries. Although she was immature and utterly dependent on her mother and me for survival, she was nonetheless a vital, complete human being—in some ways more entire than she would ever be again.

As adults, we seem to have a fleeting memory of this state of original wholeness, a sensation that is as hard to recapture as a dream. We seem to recall a distant time when we were more unified and connected to the world. This feeling is described over and over again in the myths of all cultures, as if words could lend it more reality. It is the story of the Garden of Eden, and it strikes us with compelling force.

But what does this have to do with marriage? For some reason, we enter marriage with the expectation that our partners will magically restore this feeling of wholeness. It is as if they hold the key to a long-ago kingdom, and all we have to do is persuade them to unlock the door. Their failure to do so is one of the main reasons for our eventual unhappiness.

You and I Are One

THE FEELING OF UNITY that a child experiences in the womb and in the first few months of life gradually fades, giving way to a drive to be a distinct self. The essential state of unity remains, but there is a glimmer of awareness of the external world. It is during this stage of development that the child makes the monumental discovery that its mother, the gentle giant who holds it and feeds it and makes such comforting sounds, is not always there. The child still feels connected to its mother but has a primitive awareness of self.

When babies are in this symbiotic stage, development psychologists tell us that they experience a yearning to be connected with their caretakers. They label this the drive for attachment. The child's life energy is directed outward toward the mother in an effort to recapture its earlier sense of physical and spiritual union. A term that describes this yearning is "eros," a Greek word that we normally equate with romantic or sexual love but that originally had the broader meaning of "the life force."[3]

A child's success at feeling both distinct from and connected to its mother has a profound impact on all later relationships. If the child is fortunate, he will be able to make clear distinctions between himself and other people but still feel connected to them; he will have fluid boundaries that he can open or close at will. A child who has painful experiences early in life will either feel cut off from those around him or will attempt to fuse with them, not knowing where he leaves off and others begin. This lack of firm boundaries will be a recurring problem in marriage.

As a child grows older, eros is directed not only to the mother but also to the father, siblings, and the world as a whole. I remember when my daughter Leah was three years old and wanted to explore everything around her. She had so much vitality that she could run all day long and not be tired. "Run with me, Daddy! Somersault!" She twirled in circles and got so dizzy that she would fall down and laugh and laugh. She would chase fireflies, talk to leaves, swing from her knees on the monkey bars, and pet every dog she saw. Like Adam, she enjoyed naming objects, and developed a keen ear for words. When I looked at Leah, I saw eros, the full pulsation of life. I envied her and yearned for what I had lost.

Helen and I strive to keep eros alive in Leah, to sustain the brightness of her eyes and the thrill of her contagious laughter. But, despite our best intentions, we do not meet all of her needs. Sometimes it seems as if life itself is making her turn inward. Once she was frightened by a large dog and learned to be wary of strange animals. One day she slipped in a pool and developed a fear of water. But sometimes Helen and I are more directly to blame. We have five other children besides Leah, and there are times when she feels left out. There are days when we come home from work too tired to listen to what she is saying, too distracted to understand what she wants. Tragically, we also wound her by unwittingly passing on our own childhood wounds, the emotional inheritance of generations. We either overcompensate for what we didn't get from our parents or blindly re-create the same painful situations.

For whatever reasons, when Leah's desires are not satisfied a questioning look comes over her face; she cries; she is afraid. She no longer talks to leaves or notices the fireflies darting about the bushes. Eros is blunted and turns in on itself.

THE PERILOUS PILGRIMAGE

LEAH'S STORY is my story and your story. We all started out life whole and vital, eager for life's adventures, but we all had a perilous pilgrimage through childhood. In fact, some wounding took place in the first few months of our lives. Think for a moment about the ceaseless demands of an infant. When an infant wakes up in the morning, it cries to be fed. Then its diapers are wet and it cries to be changed. Then the baby wants to be held, a physical craving as powerful as its need for food. Then the baby is hungry again and once more cries to be fed. A bubble of gas forms in its stomach, and the baby cries out in anguish. It signals distress the only way it knows how—with an undifferentiated cry—and if its caretakers are perceptive enough, the infant is fed, changed, held, or rocked, and experiences momentary satisfaction. But if the caretakers can't figure out what is wrong, or if they withhold their attentions for fear of spoiling the baby, the child experiences a primitive anxiety: the world is not a safe place. Since it has no way of taking care of itself and no sense of delayed gratification, it believes that getting the outside world to respond instantly to its needs is truly a matter of life and death.

Although you and I have no recollection of these first few months of life, our old brains are still trapped in an infantile perspective. Although we are now adults, capable of keeping ourselves fed and warm and dry, a hidden part of us still expects the outside world to take care of us. When our partners are hostile or merely unhelpful, a silent alarm is triggered deep in our brains that fills us with the fear of death. As you will soon see, this automatic alarm system plays a key role in marriage.

As a child grows out of infancy, new needs emerge, and each new need defines a potential area of wounding. When a baby is about eighteen months old, for example, it has a clearer sense of where it leaves off and others begin. This is a stage of development referred to as the stage of "autonomy and independence." In this period the child has a growing interest in exploring the world beyond its primary caretaker. If a toddler had an adult's command of language, he would say something like this: "I'm ready to spend some time off your lap now. I'm ready to let go of the nipple and wander away by myself. I'm a little insecure about leaving you, however, and I'll be back in a few minutes to make sure you haven't disappeared." But since the child has only a limited vocabulary, he simply climbs down from his mother's lap, turns his back, and toddles out of the room.

Now, ideally, the mother smiles and says something like this: "Bye, sweetie. Have a good time. I'll be right here when you need me." And when the toddler comes back a few minutes later, suddenly aware of how dependent he really is, his mother says, "Hi! Did you have fun? Come sit in my lap for a minute." She lets the child know that it is OK to leave her side and venture off on his own, yet she is available whenever he needs her. The little boy learns that the world is a safe, exciting place to explore.

FUSERS AND ISOLATERS

MANY CHILDREN ARE FRUSTRATED at this crucial stage of development. Some have a caretaker who thwarts their independence. The mother or father is the one who feels insecure when the child is out of sight, not the child. For some reason—

one that is rooted in the parent's own childhood—the parent needs the child to remain dependent. When a little girl wanders out of the room, her insecure mother might call out, "Don't go into the next room! You might get hurt!" The child dutifully comes back to her mother's lap. But inside her shell of conformity she is afraid. Her inner drive for autonomy is being denied. She fears that, if she always comes running back to her mother, she will be engulfed; she will be trapped in a symbiotic union forever.

Without the child's knowing it, this fear of engulfment becomes a key part of her character, and in later years she becomes what I call an "isolater," a person who unconsciously pushes others away. She keeps people at a distance because she needs to have "a lot of space" around her; she wants the freedom to come and go as she pleases; she doesn't want to be "pinned down" to a single relationship. All the while underneath this cool exterior is a two-year-old girl who was not allowed to satisfy her natural need for independence. When she marries, her need to be a distinct "self" will be on the top of her hidden agenda.

Some children grow up with the opposite kind of parents, ones who push them away when they come running to them for comfort: "Go away, I'm busy." "Go play with your toys." "Stop clinging to me!" The caretakers are not equipped to handle any needs but their own, and their children grow up feeling emotionally abandoned. Eventually they grow up to become what I call "fusers," people who seem to have an insatiable need for closeness. Fusers want to "do things together" all the time. If people fail to show up at the appointed time, they feel abandoned. The thought of divorce fills them with terror. They crave physical affection and reassurance, and they often need to stay in constant verbal contact. Underneath all this clinging behavior is a young child who needed more time on a parent's lap.

Ironically, for reasons I will explore in later chapters, fusers and isolaters tend to grow up and marry each other, thus beginning an infuriating game of push and pull that leaves neither partner satisfied.

As you journeyed through childhood, you went through one developmental stage after another, and the way your caretakers responded to your changing needs greatly affected your emotional health. More than likely, they coped with one stage of your growth better than another. They may have taken excellent care of you when you were an infant, for example, but fallen apart at your first temper tantrum. Or they may have been delighted by your inquisitive nature as a toddler but been threatened by your attraction to your opposite-sex parent when you were five or six. You may have grown up with caretakers who met most of your needs, or only some of them, but, like all children, you grew up knowing the anguish of unmet needs and these needs followed you into your marriage.

The Lost Self

WE HAVE NOW EXPLORED one important feature of the vast hidden world I call the "unconscious marriage," and that is our storehouse of unmet childhood needs, our unfulfilled desire to be nurtured and protected and allowed to proceed unhindered along a path to maturity. Now we will turn to another kind of childhood wound, an even subtler kind of psychic injury called "socialization," all those messages we receive from our caretakers and from society at large that tell us who we are and how we have to behave. These, too, play a compelling but hidden role in marriage.

At first it may seem strange to equate socialization with emotional injury. To help explain why this is so, I want to describe one of my clients. (As is true for most of the people I mention in this book, names and certain identifying characteristics have been changed to preserve anonymity.) Sarah is an attractive, personable woman in her mid-thirties. A main concern in her life is her apparent inability to think clearly and logically. "I can't think," she has told me over and over again, "I just can't think." She is a lower-level manager in a computer firm, where she has worked diligently for fifteen years. She would have advanced much further in the company if she were an effective problem-solver, but whenever she is presented with a difficult situation, she panics and runs to her supervisor for support. Her supervisor gives her sage advice, reinforcing Sarah's belief that she is incapable of making decisions on her own.

It didn't take much probing to discover part of the reason for Sarah's anxiety. From a very early age, she received from her mother the explicit message that she was not very intelligent. "You're not as smart as your older brother," her mother would say, and "You'd better marry a smart man, because you're going to need a lot of help. But I doubt if a smart man would marry you." As blatant as these messages were, they didn't fully account for Sarah's perceived inability to think. Amplifying her mother's message was the prevalent view of the 1950s that little girls were sweet, pretty, and compliant, but not especially bright; the girls in Sarah's grade school dreamed of being wives, nurses, and teachers, not executives, astronauts, and doctors.

Another influence on Sarah's problem-solving capacity was the fact that her mother had very little confidence in her own reasoning ability. She managed the house and took care of her children's needs, but she deferred all major decisions to her husband. This dependent, passive model defined "womanhood" for Sarah.

When Sarah was fifteen, she was fortunate enough to have a teacher who recognized her natural abilities and encouraged her to work harder on her schoolwork. For the first time in her life, Sarah came home with a report card that was mostly A's. She will never forget her mother's reaction: "How on earth did that happen? I bet you can't do that again." And Sarah couldn't, because she finally gave in and put to sleep the part of her brain that thinks calmly and rationally.

The tragedy was not only that Sarah lost her ability to reason, but also that she acquired the unconscious belief that thinking was dangerous. Why was that? Since Sarah's mother had strongly rejected her intellectual capabilities, she believed that if she were to think clearly she would be defying her mother; she would be contradicting her mother's definition of her. She couldn't risk alienating her mother, because she was dependent on her mother for survival. It was dangerous, therefore, for Sarah to know that she had a mind. Yet she couldn't fully disown her intelligence. She envied people who could think, and when she married she chose a man who was exceptionally bright, an unconscious ploy to make up for the psychological damage of childhood.

Like Sarah, we all have parts of ourselves that we have hidden from consciousness. I call these missing elements the "lost self." Whenever we complain that we "can't think" or that we "can't feel anything" or "can't dance" or "can't have orgasms" or "aren't very creative," we are identifying natural abilities, thoughts, or feelings that we have surgically removed from our awareness. They are not gone; we still possess them. But for the moment they are not a part of our consciousness, and it is as if they do not exist.

As in Sarah's case, our lost self was formed early in childhood—largely as a result of our caretakers' well-intentioned efforts to teach us to get along with others. Each society has a unique collection of practices, laws, beliefs, and values that children need to absorb, and mothers and fathers are the main conduit through which they are transmitted. This indoctrination process goes on in every family in every society. There seems to be a universal understanding that, unless limits are placed on the individual, the individual becomes a danger to the group. In the words of Freud, "The desire for a powerful and uninhibited ego may seem to us intelligible, but, as is shown by the times that we live in, it is in the profoundest sense antagonistic to civilization."

But even though our parents often had our best interests at

heart, the overall message handed down to us was a chilling one. There were certain thoughts and feelings we could not have, certain natural behaviors that we had to extinguish, and certain talents and aptitudes we had to deny. In thousands of ways, both subtly and overtly, our parents gave us the message that they approved of only a part of us. In essence, we were told that we could not be whole and exist in this culture.

Body Taboos

ONE OF THE AREAS in which we were most restricted was our bodies. At a very young age, we were taught to cover our bodies in gender-specific ways and not to talk about or touch our genitals. These prohibitions are so universal that we tend to notice them only when they are broken. A friend of mine told me a story that illustrates how startling it can be when parents fail to pass on these unspoken taboos. A friend of hers named Chris and her eleven-month-old son happened to drop by her house one day. Soon my friend and Chris and the baby were sitting out on the back deck, sipping ice tea. Since the May sunshine was pleasantly warm, Chris took off the baby's clothes so he could sunbathe. The two women chatted while the little boy crawled around on the deck, happily digging his fingers into the warm soil of the flowerpots. After about half an hour, the baby became hungry, and Chris put him to her breast. My friend noticed that as the baby nursed he developed a miniature erection. Apparently nursing was such a sensual experience that he felt pleasure throughout his body. Instinctively, the little boy reached down to touch his genitals. Unlike most mothers, Chris did not pull his hand away. Her baby was allowed to feel the warm sun on his naked skin, nurse from his mother's breasts, have an erection, and add to his pleasure by holding on to his penis.

It is normal and natural for an infant to want to have those good feelings, but we rarely allow it. Think about all the rules his mother was breaking. First of all, society tells us that women can nurse their babies but that if they do so it should be discreetly, so that no one might catch a fleeting glimpse of a naked breast. Second, infants should be clothed at all times—at least in a diaper—even when they are outside and the day is mild and sunny. Third, little boys and girls should not experience any form of genital arousal, but if for some reason they do they should not be permitted to enjoy it. By allowing her baby to revel in all of his senses, Chris was violating three potent taboos.

It is not my purpose to attack or defend society's prohibitions against bodily pleasure. That would be an entire book in itself. (Nor do I want to simplify the problem that having a body, much less enjoying it, has been in the Western world.) But to understand the hidden desires that permeate your marriage, it's important to know this simple fact: when you were young, there were many, many times when limits were placed on your sensuality. Like most children growing up in this culture, you were probably made to feel embarrassed or guilty or naughty that you had a body that was capable of exquisite sensation. To be a "good" boy or girl, you had to psychologically cut off or disown that part of yourself.

FORBIDDEN FEELINGS

YOUR EMOTIONS WERE another prime candidate for socialization. Some feelings, of course, were not just permitted, they were encouraged. Oh, how hard your parents worked to get you to smile when you were an infant! And a few weeks later, when you laughed out loud, everyone had a marvelous time. Anger, however, was another matter. Temper tantrums are noisy and unpleasant, and most parents try to discourage them. They do this in a number of ways. Some parents tease their children: "You look so cute when you're mad. I see a smile coming on.

Give us a smile." Others discipline them: "You stop that right now! Go to your room. I'll have none of this back talk!" Insecure parents often give in to their children: "OK. Have it your way. But the next time you'd better behave!"

It is the rare parent who validates a child's anger. Imagine a little girl's relief if her parents were to say something like this: "I can see that you're mad. You don't want to do what I ask. But I am the parent and you are the child and you need to do what I say." Having her anger acknowledged would contribute to her sense of self. She would be able to tell herself, "I exist. My parents are aware of my feelings. I may not always get my way, but I am listened to and respected." She would be allowed to stay in touch with her anger and retain an essential aspect of her wholeness.

But such is not the fate of most children. The other day I was in a department store and happened to witness how abruptly a child's anger can be put off—especially when it's anger directed at a parent. A woman was doing some clothes shopping while her little boy, about four years old, tagged along. She was preoccupied, and the little boy kept up an insistent monologue in an effort to get her attention. "I can read these letters," he said, pointing to a sign, "M-A-D-E." He got no reaction. "Are you going to try on more clothes?" he asked. No response. The whole time I was watching, she gave him only a few seconds of attention, and when she did she sounded annoyed and depressed. Finally I heard him say loud and clear to a store clerk, "My mommy was hurt in a car crash. She got killed." This pronouncement got his mother's instant attention. She shook her son by the shoulders, spanked him, and forcibly shoved him down on a chair. "What do you mean? I wasn't killed in a car crash! Stop talking like that. Go over and sit on that chair and be quiet. Not another word out of you." The boy was white-faced and sat without moving until his mother was done with her shopping.

Inside his head, the little boy's anger at his mother had been transformed into a vengeful fantasy in which she was killed in a highway accident. He hadn't been the one to hurt her. At four, he had already been taught to disown his angry thoughts and feelings. Instead he imagined that she had simply gotten in the way of a car driven by somebody else.

When you were young, there were probably many times when you, too, were angry at your caretakers. More than likely, it was a sentiment that got little support. Your angry feelings, your sexual feelings, and a host of other "antisocial" thoughts and feelings were pushed deep inside of you and were not allowed to see the light of day.

A few parents take this invalidation process to the extreme. They deny not only their children's feelings and behaviors, but the entire child as well. "*You* do not exist. You are not important in this family. Your needs, your feelings, your wishes are not important to us." I worked with one young woman I'll call Carla whose parents denied her existence to the point where they made her feel invisible. Her mother was an immaculate housekeeper, and her instructions to her daughter were to "clean up after yourself so well that no one can tell you live here." Plastic runners placed on the carpets determined where Carla could walk. The professionally landscaped yard had no room for tricycles or swings or sandboxes. Carla has a strong memory of sitting in the kitchen one day when she was about ten years old, feeling so depressed she wanted to die. Her mother and father walked in and out of the kitchen numerous times without even acknowledging her presence. Carla began to feel that she had no bodily reality. It is no wonder that when she turned thirteen she complied with her parents' unspoken directive to disappear and became anorexic, literally trying to starve herself out of existence.

TOOLS OF REPRESSION

IN THEIR ATTEMPTS to repress certain thoughts, feelings, and behavior, parents use various techniques. Sometimes they issue clear-cut directives: "You don't really think that." "Big boys don't cry." "Don't touch yourself there!" "I never want to hear you say that again!" "We don't act like that in this family!" Or, like the mother in the department store, they scold, threaten, or spank. Much of the time, they mold their children through a subtler process of invalidation—they simply choose not to see or reward certain things. For example, if parents place little value on intellectual development, they give their children toys and sports equipment but no books or science kits. If they believe that girls should be quiet and feminine, and boys should be strong and assertive, they only reward their children for gender-appropriate behavior. For example, if their little boy comes into the room lugging a heavy toy, they might say, "What a strong little boy you are!" But if their daughter comes in carrying the same toy, they might caution, "Be careful of your pretty dress."

The way that parents influence their children most deeply, however, is by example. Children instinctively observe the choices their parents make, the freedoms and pleasures they allow themselves, the talents they develop, the abilities they ignore, and the rules they follow. All of this has a profound effect on children: "This is how we live. This is how to get through life." Whether children accept their parents' model or rebel against it, this early socialization plays a significant role in mate selection and, as we will soon see, is often a hidden source of tension in married life.

A child's reaction to society's edicts goes through a number of predictable stages. Typically, the first response is to hide forbidden behaviors from the parents. The child thinks angry thoughts but doesn't speak them out loud. He explores his body in the privacy of his room. He teases his younger sibling when his parents are away. Eventually the child comes to the conclusion that some thoughts and feelings are so unacceptable that they should be eliminated, so he constructs an imaginary parent in his head to police his thoughts and activities, a part of the mind that psychologists call the "superego." Now, whenever the child has a forbidden thought or indulges in an "unacceptable" behavior, he experiences a self-administered jolt of anxiety. This is so unpleasant that the child puts to sleep some of those forbidden parts of himself—in Freudian terms, he represses them. The ultimate price of his obedience is a loss of wholeness.

THE FALSE SELF

TO FILL THE VOID, the child creates a "false self," a character structure that serves a double purpose: it camouflages those parts of his being that he has repressed and protects him from further injury. A child brought up by a sexually repressive, distant mother, for instance, may become a "tough guy." He tells himself, "I don't care if my mother isn't very affectionate. I don't need that mushy stuff. I can make it on my own. And another thing—I think sex is dirty!" Eventually he applies this patterned response to all situations. No matter who tries to get close to him, he erects the same barricade. In later years, when he overcomes his reluctance to getting involved in a love relationship, it is likely that he will criticize his partner for her desire for intimacy and her intact sexuality: "Why do you want so much contact and why are you so obsessed with sex? It's not normal!"

A different child might react to a similar upbringing in an opposite manner, exaggerating his problems in the hope that someone will come to his rescue: "Poor me. I am hurt. I am deeply wounded. I need someone to take care of me." Yet another child might become a hoarder, striving to hold on to every bit of love and food and material goods that comes his way out of the certain knowledge that there is never enough. But, whatever the nature of the false self, its purpose is the same: to minimize the pain of losing part of the child's original, God-given wholeness.

The Disowned Self

AT SOME POINT in a child's life, however, this ingenious form of self-protection becomes the cause of further wounding as the child is criticized for having these negative traits. Others condemn him for being distant or needy or self-centered or fat or stingy. His attackers don't see the wound he is trying to protect, and they don't appreciate the clever nature of his defense: all they see is the neurotic side of his personality. He is deemed inferior; he is less than whole.

Now the child is caught in a bind. He needs to hold on to his adaptive character traits, because they serve a useful purpose, but he doesn't want to be rejected. What can he do? The solution is to deny or attack his critics: "I'm not cold and distant," he might say in self-defense, "what I really am is strong and independent." Or "I'm not weak and needy, I'm just sensitive." Or "I'm not greedy and selfish, I'm thrifty and prudent." In other words, "That's not me you're talking about. You're just seeing me in a negative light."

In a sense, he is right. His negative traits are not a part of his original nature. They are forged out of pain and become a part of an assumed identity, an alias that helps him maneuver in a complex and sometimes hostile world. This doesn't mean, however, that he doesn't have these negative traits; there are any number of witnesses who will affirm that he does. But in order to maintain a positive self-image and enhance his chances for survival, he has to deny them. These negative traits became what is referred to as the "disowned self," those parts of the false self that are too painful to acknowledge.

Let's stop for a moment and sort out this proliferation of self parts. We have now succeeded in fracturing your original wholeness, the loving and unified nature that you were born with, into three separate entities:

1. Your "lost self," those parts of your being that you had to repress because of the demands of society.
2. Your "false self," the facade that you erected in order to fill the void created by this repression and by a lack of adequate nurturing.
3. Your "disowned self," the negative parts of your false self that met with disapproval and were therefore denied.

The only part of this complex collage that you were routinely aware of was the parts of your original being that were still intact and certain aspects of your false self. Together these elements formed your "personality," the way you would describe yourself to others. Your lost self was almost totally outside your awareness; you had severed nearly all connections with these repressed parts of your being. Your disowned self, the negative parts of your false self, hovered just below your level of awareness and was constantly threatening to emerge. To keep it hidden, you had to deny it actively or project it onto others: "I am *not* self-centered," you would say with great energy. Or "What do you mean, I'm lazy? *You're* lazy."

PLATO'S ALLEGORY

THERE IS AN ALLEGORY in Plato's *Symposium* that serves as a mythical model for this state of split existence.[4] Human beings, the story goes, were once composite creatures that were both male and female. Each being had one head with two faces, four hands and four feet, and both male and female genitals. Being unified and whole, our ancestors wielded tremendous force.

In fact, so magnificent were these androgynous beings that they dared to attack the gods. The gods, of course, would not tolerate this insolence, but they didn't know how to punish the humans. "If we kill them," they said to one another, "there will be no one to worship us and offer up sacrifices." Zeus pondered the situation and finally came up with a solution. "Men shall continue to exist," he decreed, "but they will be cut in two. Then they will be diminished in strength so we need not fear them." Zeus proceeded to split each being in two, asking Apollo's help to make the wounds invisible. The two halves were then sent in opposite directions to spend the rest of their lives searching frantically for the other half-creature, the reunion with whom would restore their wholeness.

Just like Plato's mythical creatures, we, too, go through life truncated, cut in half. We cover our wounds with healing ointment and gauze in an attempt to heal ourselves, but despite our efforts an emptiness wells up inside us. We try to fill this emptiness with food and drugs and activities, but what we yearn for is our original wholeness, our full range of emotions, the inquisitive mind that was our birthright, and the Buddha-like joy that we experienced as very young children. This becomes a spiritual yearning for completion, and, as in Plato's myth, we develop the profound conviction that finding the right person—that perfect mate—will complete us and make us whole. This special person can't be just anyone. It can't be the first man or woman who comes along with an appealing smile or a warm disposition. It has to be someone who stirs within us a deep sense of recognition: "This is the one I've been looking for! This is the one who will make up for the wounds of the past!" And for reasons we will explore in greater depth in the next chapter, this person is invariably someone who has both the positive and the negative traits of our parents!

YOUR IMAGO

In literature, as in love, we are astonished
at what is chosen by others.

—ANDRÉ MAUROIS

MANY PEOPLE HAVE A HARD TIME accepting the idea that they have searched for partners who resembled their caretakers. On a conscious level, they were looking for people with only positive traits—people who were, among other things, kind, loving, good-looking, intelligent, and creative. In fact, if they had an unhappy childhood, they may have deliberately searched for people who were radically different from their caretakers. They told themselves, "I'll never marry a drunkard like my father," or "There's no way I'm going to marry a tyrant like my mother." But, no matter what their conscious intentions, most people are attracted to mates who have their caretakers' positive *and* negative traits, and, typically, the negative traits are more influential.

I came to this sobering conclusion only after listening to hundreds of couples talk about their partners. At some point during the course of therapy, just about every person would turn angrily to his or her spouse and say, "You treat me just the way my mother did!" Or "You make me feel just as helpless and frustrated as my stepfather did!" This idea gained further validity when I assigned all my clients an exercise that asked them to compare the personality traits of their spouses with the personality traits of their primary caretakers. In most cases, there was a close correlation between parents and partners, and with few exceptions *the traits that matched up the most closely were the negative traits!* (You will be able to do this exercise yourself when you turn to Part III of this book, which includes all the exercises mentioned in this chapter and those that follow. I suggest that you read all of the text before you attempt the written work.)

Why do negative traits have such an appeal? If people chose mates on a logical basis, they would look for partners who compensated for their parents' inadequacies, rather than duplicated them. If your parents wounded you by being unreliable, for example, the sensible course of action would be to marry a dependable person, someone who would help you overcome your fear of abandonment. If your parents wounded you by being overprotective, the practical solution would be to look for someone who allowed you plenty of psychic space so that you could overcome your fear of absorption. The part of your brain that directed your search for a mate, however, was not your logical, orderly new brain; it was your time-locked, myopic old brain. And what your old brain was trying to do was re-create the conditions of your upbringing, in order to correct them. Having received enough nurturing to survive but not enough to feel satisfied, it was attempting to return to the scene of your original frustration so that you could resolve your unfinished business.[1]

SEARCH FOR THE LOST SELF

WHAT ABOUT YOUR OTHER UNCONSCIOUS DRIVE, your need to recover your lost self, those thoughts and feelings and behaviors that you had to repress to adapt to your family and to society? What kind of person would help you regain your sense of wholeness? Would it be someone who actively encouraged you to develop these missing parts? Would it be someone who shared your weaknesses and therefore made you feel less inadequate? Or, on the other hand, would it be someone who complemented your weaknesses? To find the answer, think for a minute about some part of your being that you feel is deficient. Maybe you feel that you lack artistic talent, or strong emotions, or, like Sarah in the last chapter, the ability to think clearly and rationally. Years ago, when you were around people who were especially strong in these areas, you probably were even more aware of your shortcomings. But if you managed to form an intimate relationship with one of these "gifted people," you experienced quite a different reaction. Instead of feeling awestruck or envious, you suddenly felt more complete. Being emotionally attached to this person—this is "my" boyfriend or "my" girlfriend—made his or her attributes feel a part of a larger, more fulfilled you. It was as if you had merged with the other person and become whole.

Look around you, and you will find ample evidence that people choose mates with complementary traits. Dan is glib and talkative; his wife, Gretchen, is thoughtful and introverted. Janice is an intuitive thinker; her husband, Patrick, is very logical. Rena is a dancer; her boyfriend, Matthew, has a stiff and rigid body. What people are doing in these yin/yang matches is trying to reclaim their lost selves by proxy.

The Imago

TO GUIDE YOU in your search for the ideal mate, someone who both resembled your caretakers and compensated for the repressed parts of yourself, you relied on an unconscious image of the opposite sex that you had been forming since birth. I have given this inner picture the name "imago," which is a Latin term for "image."[2] Essentially, your imago is a composite picture of the people who influenced you most strongly at an early age. This may have been your mother and father, one or more siblings, or maybe a baby-sitter or close relative. But whoever they were, a part of your brain recorded everything about them—the sound of their voices, the amount of time they took to answer your cries, the color of their skin when they got angry, the way they smiled when they were happy, the set of their shoulders, the way they moved their bodies, their characteristic moods, their talents and interests. Along with these impressions, your brain recorded all your significant interactions with them. Your brain didn't interpret these data; it simply etched them onto a template.

It may seem improbable that you have such a detailed record of your caretakers somewhere inside your head when you have only a dim recollection of those early years. In fact, many people have a hard time remembering anything that happened to them before the age of five or six—even dramatic events that should have made a deep impression. But scientists report that we have incredible amounts of hidden information in our brains. Neurosurgeons discovered this fact while performing brain surgery on patients who were under local anesthesia.[3] They stimulated portions of the patients' brains with weak electrical currents, and the patients were suddenly able to recall hundreds of forgotten episodes from childhood in astonishing detail. Our minds are vast storehouses of forgotten information. There are those who suggest that everything that we have ever experienced resides somewhere in the dark, convoluted recesses of our brains.

Not all of these experiences are recorded with equal intensity, however. The most vivid impressions seem to be the ones that we formed of our caretakers early in life. And of all the interactions that we had with these key people, the ones that were most deeply engraved were the ones that were the most wounding, because these were the encounters that seemed to threaten our existence. Gradually, over time, these hundreds of thousands of bits of information about our caretakers merged together to form a single image. The old brain, in its inability to make fine distinctions, simply filed all this information under one heading: the people responsible for our survival. You might think of the imago as a silhouette with few distinguishing physical characteristics but with the combined character traits of all of your primary caretakers.

To a large degree, whether or not you have been romantically attracted to someone depended on the degree to which that person matched your imago. A hidden part of your brain ticked and hummed, coolly analyzing that person's traits, and then compared them with your rich data bank of information. If there was little correlation, you felt no interest. This person was destined to be one of the thousands of people who come and go in your life with little impact. If there was a high degree of correlation, you found the person highly attractive.

This imago-matching process bears some resemblance to the way soldiers were trained to identify flying aircraft during World War II. The soldiers were given books filled with silhouettes of friendly and enemy aircraft. When an unidentified plane came into view, they hurriedly compared the plane with these illustrations. If it turned out to be a friendly plane, they relaxed and went back to their posts. If it was an enemy aircraft, they leaped into action. Unconsciously you have compared every man or woman that you have met to your imago. When you identified a close match, you felt a sudden surge of interest.

As with all aspects of the unconscious mind, you had no awareness of this elaborate sorting mechanism. The only way you can glimpse your imago is in dreams. If you reflect on your dreams, one thing you will notice is that your old brain capriciously merges people together. A dream that starts out with one person playing a part suddenly has another person filling that role; the unconscious has little regard for corporeal boundaries. You may be able to recall a dream where your spouse suddenly metamorphosed into your mother or father, or a dream in which your spouse and a parent played such similar roles or treated you in such a similar manner that they were virtually indistinguishable. This is the closest you will ever come to directly verifying the existence of your imago. But when you do the exercises in Part III and have a chance to compare the dominant character traits of your mate with the dominant character traits of your primary caretakers, the parallel that your unconscious mind draws between spouses and caretakers will become unmistakably clear.

THE IMAGO AND ROMANTIC LOVE

LET'S TAKE THIS INFORMATION about the imago and see how it adds to our earlier theories of romantic attraction. As an illustration, let me tell you about a client named Lynn and her search for love. Lynn is forty years old and has three school-age children. She lives in a mid-sized New England town, where she works for the city government. Peter, Lynn's husband, is a graphics designer.

In the initial counseling sessions I had with Lynn and Peter, I learned that Lynn's father had had a profound influence on her. Apparently he was a good provider and spared no expense in her behalf. But he could also be very insensitive. When he was, Lynn felt angry and threatened. She told me about the relentless way he would tickle her, even though he knew she hated it. When she finally broke down and cried, he would laugh at her and call her a crybaby. An incident that she will never forget is the time he threw her into a river to "teach her how to swim." When Lynn told me this story, her throat was tight and her hands gripped the seat of her chair. "How could he have done that?" she asked. "I was only four years old! I remember looking at my daughter when she was four years old and being amazed that he could have done that to me. It's such a trusting, vulnerable age."

Although she wasn't aware of it, Lynn had much earlier images of her father stored deep in her unconscious, ones that affected her even more deeply. As a hypothetical example, let's suppose that, when she was an infant, her father would neglect to warm the bottle when it was his turn to feed her, and she learned to associate lying in his arms with the shock of cold milk. Or maybe, when she was a few months old, he would toss her high into the air, misreading her frantic cries as an indication of excitement. She has no memory of incidents like these, but every one of her significant experiences with her father is recorded somewhere in her mind.

Lynn's mother was an equally potent source of images. On the plus side, she was generous with her time and attention and consistent with her discipline. Unlike Lynn's father, she was sensitive to her daughter's feelings. When she tucked Lynn into bed at night, she would ask her about her day and was sympathetic if Lynn reported any emotional difficulties. But Lynn's mother was also overly critical. Nothing Lynn said or did seemed to be quite good enough. Her mother was always correcting her grammar, combing her hair, double-checking her homework. Lynn felt on stage around her, and she had the feeling that she was always flubbing her lines.

Another important thing about her mother was that she was not comfortable with her own sexuality. Lynn remembers that her mother always wore long-sleeved blouses buttoned up to the top button and covered the blouses with loose, concealing sweaters. She never allowed anyone in the bathroom with her, even though the house had only one bathroom. When Lynn was a teenager, her mother never talked to her about menstruation, boyfriends, or sex. It's not surprising that one of Lynn's problems is that she is sexually inhibited.

Other people had a strong influence on Lynn, too, and one of them was her older sister, Judith. Judith, only fourteen months older, was her idol. Tall and talented, she seemed to succeed at everything she did. Lynn admired her older sister and wanted to spend as much time as possible around her, but when she did she always felt inferior.

Gradually the personality traits of these key people—Lynn's mother, her father, and her older sister—merged together in Lynn's unconscious mind to form a single image, her imago. Her imago was a picture of someone who was, among other things, affectionate, devoted, critical, insensitive, superior, and generous. The character traits that stood out in bold relief were the negative ones—the tendency to be critical, insensitive, and superior—because these were the ones that had wounded her; this is where she had unfinished business.

Lynn first met Peter at a friend's house. Her main memory of this meeting is that, when she was introduced to him, she looked in his face and felt as if she already knew him. It was a curious sensation. The next week she kept finding excuses to go over to her friend's house, and she was glad when Peter was there. Gradually she became aware of an even stronger attraction, and realized that she wasn't really happy unless she was around him. In these first encounters, Lynn wasn't consciously comparing Peter with anyone she knew—certainly not with her parents or her sister—she just found him a wonderfully appealing person who seemed easy to talk to.

In the course of their therapy, I grew to appreciate what a good imago match Peter was for Lynn. He was outgoing and confident, traits that he shared with Lynn's father and sister. But he also had a critical nature, like Lynn's mother. He kept telling Lynn that she should lose weight, loosen up, and be more playful at home—especially in bed—and be more assertive at work. The parent trait that was most marked in him, however, was his lack of compassion for her feelings, just like Lynn's father. Lynn had frequent bouts of depression, and Peter's advice to her was

"Talk less and do more. I'm tired of hearing about your problems!" This was consistent with his own approach to unhappy feelings, which was to cover them up with frantic activity.

Another reason Lynn was attracted to Peter was that he was so at home in his body. When I looked at the two of them, I was often reminded of the words of one of my professors: "If you want to know what kind of person a client is married to, imagine his or her opposite." Lynn would sit with her arms and legs crossed, while Peter would sprawl in his chair with complete abandon. Sometimes he would kick off his shoes and sit cross-legged. Other times he would swing one leg up and hook it across the arm of the chair. Lynn wore tailored clothes buttoned to the top button, or a business suit with a silk scarf knotted securely around her neck. Peter wore loose-fitting corduroy pants, shirts open at the neck, and loafers without socks.

Now we have some clues to why Lynn was attracted to Peter. Why was Peter attracted to Lynn? The fact that she had an emotional nature was one of the reasons. Although his parents had accepted Peter's body, they had rejected his feelings. When he was with Lynn, he felt more connected to his repressed emotions; she helped him regain contact with his lost self. In addition, she had numerous character traits that reminded him of his parents. Her sense of humor reminded him of his mother, and her dependent, self-effacing manner reminded him of his father. Because Lynn matched Peter's imago and Peter matched Lynn's, and because they had numerous complementary traits, they had "fallen in love."

The question that I'm frequently asked when I talk about the unconscious factors in mate selection is this: how can people tell so much about each other so quickly? While certain characteristics may be right on the surface—Peter's sexuality, for example, or Lynn's sense of humor—others are not so apparent.

The reason that we are such instant judges of character is that we rely on what Freud called "unconscious perception." We intuitively pick up much more about people than we are aware of. When we meet strangers, we instantly register the way they move, the way they seek or avoid eye contact, the clothes they wear, their characteristic expressions, the way they fix their hair, the ease with which they laugh or smile, their ability to listen, the speed at which they talk, the amount of time it takes them to respond to a question—we record all of these characteristics and a hundred more in a matter of minutes.

Just by looking at people, we can absorb vast amounts of information. When I walk to work each morning, I automatically appraise the people on the crowded Manhattan sidewalks. My judgment is instantaneous: this person is someone I wish I knew; that person is someone I have no interest in. I find myself attracted or repulsed with only a superficial glance. When I walk into a party, one glance around the room will often single out the people that I want to meet. Other people report similar experiences. A truck driver told me that he could tell whether or not he wanted to pick up a particular hitchhiker even though he was cruising at sixty-five miles an hour. "And I'm rarely wrong," he said.

Our powers of observation are especially acute when we are looking for a mate, because we are searching for someone to satisfy our fundamental unconscious drives. We subject everyone to the same intense scrutiny: is this someone who will nurture me and help me recover my lost self? When we meet someone who appears to meet these needs, the old brain registers instant interest. In all subsequent encounters, the unconscious mind is fully alert, searching for clues that this might indeed be the perfect mate. If later experiences confirm the imago match, our interest climbs even further. On the other hand, if later experiences show the match to be superficial, our interest plummets, and we look for a way to end or reduce the importance of the relationship.

Unbeknown to them, this was the psychological process that Lynn and Peter were engaged in when they met that day at a friend's house. Because Peter seemed to match Lynn's imago, she went out of her way to see him again. Because Lynn, in turn, was a reasonably good imago match for Peter, her interest was returned; this was not just another case of unrequited love. After a few weeks, Peter and Lynn had accumulated enough data about each other to realize that they were in love.

Not everyone finds a mate who conforms so closely to the imago. Sometimes only one or two key character traits match up, and the initial attraction is likely to be mild. Such a relationship is often less passionate and less troubled than those characterized by a closer match. The reason it is less passionate is that the old brain is still looking for the ideal "gratifying object," and the reason it tends to be less troubled is that there isn't the repetition of so many childhood struggles. When couples with weak imago matches terminate their relationships, it's often because they feel little interest in each other, not because they are in great pain. "There wasn't all that much going on," they say. Or "I just felt restless. I knew that there was something better out there."

At this point in our discussion of marriage, we have a more complete understanding of the mystery of romantic attraction. To the biological theory and the exchange theory and the persona theory discussed in chapter 1, we have added the idea of the unconscious search for a person who matches our imago. Our motivation for seeking an imago match is our urgent desire to heal childhood wounds. We also have new insight into marital conflict: if the primary reason we select our mates is that they resemble our caretakers, it is inevitable that they are going to reinjure some very sensitive wounds. But before we sink into this quagmire of pain and confusion called "the power struggle," I would like to focus on the ecstasy of romantic love, those first few months or years of a relationship when we are filled with the delicious expectation of wish fulfillment.

4

ROMANTIC LOVE

We two form a multitude.

— OVID

I KNOW FROM MY OWN EXPERIENCE, and from listening to others, that lovers believe their time together is special and separate from the experiences of all the other people of the world. It is a time they savor and return to in their memories again and again. When I ask couples to describe these idyllic first days to me, they describe a world transformed. People seemed friendlier, colors were brighter, food tasted better—everything around them shimmered with a pristine newness, just as it did when they were young.

But the biggest change was in the way they felt about themselves. Suddenly they had more energy and a healthier outlook on life. They felt wittier, more playful, more optimistic. When they looked in the mirror, they had a new fondness for the face that looked back at them—maybe they were worthy of their lovers' affection, after all. Some people felt so good about themselves that for a time they were even able to give up their substitute forms of gratification. They no longer needed to indulge themselves with sweets or drugs or alcohol, or tranquilize themselves with TV, or spice up their lives with recreational sex. Working overtime lost its appeal, and scrabbling after money and power seemed rather pointless. Life had meaning and substance, and it was standing right there beside them.

At the peak of their love relationships, these intense good feelings radiated outward, and people felt more loving and accepting of everyone. Some were even blessed with a heightened spiritual awareness, a feeling of inner unity and a sense of being connected with nature that they hadn't experienced since childhood. For a brief time, they saw the world not through the fractured lens of their split-off state but through the smooth, polished lens of their original nature.[1]

Lynn and Peter, the couple I introduced to you at the end of the previous chapter, told me that, when they were very much in love, they spent a day sightseeing in New York City. After dinner they impulsively took the elevator to the top of the Empire State Building so they could see the sun set from the observation deck. They held hands and looked down on the thousands of people milling below them with a feeling of compassion—how tragic that these people were not sharing their moment of ecstasy.

This timeless sentiment is beautifully expressed in a letter from Sophia Peabody to Nathaniel Hawthorne, dated December 31, 1839:[2]

Best Beloved,—
... What a year has this been to us! My definition of Beauty is, that it is love, and therefore includes both truth and good. But those only who love as we do can feel the significance and force of this.

My ideas will not flow in these crooked strokes. God be

with you. I am very well, and have walked far in Danvers this cold morning. I am full of the glory of the day. God bless you this night of the old year. It has proved the year of our nativity. Has not the old earth passed away from us?—are not all things new?

Your Sophie

The Chemistry of Love

WHAT CAUSES THE RUSH of good feeling that we call romantic love? Psychopharmacologists have learned that lovers are literally high on drugs—natural hormones and chemicals that flood their bodies with a sense of well-being.[3] During the attraction phase of a relationship, the brain releases dopamine and norepinephrine, two of the body's many neurotransmitters. These neurotransmitters help contribute to a rosy outlook on life, a rapid pulse, increased energy, and a sense of heightened perception. During this phase, when lovers want to be together every moment of the day, the brain increases its production of endorphins and enkephalins, natural narcotics, enhancing a person's sense of security and comfort. Dr. Michael R. Liebowitz, associate professor of clinical psychiatry at Columbia University, takes this idea one step further and suggests that the mystical experience of oneness that lovers undergo may be caused by an increase in the production of the neurotransmitter serotonin.

But, as intriguing as it is to look at love from a pharmacological point of view, scientists can't explain what causes the release of these potent chemicals, or what causes them to diminish. All they can do is document the fact that romantic love is an intense physical experience with measurable biological components. To gain additional insight, we need to return to the field of psychology, and to the view that romantic love is a creation of the unconscious mind.[4]

The Universal Language of Love

IN THE PREVIOUS CHAPTER, I offered an explanation of romantic love. The reason we have such good feelings at the beginning of a relationship, I asserted, is that a part of the brain believes that finally we have been given a chance to be nurtured and to regain our original wholeness. If we look in the right places, we can find plenty of evidence that this is indeed what happens. One place to look is in the universal language of lovers. By listening to popular songs, reading love poems, plays, and novels, and listening to hundreds of couples describe their relationships, I have come to the conclusion that all the words exchanged between lovers since time began can be reduced to four basic sentences—the rest is elaboration. And these four sentences offer a rare glimpse into the unconscious realm of romantic love.

The first of these sentences occurs early in a relationship, maybe during the first or second encounter, and it goes something like this: "I know we've just met, but somehow I feel as though I already know you." This isn't just a line lovers hand each other. For some unaccountable reason, they feel at ease with each other. They feel a comfortable resonance, almost as if they had known each other for years. *I call this the "phenomenon of recognition."*

Somewhat later, lovers get around to the second significant exchange of information. "This is peculiar," they say to each other, "but even though we've only been seeing each other for a short time, I can't remember when I didn't know you." Even though they met only a few days or weeks ago, it seems as though they've always been together; their relationship has no temporal boundaries. *I call this the "phenomenon of timelessness."*

When a relationship has had time to ripen, lovers look in each other's eyes and proclaim the third meaningful sentence: "When

I'm with you, I no longer feel alone; I feel whole, complete."
One of my clients, Patrick, expressed the feeling in these words:
"Before I knew Diane, I felt as though I had been spending all of
my life wandering around in a big house with empty rooms.
When we met, it was like opening a door and finding someone
home." Being together seemed to put an end to his relentless
search for completion. He felt fulfilled, filled up. *I call this the
"phenomenon of reunification."*

Finally, at some point, lovers utter a fourth and final declaration of love. They tell each other: "I love you so much, I can't
live without you." They have become so involved with each
other that they can't imagine a separate existence. *I call this the
"phenomenon of necessity."*

Whether lovers actually say words like these or merely experience the feelings behind them, they underscore what I have
been saying so far about romantic love and the nature of the unconscious.

The first sentence—in which lovers report an eerie sense of
recognition—loses some of its mystery when we recall that the
reason people "choose" their lovers is that the lovers resemble
their caretakers. No wonder they have a sense of déjà vu, a feeling of familiarity. On an unconscious level, they feel connected
once again with their caretakers, only this time they believe
their deepest, most fundamental, most infantile yearnings are
going to be satisfied. Someone is going to take care of them;
they are no longer going to be alone.

The second statement, "I can't remember when I didn't know
you," is a testimony to the fact that romantic love is an old-
brain phenomenon. When people fall in love, their old brain
fuses the image of their partners with the image of their caretakers, and they enter the realm of the eternal now. To the unconscious, being in an intimate love relationship is very much like
being an infant in the arms of your mother. There is the same illusion of safety and security, the same total absorption.

In fact, if we could observe a pair of lovers at this critical juncture of their relationship, we would make an interesting observation: the two of them are taking part in an instinctual bonding process that mimics the way mothers bond with their newborn infants. They coo, prattle, and call each other diminutive names that they would be embarrassed to repeat in public. They stroke, pet, and delight in every square inch of each other's bodies—"What a cute little navel!" "Such soft skin!"—just the way a mother adores her baby. Meanwhile, they add to the illusion that they are each other's surrogate parents by saying, "I'm going to love you the way nobody ever has," which the unconscious mind interprets to mean "more than Mommy and Daddy." Needless to say, the old brain revels in all of this delightfully regressive behavior. The lovers believe they are going to be healed—not by hard work or painful self-realization—but by the simple act of merging with someone the old brain has confused with their caretakers.

What about the third sentence—that feeling of wholeness and oneness that envelops lovers? When lovers tell each other, "When I'm with you, I feel whole, complete," they are acknowledging that they have unwittingly chosen someone who manifests the very parts of their being that were cut off in childhood; they have rediscovered their lost self. A person who grew up repressing his or her feelings will choose someone who is unusually expressive. A person who was not allowed to be at ease with his or her sexuality will choose someone who is sensual and free. When people with complementary traits fall in love, they feel as if they've suddenly been released from repression. Like Plato's truncated, androgynous beings, each of them had been half a person; now they are whole.

And what about that last sentence—the feeling that lovers have that they will die if they part? What can this tell us about the nature of romantic love? First, it documents the fact that lovers unknowingly transfer responsibility for their very survival from their parents to their partners. This same marvelous being who has awakened eros is now going to protect them from thanatos, the ever-present fear of death. By attending to their unmet childhood needs, their partners are going to become allies in their struggle for survival. On a deeper level, this sentence reveals the fear that, if the lovers were to part, they would lose their rediscovered sense of wholeness. They would once again be fractured, half-whole creatures, separated from the fullness of existence. Loneliness and anxiety would well up inside them, and they would no longer feel connected to the world around them. Ultimately, to lose each other would be to lose their new sense of self.

A BRIEF INTERLUDE

FOR A WHILE, however, these fears are held at bay, and to the lovers it seems as though romantic love is actually going to heal them and make them whole. Companionship alone is a soothing balm. Because they are spending so much time together, they no longer feel lonely or isolated. And as their level of trust increases, they deepen their level of intimacy. They may even talk about some of the pain and sorrow of their childhood, and if they do they are rewarded for their openness by their lovers' heartfelt sympathy: "Oh, I feel so sad that you had to go through that." "How awful that you had to suffer so much." They feel as if no one, not even their own parents, has cared so deeply about their inner world. As they share these intimacies, they may even experience moments of true empathic communion and become absorbed in each other's world. During these rare moments, they aren't judging each other, or interpreting what their lovers are saying, or even comparing their various experiences. They are doing much more: for a short time, they are letting go of their lifelong self-absorption and sharing in the reality of another human being.

But romantic love brings more than kind words and empathic

moments to heal their wounds. With a sixth sense that is often lamentably lacking in later stages of a relationship, lovers seem to divine exactly what their partners are lacking. If the partner needs more nurturing, they gladly play the role of Mommy or Daddy. If the partner wants more freedom, they grant him or her independence. If the partner needs more security, they become protective and reassuring. They shower each other with spontaneous acts of caring that seem to erase their earlier, childhood deprivations. Being in love is like suddenly becoming the favored child in an idealized family.

FOSTERING AN ILLUSION

FOR A WHILE, lovers cling to the illusion of romantic love. However, this requires a good deal of unconscious playacting. One bit of make-believe in which virtually all lovers engage is trying to appear to be more emotionally healthy than they really are. After all, if you don't appear to have many needs of your own, your partner is free to assume that your goal in life is to nurture, not to be nurtured, and this makes you very desirable indeed. One woman, Louise, described to me the efforts she went to to appear to be the perfect mate for her future husband, Steve. A few weeks after they met, Louise invited Steve over to her house for dinner. "I wanted to display my domestic talent," she said. "He saw me as a career woman, and I wanted him to see I could cook, too." To make her life seem as simple and uncomplicated as possible, she arranged to have her eleven-year-old son from a previous marriage stay the night with a friend—no reason to reveal all of life's complexities at this stage of the game. Then she thoroughly cleaned the house, planned the menu around the only two things she could cook really well—quiche and Roquefort salad—and arranged fresh flowers in all the rooms. When Steve walked into the house, dinner was ready, her makeup was fresh, and classical music was on the stereo. Steve, in turn, came as his most charming, helpful self, and when dinner was over he insisted on washing the dishes and fixing the broken porch light. That night they declared their love for each other, and for several months they were both able to orchestrate their lives so that they had few, if any, needs of their own.

This degree of make-believe is quite common; most of us go to a lot of trouble in the early stages of a relationship to appear to be ideal mates. In some cases, however, the deception is more extreme.

One of my clients, a woman I'll call Jessica, had a history of becoming involved with unreliable men. She had two failed marriages and a string of painful relationships. The relationship that finally convinced Jessica she needed therapy was with Brad, a man who at first seemed totally devoted to her. Once he had gained her trust, she told him all about her previous difficulties with men. Brad was sympathetic and assured her that he would never leave her. "If anyone leaves, it will be you," he said. "I will always be here." He seemed for all the world like a stable, trustworthy mate.

The two of them were together constantly for about six months, and Jessica began to relax into the security of the relationship. Then, one day, she came home from work to find a note from Brad pinned to the door. In the note he explained that he had been offered a higher-paying job in another town and couldn't turn it down. He had wanted to tell her about it in person, but he had been afraid she'd be too upset. He hoped that she would understand.

When Jessica recovered from shock, she called Brad's best friend and demanded that he tell her what he knew. As she listened to him talk, a shockingly different portrait of Brad began to emerge. Apparently he never stayed in one place very long. In the previous fifteen years, he had moved six times and been married three times. All this was news to Jessica. Sensing her need for security, Brad had done his best to appear to be a reliable lover. This is a psychological process known as "projective identification." He had unconsciously identified himself with Jessica's vision of the ideal man. My suspicion is that at first his subterfuge was well intentioned. He probably didn't begin the relationship with the purpose of gaining her trust and affection and then leaving her; he just couldn't keep up the charade.

When Brad left her, Jessica had every reason to fly into a rage, but instead she fabricated an illusion that he was planning to send for her as soon as he saved up some money. She stayed by the phone for hours in case he called, and waited anxiously for a letter. But she never heard from him again. "And I'm glad I didn't," she told me one day, "because I would have taken him back—no matter what he had done. That's how badly I needed him."

Jessica was demonstrating a classic case of denial; she was refusing to believe that Brad was in fact an immature, unreliable man. Her memory of the role he had obligingly played for her was more real to her than the truth of his actual behavior.

DENIAL

TO SOME DEGREE, we all use denial as a coping tool. Whenever life presents us with a difficult or painful situation, we have a tendency to want to ignore reality and create a more palatable fantasy. But there is no time in our lives when our denial mechanism is more fully engaged than in the early stages of our love relationships.

John, a man in his thirties who came to me for counseling, was particularly adept at denial. He was a computer programmer who had designed a software program that was so successful he used it to start his own company. For the first ten or fifteen minutes of each session, he would talk about his company and how well it was doing. Then the conversation would grind to a halt, he would avert his eyes, and he would get around to the real topic of conversation, which was Cheryl, the woman he loved. He was utterly bewitched by her and would marry her in a second if she would only say yes. But Cheryl kept refusing to make a commitment.

When John first met Cheryl, she appeared to be everything he wanted in a woman. She was attractive, intelligent, and delightfully sensual. But, a few months into the relationship, he began to be aware of some of her negative traits. When they went out to dinner, for example, he noticed that she always complained about the food or the service, no matter how good it was. He also noticed that she would complain endlessly about her job but would do nothing to improve her working conditions.

To avoid being put off by these negative traits, John engaged in strenuous mental gymnastics. When he went out to dinner with her, he would focus on her discriminating tastes, not on her complaining attitude. When she ranted and raved about her job, he thought about what a trooper she was to put up with such terrible working conditions. "Other people would have quit long ago," he told me with a note of pride.

The only thing that really bothered him about Cheryl was her unavailability. She always seemed to be pushing him away. The situation worsened after they had been seeing each other for about six months, when Cheryl demanded that he not see her during the week so that she could have "a little breathing room." John reluctantly agreed to her terms, even though he knew that one of the reasons she wanted this time off was so that she could date other men. She made it clear to him that he had no choice but to grant her more freedom.

As compensation, John started spending time with a woman named Patricia, who was very unlike Cheryl. Devoted, compliant, and patient, she was crazy about him. "She'd marry me in a minute," John told me one day, "just the way I'd marry Cheryl in a minute. But I don't care that much about Patricia. Even though she's nicer to be around, I never think about her when I'm away from her. It's almost as if she doesn't exist. Sometimes I feel that I'm taking advantage of her, but I don't like to be alone. She fills up the hole." Meanwhile, unavailable, critical Cheryl occupied his every waking moment. "Whenever I'm not thinking about work," he told me, "I'm dreaming about Cheryl."

Why was John so immune to Patricia's charms and so willing to overlook Cheryl's faults? It should come as no surprise that John's mother had a critical, distant nature, very much like Cheryl's. A worried look would often come over his mother's face, and she would tune him out. John had no idea what was going on in her mind. Like all children, he had no knowledge of—or interest in—his mother's subjective state. All he knew was that she was frequently unavailable to him and this filled him with anxiety. When he recognized that distracted look, he would become angry and strike out at her. She would push him away and send him to his room. If he became very angry at her, she would spank him and not talk to him for hours.

Eventually John learned to suffer in silence. He has a vivid memory of the day he learned to adopt a stoical attitude. His mother had yelled at him and spanked him with a hairbrush. He doesn't remember what had made her so angry. All he remembers is that he felt his punishment was unjustified, and he ran sobbing to his room. When he got to his room, he went into his closet and closed the door. The closet had a mirror on the inside of the door, and he remembers turning on the light and staring at his tear-streaked face. "Nobody cares that I'm in here crying," he told himself. "What good is it to cry?" After a while, he stopped crying and wiped away his tears. The remarkable thing is that he never cried again. That very day he began to cover over his sadness and his anger with an unchanging mask.

John's childhood experiences help explain his mysterious attraction to Cheryl. When Cheryl ignored his advances by going out with other men or by asking him not to call her for a few days, he was filled with the same primitive yearning for closeness that he had experienced with his mother. In fact, there was so much in common between the two women that on an unconscious level he could not distinguish between them. Cheryl's coldness activated in him the same intense longing he had felt for his mother. As far as his old brain was concerned, Cheryl *was* his mother, and his efforts to win her favor were a grownup version of the crying and yelling he had done as a child to attract his mother's attention. The psychological term for this case of mistaken identity is "transference," taking the attributes of one person and overlaying them on another. It is especially easy for people to transfer their feelings about their parents onto their partners, because, through a process of unconscious selection, they have chosen partners who resemble their caretakers. All they have to do is exaggerate the similarities between them and diminish the differences.

John had other reasons to be drawn to Cheryl besides her resemblance to his mother. Another source of his attraction was that she had an artistic flair. Since he was a rather "dull businessman" (his own words), her refined sense of aesthetics opened up whole new dimensions to him. "We'll be driving in the car and I'll have my head full of business plans," he told me, "and Cheryl will draw my attention to an interesting building or a beautiful tree, and it will suddenly materialize before my eyes. I wouldn't have seen it at all if she hadn't called it to my attention. It's almost as if she creates it. When I'm alone, my world seems gray and two-dimensional."

Something else about Cheryl that attracted him—though he would have vehemently denied it—was the fact that she had a caustic, critical nature. This dark side of her personality appealed to him for two reasons. First, as we've already discussed, it reminded him of his mother, who was an angry, emotional person. Second, and perhaps more important, Cheryl's bad temper helped him get in touch with his own denied emotions. Even though he had just as much anger as Cheryl, he had learned to mask his hostility behind a compliant, accepting manner. In childhood this had been a useful adaptation, because it protected him from his mother's temper. But now that he was an adult, this repression left him half a person. Without being able to feel and express strong emotions, he felt empty inside. He discovered that, when he was with Cheryl, he experienced a much-needed emotional catharsis. He didn't have to be angry himself—that would have aroused his superego, the parent-cop inside his head, which carried on his mother's prohibitions. Instead he could have the illusion of being a whole person once again just by associating himself with her.

Home Movies

"PROJECTION" IS THE TERM that describes the way John took a hidden part of himself—his anger—and attributed it to his lover. He projected his repressed anger onto Cheryl's visible anger. Like John, we project whenever we take a part of the disowned self or the lost self and send it out like a picture onto another person. We project all the time, not just in our primary love relationships. I remember one time in Dallas, when I was sharing a suite with a psychiatrist whose first name was James. We had an extra room, and we were looking for another person to share the rent. James had a friend who had finished medical school and was going into private practice, so he suggested that we consider him for a suite mate. Since that sounded fine to me, James agreed to invite his friend over so I could meet him.

A few days later, I opened my office door and happened to see a man walking down the hall. He was walking away from me, so all I saw was his back, but there was something about his walk that I found extremely irritating. He was swinging his hips and his head as if he owned the whole world. He sauntered instead of walked. "That has got to be one of the most arrogant men in the world," I told myself. "I wonder who that is. He must be a client of James's."

I went back into my room and forgot about the incident. A little while later, there was a knock at my door. It was James, and with him was the very man I had seen walking down the hall. "Harville," James said, "this is Robert Jenkins. He's the psychiatrist friend that I told you about who would like to rent the extra room. I thought that you and he might like to go out to lunch together."

I took a look at Robert and saw a man with a smiling, pleasant face. He had neatly trimmed hair, a well-groomed salt-and-pepper beard, horn-rimmed glasses, and large brown eyes. He reached out his hand to me. "Hello, Harville. I've heard so much about you. I hear you're involved in some really interesting things. I'd love to talk with you about it."

Such a nice, humble speech, I thought. Could this be the same man that I thought was so arrogant? Robert and I went out to lunch, and we had an interesting conversation. Later that day, I told James that I thought Robert would be an excellent person to share the suite with us. Eventually Robert became a good friend and a trusted colleague. Although he did have his prideful moments—just like me and everyone else I knew—the negative trait that had seemed so intense when I first saw him was really a part of me. I had taken the part of me that is arrogant—the part of me that does not fit with my image of myself as a sensitive, caring therapist—and thrust it onto Robert.

People in love are masters at projection. Some couples go through their whole marriages as if they were strangers sitting in a darkened movie theater, casting flickering images on each other. They don't even turn off their projectors long enough to see who it is that serves as the screen for their home movies. In just such a way, John projected his repressed anger onto Cheryl. Although she was indeed an angry person, he was also seeing in her a part of his own nature, a part of his being that was "ego-dystonic"—that is, incompatible with his self-image.

ROMANTIC LOVE DEFINED

IF WE WERE TO TRANSLATE John's love for Cheryl into dry psychological terms, it could be described as a mixture of denial, transference, and projection. John was "in love with Cheryl" because:

1. He had transferred his feelings about his mother onto her.
2. He had projected his hidden rage onto her visible rage.
3. He was able to deny the pain that she caused him.

He thought he was in love with a person, when in fact he was in love with an image projected upon that person. Cheryl was not a real person with needs and desires of her own; she was a resource for the satisfaction of his unconscious childhood longings. He was in love with the idea of wish fulfillment and—like Narcissus—with a reflected part of himself.

PSYCHE AND EROS

THE ILLUSORY NATURE of romantic love is beautifully illustrated in the myth of Psyche and Eros, an archetypal legend that was first recorded in the second century A.D.[5] According to this legend, the goddess Aphrodite was jealous of a beautiful young mortal named Psyche, and resented the adoration shown her by her countrymen. In a fit of pique, Aphrodite decreed that Psyche be carried to the top of a mountain, where she was to become the bride of a horrible monster (in some versions of the myth, this monster is called Death). Psyche's parents and the local villagers sadly escorted the young virgin up the mountain, chained her to a rock, and left her to her fate. But before Psyche could be claimed by the monster, the West Wind took pity on her and gently wafted her down the mountain to a valley that happened to be the home of Aphrodite's son, Eros, the god of love.

Psyche and Eros promptly fell in love, but Eros did not want Psyche to know that he was a god, so he kept his true identity concealed by coming to her only in darkness. At first Psyche agreed to this strange condition and enjoyed her new love, the splendid palace, and the beautiful grounds. Then, one day, her two sisters paid her a visit and, envious of her good fortune, began to ask prying questions about Eros. When Psyche couldn't answer them, they planted the suspicion in her mind that her lover might be a loathsome serpent intent on devouring her.

That night, before Eros came to her, Psyche hid a lamp and a sharp knife under their bed. If her lover turned out to be an evil creature, she was determined to lop off his head. She waited until Eros was sound asleep, then quietly lit the lamp. But as she leaned over to get a closer look at him, a drop of hot oil spilled from the lamp onto his shoulder. Eros quickly awoke and, when he saw the lamp and the knife, flew out the open window, vowing to punish Psyche for discovering the truth by leaving her forever. In anguish, Psyche ran after him, crying out his name, but she couldn't keep up with him and tripped and fell. Instantly the heavenly palace and the exquisite countryside vanished, and she was once more chained to a rock on the lonely, craggy mountaintop.

As with all fairy tales, there is truth to this legend. Romantic love does indeed thrive on ignorance and fantasy. As long as lovers maintain an idealized, incomplete view of each other, they live in a Garden of Eden. But the myth also contains some fiction. When Psyche lit the lamp and saw Eros clearly for the first time, she discovered that he was a magnificent god with golden wings. When you and I lit our lamps and took our first objective look at our lovers, we discovered that they weren't gods at all—they were imperfect humans, full of warts and blemishes, all those negative traits that we had steadfastly refused to see.

THE POWER STRUGGLE

I can't live either without you or with you.

— OVID

WHEN DOES ROMANTIC LOVE END and the power struggle begin? As in all attempts to map human behavior, it's impossible to define precisely when these stages occur. But for most couples there is a noticeable change in the relationship about the time they make a definite commitment to each other. Once they say, "Let's get married" or "Let's get engaged" or "Let's be primary lovers, even though we still see other people," the pleasing, inviting dance of courtship draws to a close, and lovers begin to want not only the expectation of need fulfillment—the illusion that was responsible for the euphoria of romantic love—but the reality as well. Suddenly it isn't enough that their partners be affectionate, clever, attractive, and fun-loving. They now have to satisfy a whole hierarchy of expectations, some conscious, but most hidden from their awareness.

What are some of these expectations? As soon as they start

living together, most people assume that their mates will conform to a very specific but rarely expressed set of behaviors. For example, a man may expect his new bride to do the housework, cook the meals, shop for groceries, wash the clothes, arrange the social events, take on the role of family nurse, and buy everyday household items. In addition to these traditional role expectations, he has a long list of expectations that are peculiar to his own upbringing. On Sundays, for example, he may expect his wife to cook a special breakfast while he reads the Sunday paper, and then join him for a leisurely stroll in the park. This is the way his parents spent their Sundays together, and the day wouldn't feel "right" unless it echoed these dominant chords.

Meanwhile, his wife has an equally long, and perhaps conflicting, set of expectations. In addition to wanting her husband to be responsible for all the "manly" chores, such as taking care of the car, paying the bills, figuring the taxes, mowing the lawn, and overseeing minor and major home repairs, she may expect him to help with the cooking, shopping, and laundry as well. Then, she, too, has expectations that reflect her particular upbringing. An ideal Sunday for her may include going to church, going out to a restaurant for brunch, and spending the afternoon visiting relatives. Since neither of them shared expectations before getting married, these could develop into a significant source of tension.

But far more important than these conscious or semiconscious expectations are the unconscious ones people bring to marriage, and the primary one is that their partners, the ones they've winnowed out of long lists of candidates, are going to love them the way their parents never did.[1] Their partners are going to do it all—satisfy unmet childhood needs, complement lost self-parts, nurture them in a consistent and loving way, and be eternally available to them. These are the same expectations that fueled the excitement of romantic love, but now there is less of a desire to reciprocate. After all, people don't get married to take care of their partner's needs—they get married to further their own psychological and emotional growth. Once a relationship seems secure, a psychological switch is triggered deep in the old brain that activates all the latent infantile wishes. It is as if the wounded child within takes over. Says the child, "I've been good enough long enough to ensure that this person is going to stay around for a while. Let's see the payoff." So husbands and wives take a big step back from each other and wait for the dividends of togetherness to start rolling in.

The change may be abrupt or gradual, but at some point husbands and wives wake up to discover that they've migrated to a colder climate. Now there are fewer back rubs; shorter, more cryptic love notes; less lovemaking. Their partners have stopped looking for excuses to be with them and are spending more time reading, watching television, socializing with friends, or just plain daydreaming.

WHY HAVE YOU CHANGED?

THIS BLEAK RATIONING OF LOVE is partly the result of a disturbing revelation. At some point in their relationships, most people discover that some aspect of their partners' character, a personality trait they once thought highly desirable, is beginning to annoy them. A man finds that his wife's conservative nature— one of the primary reasons he was attracted to her—is now making her seem staid and prudish. A woman discovers that her husband's tendency to be quiet and withdrawn—a trait she once thought was an indication of his spiritual nature—is making her feel lonely and isolated. A man finds his wife's impulsive, outgoing personality—once so refreshing—is now making him feel invaded.

What is the explanation for these disturbing reversals? If you will recall, in our desire to be spiritually whole—to be as complete and perfect as God had intended—we chose marriage partners who made up for the parts of our being that were split off in childhood. We each found someone who compensated for our lack of creativity or inability to think or to feel. Through union with our partners, we felt connected to a hidden part of ourselves. At first this arrangement seemed to work. But as time passed, our partners' complementary traits began to stir up feelings and attributes in us that were still taboo.

To see how this drama plays out in real life, let's continue with the story of John, the successful businessman from the previous chapter who was spending time with Patricia but desperately wanting to be with Cheryl. John came in for a therapy session one day in an ebullient mood. This time he didn't spend the customary fifteen minutes talking about his software business; he plunged right in and told me his good news. Cheryl, in a rare, conciliatory gesture, had decided to let him move in with her for a six-month trial period. This was the answer to his dreams.

John's euphoria lasted several months, during which time he decided that he no longer needed therapy. (As is true for most of my clients, he had little interest in working on his problems as long as he was feeling happy.) But one day he called and asked for an appointment. When he came in he reported that he and Cheryl were beginning to have difficulties. One of the things he mentioned was that Cheryl's vibrant personality was beginning to grate on him. He could tolerate her "emotional excesses" (as he now described them) when she directed them at others—for example, when she was berating a clerk or talking excitedly with a girlfriend—but when she beamed her high-voltage emotions at him, he had a fleeting sensation of panic. "I feel like my brain is about to short-circuit," he told me.

The reason John was feeling so anxious around Cheryl was that she was beginning to stir his own repressed anger. At first being around her had given him the comforting illusion that he was in touch with his feelings. But after a time her free emotional state stimulated his own feelings to such a degree that they threatened to emerge. His superego, the part of his brain that was carrying out his mother's injunction against anger, sent out frantic error messages warning him to keep his repression intact. John tried to reduce his anxiety by dampening Cheryl's personality: "For God's sake, Cheryl! Don't be so emotional! You're behaving like an idiot." And "Calm down, and then talk to me. I can't understand a word that you're saying." The very character trait that had once been so seductive to him was now perceived by his own brain as a threat to his existence.

In a similar way, there probably came a time in your marriage when you began to wish that your partner was less sexy or less fun-loving or less inventive—somehow less whole—because these qualities called forth repressed qualities in you, and your hidden self was threatening to make an unscheduled reappearance. When it did, it ran headlong into the internal police force that had severed those self parts in the first place, and you were filled with anxiety. This was such an unpleasant experience that you may have tried to repress your partner the same way your parents repressed you. In an effort to protect your existence, you were trying to diminish your partner's reality.

Your growing discomfort with your partner's complementary traits was only part of the rapidly brewing storm. Your partner's negative traits, the ones that you had resolutely denied during the romantic phase of your relationship, were also beginning to come into sharp focus. Suddenly your partner's chronic depression or drinking problem or stinginess or lack of responsibility became evident. This gave you the sickening realization that not only were you not going to get your needs met, but your partner was destined to wound you in the very same way you were wounded in childhood!

A GLIMPSE AT A PAINFUL REALITY

I MADE THIS PAINFUL DISCOVERY early on in my first marriage—in fact, on the second day of our honeymoon. My new bride and I were spending a week on an island off the shores of South Georgia. We were walking along the beach. I was poking through piles of driftwood, and my wife was down by the water, two or three hundred feet in front of me, head down, totally absorbed in the task of looking for shells. I happened to glance up and saw her silhouetted against the rising sun. To this day I can remember exactly what she looked like. She had her back to me. She was wearing black shorts and a red top. Her shoulder-length blonde hair was blowing in the wind. As I gazed at her, I noticed a slight droop to her shoulders. At that instant I felt a jolt of anxiety. This was immediately followed by the sick, sinking realization that I had married the wrong person. It was a strong feeling—I had to check an impulse to run back to the car and drive away. While I was standing there transfixed, my wife turned to me, waved, and smiled. I felt as though I were awakening from a nightmare. I waved back and rushed up to meet her.

It was as if a veil had lifted for a moment, and then dropped back down. It took me years to figure out exactly what had happened. The connection was finally made one day while I was in therapy. My therapist was guiding me through a regressive exercise, an exercise designed to take me back to my childhood, and with his help I was able to picture myself playing on the floor in my mother's kitchen. I was only one or two years old. I visualized my mother busy at the stove, with her back to me. This must have been a typical scene, because I was her ninth child, and she probably spent four or five hours a day in the kitchen, cooking and cleaning. I could see my mother's back quite clearly. She was standing at the stove wearing a print dress, and she had apron strings tied around her waist. She was tired and depressed and her shoulders sagged.

As an adult viewing this imaginary scene, I was flooded with the awareness that she didn't have any physical or emotional energy for me. My father had died only a few months before from a head injury, and she was left alone with her grief, very little money, and a houseful of children to look after. I felt like an unwanted child. Not that my mother didn't love me—she was an affectionate, caring woman—but she was physically and emotionally worn out. She was so wrapped up in her own worries, she could only look after me mechanically.

This was a new discovery for me. Until that point in my therapy, I had attributed my anxiety to the fact that both my parents had died by the time I was six years old. But that day I learned that my feelings of abandonment had started much earlier. In my regressed state, I called to my mother, but she would not answer. I sat in the psychiatrist's office and cried in deep pain. Then I had a second revelation. I suddenly realized what had happened to me that day on my honeymoon. When I had seen my wife so far away from me, so absorbed in herself, and with the same slump to her shoulders, I had had the eerie premonition that my marriage was going to be a repetition of my early days with a depressed mother. The emptiness of the early days of my childhood was going to continue. It had been too much for me to absorb, and I had quickly drawn the curtain.

At some point in their marriages, most people discover that something about their husbands or wives awakens strong memories of childhood pain. Sometimes the parallels are obvious. A woman with abusive parents, for example, may discover a violent streak in her spouse. A man with alcoholic parents may wake up to find himself married to an incipient alcoholic or drug addict. A woman who grew up in a contorted Oedipal relationship with her parents may be enraged to discover that her husband is having a secret affair.

But the similarities between parents and partners are often subtler. This was the case for Bernard and Kathryn, clients of mine who had been married for twenty-eight years. Bernard was a manager of a public utility; Kathryn was going back to school to get a degree in counseling. They had three children and one grandchild.

One evening as they walked into my office for their weekly appointment, they both looked downtrodden and defeated. I guessed right away that they had recently had one of the "core" scenes, a fight that they had had over and over again throughout the last twenty years of their marriage in countless subtle variations. Most couples have such a core scene, a fight they have so many times that they know their parts by heart.

They told me that the fight had taken place while they were decorating the house for Christmas. Bernard had been characteristically quiet, absorbed in his own thoughts, and Kathryn had been issuing orders. All three of their children and their spouses were coming to stay for the holidays, and Kathryn wanted everything to be perfect. Bernard dutifully performed whatever task was asked of him and went on pondering his own thoughts. After an hour or so, his silence became deafening to Kathryn, and she tried to involve him in a conversation about their children. He volunteered only a few sentences. She became more and more annoyed with him. Finally she lashed out at him for the way he was hanging the lights on the tree: "Why don't you pay attention to what you're doing? I may as well do it myself!" Bernard let her tirade wash over him, then calmly turned and walked out the back door.

Kathryn went to the kitchen window. As she watched the garage door close behind Bernard, she was filled with two primal emotions: fear and anger. Anger was uppermost: this time she wasn't going to let him retreat. She marched out after him and threw open the garage door. "For God's sake! Why don't you help me? You're always locked up in the garage. You never help me when I need you. What's the matter with you?"

To a therapist, Kathryn's use of global words like "always" and "never" would have been a clear indication that she was in a regressive state. Young children have a hard time distinguishing between past and present; whatever is happening at this moment has always happened in the past and will always happen in the future. But Bernard was not a therapist. He was her beleaguered husband, and he had just escaped from a torrent of criticism in the hopes of finding peace and quiet. His old brain responded to her attack—which in reality was nothing more than an adult version of the infant's cry—with a counterattack. "Maybe I'd help you more if you weren't so bitchy!" he retorted. "You're always hounding me. Can't I be alone for five minutes?" He seethed with anger, and Kathryn burst into tears.

As an outsider, I could easily see the step-by-step evolution of their arguments. The trigger for the fights was almost always the fact that Bernard was withdrawn. Trying to get some response from him, Kathryn would nag. Bernard would pay no attention to her until he had had all that he could stand; then he would go to another room to try to find peace and quiet. At that point Kathryn would explode in rage and Bernard would respond in kind. Finally Kathryn would burst into tears.

When they were through recounting this latest episode, I asked Kathryn to remember exactly how she had felt working on the holiday preparations with her unresponsive husband. She sat quietly for a moment, struggling to recall her feelings. Then she looked up at me with a puzzled expression and said, "I felt scared. It scared me that he wouldn't talk to me." For the first time she realized that she was actually afraid of his silences.

"What were you afraid of, Kathryn?" I asked her.

She answered quickly. "I was afraid he was going to hurt me."

Bernard looked over at her with wide-open eyes. I said, "Let's check this out with Bernard. Bernard, were you standing in the kitchen thinking about hurting Kathryn?"

"Hurting her?" he said, his surprise evident. "Hurting her?! I have never touched her in my life. I was just thinking my own thoughts. If I remember correctly, I was worrying about the fact that we would need to put a new roof on the house in the spring because of the leak. And I was probably thinking about something at the office."

"Really?" asked Kathryn. "You weren't mad at me that day?"

"No! Sure, I got annoyed when you kept criticizing me, but all I wanted to do was get away. I kept thinking about how nice it would be to be out in the garage working on my own projects instead of being nagged at all the time."

"Well, the way I see it, you're always angry at me, and eventually you can't hold it in any longer, so you blow up."

"I do blow up, but it takes about two or three hours of your nagging before I do! Anybody would get angry at that. I don't start out being angry at you."

This checked out with me. Bernard did not seem to be a violent man.

"Kathryn," I said to her, "for a moment I want you to close your eyes and think some more about what makes you afraid when Bernard doesn't respond to you."

After half a minute she replied, "I don't know. It's just the silence." She was having a hard time coming up with additional insight.

"Well, stay with that thought for a moment and try to recall something about silence in your childhood. Close your eyes."

The room was quiet. Then Kathryn gasped and opened her eyes. "It's my father! I've never seen that before. He used to sink into a deep depression and not talk for weeks. Whenever he was in one of those moods, I knew not to bother him, because, if I did one thing wrong, he would hit me. When I saw him start to sink into a depression, I would panic. I knew that I was in for a hard time."

Kathryn's father and her husband shared an important personality trait—they both were prone to long periods of silence—and this undoubtedly was one of the reasons that

Kathryn was attracted to Bernard. She had chosen someone who resembled her father so she could resolve her childhood fear of being abused. She didn't marry a talkative, outgoing person—she found someone who had her father's *negative traits* so she could re-create her childhood and continue her struggle for consistent love and kindness. But Bernard resembled Kathryn's father only superficially. He was silent because he was an introvert, not because he was depressed and given to anger. It was Kathryn's constant nagging that provoked her husband.

I have found this phenomenon in many of my clients. They react to their partners as if they were carbon copies of their parents, even though not all of their traits are the same. In their compelling need to work on unfinished business, they project the missing parental traits onto their partners. Then, by treating their partners as if they actually had these traits, they manage to provoke the desired response. A colleague of mine claims that people either "pick imago matches, project them, or provoke them."

HOME MOVIES, PART II

SO FAR IN THIS CHAPTER, we've talked about two factors that fuel the power struggle:

1. Our partners make us feel anxious by stirring up forbidden parts of ourselves.
2. Our partners have or appear to have the same negative traits as our parents, adding further injury to old wounds and thereby awakening our unconscious fear of death.

Now there is a third and final aspect of the power struggle that deserves our attention. In the previous chapter, I talked about the fact that many of our joyful feelings of romantic love come from projecting positive aspects of our imago onto our partners; in other words, we look at our partners and see all the good things about Mom and Dad and all the good but repressed parts of our own being. In the power struggle, we keep the movie projectors running, only we switch reels and begin to project our denied negative traits!

In chapter 2, I defined these denied negative traits as the "disowned self." If you will recall, I talked about the fact that all people have a dark side to their nature, a part of their being that they try to ignore. For the most part, these are creative adaptations to childhood wounds. People also acquire negative traits by observing their parents. Even though they may not like certain things about their parents, they "introject" these traits through a process called "identification." A father's judgmental nature and a mother's tendency to belittle herself, for example, become traits passed on to the children. But as the children become more self-aware, they recognize that these are the very traits they dislike in their parents, and they do their best to deny them.

Now, this is where it gets interesting. Not only do the children manifest these negative traits themselves—although disowned and thus out of awareness—but when they grow up they also look for these traits in potential mates, for they are an essential part of their imagos. *The imago is not only an inner image of the opposite sex; it is also a description of the disowned self.*

A case history might help you understand this curious and complex psychological phenomenon. I spent many years working with a young woman named Lillian. Lillian's parents divorced when she was nine years old, and her mother gained custody of both Lillian and her twelve-year-old sister, June. A year after the divorce, her mother married a man who did not get along with June. The stepfather yelled at her constantly, punishing even the smallest transgression. Several times a week his rage would escalate, and he would take the girl into her room and spank her with a belt. Lillian would stand outside the door, listening to the blows from the belt and shaking with anger and fear. She detested her stepfather. Yet, to Lillian's dismay, when she was left alone with her sister, she began to treat her with almost equal disdain. She would even call her some of the very same hurtful names she heard her stepfather use.

The fact that she was capable of hurting her sister was so painful to Lillian that she repressed these episodes. It was only after a year of therapy that she could remember those times, and it was even longer before she trusted me enough to tell me about them. When she did, I was able to help her see that it was human nature for her to absorb both the positive *and the negative* traits of her stepfather. He was the dominant influence in the household, and her unconscious mind registered the fact that the person who was most angry happened to be the most powerful. Anger and derision, therefore, must be a valuable survival skill. Gradually this character trait wormed its way into Lillian's basically kind nature.

When Lillian grew up and married, it was inevitable that she would fall in love with someone who had some of her stepfather's characteristics, notably his violent anger, because this was the part of him that had been so threatening to her. In fact, the reason she came in for therapy was that her husband had physically abused her.

After two years of therapy, she was able to see that the anger she had found so detestable in her stepfather was one of the unconscious factors behind her attraction to her husband, and— even more alarming—was also a denied part of her own personality. This particular imago trait, therefore, was not only a description of her husband but also a description of a disowned part of herself.

I see a similar tendency in virtually every love relationship. People try to exorcise their denied negative traits by projecting them onto their mates. Or, to put it another way, they look at their partners and criticize all the things they dislike and deny in themselves. Taking a negative trait and attributing it to their partners is a remarkably effective way to obscure a not-so-desirable part of the self.

Now we have defined the three major sources of conflict that make up the power struggle. As the illusion of romantic love slowly erodes, husbands and wives begin to:

1. Stir up each other's repressed behaviors and feelings.
2. Reinjure each other's childhood wounds.
3. Project their own negative traits onto each other.

All of these interactions are unconscious. All people know is that they feel confused, angry, anxious, depressed, and unloved. And it is only natural that they blame all this unhappiness on their partners. *They* haven't changed—they're the same people they used to be! It's their partners who have changed!

WEAPONS OF LOVE

IN DESPAIR, people begin to use negative tactics to force their partners to be more loving. They withhold their affection and become emotionally distant. They become irritable and critical. They attack and blame: "Why don't you . . . ?" "Why do you always . . . ?" "How come you never . . . ?" They fling these verbal stones in a desperate attempt to get their partners to be warm and responsive—or to express whatever positive traits are in their imagos. They believe that, if they give their partners enough pain, the partners will return to their former loving ways.

What makes people believe that hurting their partners will make them behave more pleasantly? Why don't people simply tell each other in plain English that they want more affection or attention or lovemaking or freedom or whatever it is that they are craving? I asked that question out loud one day as I was conducting a couples workshop. It wasn't just a rhetorical question; I didn't have the answer. But it just so happened that, a few minutes before, I had been talking about babies and their instinctual crying response to distress. All of a sudden I had the answer. Once again our old brains were to blame. When we were babies, we didn't smile sweetly at our mothers to get them to take care of us. We didn't pinpoint our discomfort by putting it into words. We simply opened our mouths and screamed. And it didn't take us long to learn that, the louder we screamed, the quicker they came. The success of this tactic was turned into an "imprint," a part of our stored memory about how to get the world to respond to our needs: "When you are frustrated, provoke the people around you. Be as unpleasant as possible until someone comes to your rescue."

This primitive method of signaling distress is characteristic of most couples immersed in a power struggle, but there is one example that stands out in my mind. A few years ago I was seeing a couple who had been married about twenty-five years. The husband was convinced that his wife was not only selfish but also vindictive. "She never thinks of me," he complained, listing numerous ways his wife ignored him. Meanwhile, his wife sat in her chair and shook her head in mute disagreement. As soon as he was through, she leaned forward in her chair and said to me in a strong and earnest voice, "Believe me, I do everything I can to please him. I spend more time with him; I spend less time with him. I even learned how to ski this winter, thinking that would make him happy—and I hate the cold! But nothing seems to work."

To help end the stalemate, I asked the husband to tell his wife one specific thing that she could do that would make him feel better—one practical, doable, measurable activity that would help him feel more loved. He hemmed and hawed and then said with a growl, "If she's been married to me for twenty-five years and still doesn't know what I want, then she hasn't been paying any attention! She just doesn't care about me!"

This man, like the rest of us, was clinging to a primitive view of the world. When he was an infant lying in the cradle, he experienced his mother as a large creature leaning over him, trying to intuit his needs. He was fed, clothed, bathed, and nurtured, even though he could not articulate a single need. A crucial lesson learned in the preverbal stage of his development left an indelible imprint on his mind: other people were supposed to figure out what he needed and give it to him without his having to do anything more than cry.[2] Whereas this arrangement worked fairly well when he was a child, in adulthood his needs were a great deal more complex. Furthermore, his wife was not a devoted mother hovering over his crib. She was an equal, with—much to his surprise—needs and expectations of her own. And although she wanted very much to make him happy, she didn't know what to do. Lacking this information, she was forced to play a grown-up version of pin-the-tail-on-the-donkey: "Is this what you want? Is this?"

When partners don't tell each other what they want and constantly criticize each other for missing the boat, it's no wonder that the spirit of love and cooperation disappears. In its place comes the grim determination of the power struggle, in which each partner tries to force the other to meet his or her needs. Even though their partners react to these maneuvers with renewed hostility, they persevere. Why? Because in their unconscious minds they fear that, if their needs are not met, they will die. This is a classic example of what Freud called the "repetition compulsion," the tendency of human beings to repeat ineffective behaviors over and over again.

Some couples stay in this angry, hostile state forever. They hone their ability to pierce each other's defenses and damage each other's psyches. With alarming frequency, the anger erupts into violence. According to recent studies, between twenty-six and thirty million spouses are abused each year; up to fifty percent of all American wives have been hit by their husbands.[3]

STAGES OF THE POWER STRUGGLE

WHEN YOU ARE IMMERSED in the power struggle, life seems chaotic. You have no reference points. You have no sense of when it all started or how it will end. But from a distant perspective the power struggle can be seen to follow a predictable course, one that happens to parallel the well-documented stages of grief in a dying or bereaved person.[4] But this death is not the death of the real person; it's the death of the illusion of romantic love.

First comes the shock, that horrifying moment of truth when a window opens and a wrenching thought invades your consciousness: "This is not the person I thought I had married." At that instant you assume that married life is going to be a continuation of the loneliness and pain of childhood; the long-anticipated healing is not to be.

After the shock comes denial. The disappointment is so great that you don't allow yourself to see the truth. You do your best to see your partner's negative traits in a positive light. But eventually the denial can no longer be sustained, and you feel betrayed. Either your partner has changed drastically since the days when you were first in love, or you have been deceived all along about his or her true nature. You are in pain, and the degree of your pain is the degree of the disparity between your earlier fantasy of your partner and your partner's emerging reality.

If you stick it out beyond the angry stage of the power struggle, some of the venom drains away, and you enter the fourth stage, bargaining. This stage goes something like this: "If you will give up your drinking, I will be more interested in sex." Or "If you let me spend more days sailing, I will spend more time with the children." Marriage therapists can unwittingly prolong this stage of the power struggle if they help couples negotiate behavioral contracts without getting to the root of the problem.[5]

The last stage of the power struggle is despair. When couples reach this final juncture, they no longer have any hopes of finding happiness or love within the relationship; the pain has gone on too long. At this point, approximately half the couples withdraw the last vestiges of hope and file for divorce. Most of those who stay married create what is called a "parallel" marriage and try to find all their happiness outside the relationship. A very few, perhaps as few as five percent of all couples, find a way to resolve the power struggle and go on to create a deeply satisfying relationship.[6]

For the sake of clarity, I would like to reduce the discussion in these first five chapters to its simplest form. First of all, we choose our partners for two basic reasons: (1) they have both the positive and the negative qualities of the people who raised us, and (2) they compensate for positive parts of our being that were cut off in childhood. We enter the relationship with the unconscious assumption that our partner will become a surrogate parent and make up for all the deprivation of our childhood. All we have to do to be healed is to form a close, lasting relationship.

After a time we realize that our strategy is not working. We are "in love," but not whole. We decide that the reason our plan is not working is that our partners are deliberately ignoring our needs. They know exactly what we want, and when and how we want it, but for some reason they are deliberately withholding it from us. This makes us angry, and for the first time we begin to see our partners' negative traits. We then compound the problem by projecting our own denied negative traits onto them. As conditions deteriorate, we decide that the best way to force our partners to satisfy our needs is to be unpleasant and irritable, just as we were in the cradle. If we yell loud enough and long enough, we believe, our partners will come to our rescue. And, finally, what gives the power struggle its toxicity is the underlying unconscious belief that, if we cannot entice, coerce, or seduce our partners into taking care of us, we will face the fear greater than all other fears—the fear of death.

What may not be immediately apparent in this brief summary is this: there is really very little difference between romantic love and the power struggle. On the surface, these first two stages of marriage appear to be worlds apart. A couple's delight in each other has turned to hatred, and their goodwill has degenerated into a battle of wills. But what's important to note is that the underlying themes remain the same. Both individuals are still searching for a way to regain their original wholeness, and they are still holding on to the belief that their partners have the power to make them healthy and whole. The main difference is that now the partner is perceived as withholding love. This requires a switch in tactics, and husbands and wives begin to hurt each other, or deny each other pleasure and intimacy, in hopes of having their partners respond with warmth and love.

What is the way out of this labyrinth of confusion? What lies beyond the power struggle? In the next chapter, "Becoming Conscious," we will talk about a new kind of relationship, "the conscious marriage," and show how it helps husbands and wives begin to satisfy each other's childhood longings.

part II

THE CONSCIOUS MARRIAGE

6

BECOMING CONSCIOUS

Seldom or never does a marriage develop into
an individual relationship smoothly without crisis.
There is no birth of consciousness without pain.

— C. G. JUNG

SCANNING THE FIRST FIVE CHAPTERS, it would be easy to
get the impression that the old brain is the cause of most of our
marriage problems. It's the old brain that causes us to choose
partners who resemble our caretakers. It's the old brain that is
the source of all our elaborate defenses—the projections, transferences, and introjections—that obscure the reality of ourselves and our partners. And it's the old brain that is responsible
for our infantile response to frustration, the "cry-or-criticize"
response that only results in further alienation.

But the old brain also plays a positive role in marriage. Although some of the tactics of the old brain may be self-defeating,
its fundamental drives are essential to our well-being. Our unconscious drive to repair the emotional damage of childhood is
what allows us to realize our spiritual potential as human beings,
to become complete and loving people capable of nurturing

others. And even though our projections and transferences may temporarily blind us to our partners' reality, they're also what *binds* us to them, setting up the preconditions for future growth.

The problem with the old brain is that it's unguided; it's like a blind animal trying to find its way to the watering hole. To achieve the valid and important objectives of the old brain, we need to enlist the aid of the new brain—the part of us that makes choices, exerts will, knows that our partners are not our parents, that today is not always, and that yesterday is not today. We need to take the rational skills that we use in other parts of our lives and bring them to bear on our love relationships. Once we forge a working alliance between the powerful, instinctual drives of the old brain and the discriminating, cognitive powers of the new brain, we can begin to realize our unconscious goals. Through the marriage of old-brain instincts and new-brain savvy, we can gradually leave the frustrations of the power struggle behind us.

New Brain–Old Brain Merger

HOW WOULD MARRIED LIFE BE different if the new brain played a more active role? Here's an example of a typical interaction between a husband and wife and how it might be handled in an unconscious marriage, a typical love relationship dominated by old-brain reactivity, and in a conscious marriage, a relationship where the old brain is tempered by reason.

Imagine that you are happily eating breakfast, and your spouse suddenly criticizes you for burning the waffles. Your old brain, the perpetual guardian of your safety, instantly prompts you to fight or flee. It cares not that the person who criticized you is your spouse; all it cares about is that you're under attack. Unless you interfere with your automatic old-brain response, you will immediately return your partner's critical remark with a scathing rejoinder—"Well, I may have burned the waffles, but *you* spilled the syrup!" Or, on the other hand, you might attempt to flee the encounter altogether by leaving the room or burying your head in the newspaper. Depending on your approach, your partner will feel either attacked or abandoned and will most likely lash out again. A perpetual-emotion machine will be set in gear, and you will have defeated the desired outcome, which is to have a pleasant, intimate breakfast together.

This is precisely the kind of situation in which the new brain could be pressed into service to come up with a less provocative response. One approach (an approach that we will explore in detail in a later chapter) might be to paraphrase your partner's statement in a neutral tone of voice, acknowledging the anger but not rushing to your own defense. For example, you might say something like this: "You're really upset that I burned the waffles again." Your partner might then respond: "Yes, I am! I'm tired of all the wasted food around here. Next time be more careful!" And, still relying on new-brain tact, you could respond once again in the same nondefensive manner: "You're right. Food does get wasted around here. I'll get an extension cord and bring the waffle iron into the dining room, where we can keep a closer eye on it." Your partner, disarmed by your rational tone of voice and your ability to think of an alternative solution, will probably calm down and become more tractable: "Good idea. And thanks for not getting upset. I guess I'm a little edgy this morning. I'm behind at work and I don't know how I'm going to manage." Because you were willing to risk a creative response to anger, you have suddenly become a trusted confidant, not a sparring partner.

Once you become skilled in this nondefensive approach to criticism, you will make an important discovery: *in most interactions with your spouse, you are actually safer when you lower your defenses than when you keep them engaged, because your partner becomes an ally, not an enemy.* By relying on your new brain, which, unlike your old brain, recognizes that being criticized for burning the waffles is not the same thing as being attacked with the bread knife, you learn to moderate your instinctual fight/flight response. Paradoxically, you do an even better job of satisfying the underlying purpose of this automatic defense, which is to keep yourself safe and unharmed.

This is only one example of how greater reliance on the flexibility and discriminating powers of the conscious brain can help you achieve your unconscious goals. Let's move on to the larger picture and get a comprehensive view of what I mean by "a conscious marriage." Let's start with a definition: a conscious marriage is a marriage that fosters maximum psychological and spiritual growth; it's a marriage created by becoming conscious and cooperating with the fundamental drives of the unconscious mind: to be safe, to be healed, and to be whole.[1]

What are some of the differences when you become conscious? The following list highlights some of the essential differences in attitude and behavior:

Ten Characteristics of a Conscious Marriage

1. *You realize that your love relationship has a hidden purpose—the healing of childhood wounds.* Instead of focusing entirely on surface needs and desires, you learn to recognize the unresolved childhood issues that underlie them. When you look at marriage with this X-ray vision, your daily interactions take on more meaning. Puzzling aspects of your relationship begin to make sense to you, and you have a greater sense of control.

2. *You create a more accurate image of your partner.* At the very moment of attraction, you began fusing your lover with your primary caretakers. Later you projected your negative traits onto your partner, further obscuring your partner's essential reality. As you move toward a con-

scious marriage, you gradually let go of these illusions and begin to see more of your partner's truth. You see your partner not as your savior but as another wounded human being, struggling to be healed.

3. *You take responsibility for communicating your needs and desires to your partner.* In an unconscious marriage, you cling to the childhood belief that your partner automatically intuits your needs. In a conscious marriage, you accept the fact that, in order to understand each other, you have to develop clear channels of communication.

4. *You become more intentional in your interactions.* In an unconscious marriage, you tend to react without thinking. You allow the primitive response of your old brain to control your behavior. In a conscious marriage, you train yourself to behave in a more constructive manner.

5. *You learn to value your partner's needs and wishes as highly as you value your own.* In an unconscious marriage, you assume that your partner's role in life is to take care of your needs magically. In a conscious marriage, you let go of this narcissistic view and divert more and more of your energy to meeting your partner's needs.

6. *You embrace the dark side of your personality.* In a conscious marriage, you openly acknowledge the fact that you, like everyone else, have negative traits. As you accept responsibility for this dark side of your nature, you lessen your tendency to project your negative traits onto your mate, which creates a less hostile environment.

7. *You learn new techniques to satisfy your basic needs and desires.* During the power struggle, you cajole, harangue, and blame in an attempt to coerce your partner to meet your needs. When you move beyond this stage, you realize that your partner *can indeed be a resource for you—* once you abandon your self-defeating tactics.

8. *You search within yourself for the strengths and abilities*

you are lacking. One reason you were attracted to your partner is that your partner had strengths and abilities that you lacked. Therefore, being with your partner gave you an illusory sense of wholeness. In a conscious marriage, you learn that the only way you can truly recapture a sense of oneness is to develop the hidden traits within yourself.

9. *You become more aware of your drive to be loving and whole and united with the universe.* As a part of your God-given nature, you have the ability to love unconditionally and to experience unity with the world around you. Social conditioning and imperfect parenting made you lose touch with these qualities. In a conscious marriage, you begin to rediscover your original nature.

10. *You accept the difficulty of creating a good marriage.* In an unconscious marriage, you believe that the way to have a good marriage is to pick the right partner. In a conscious marriage you realize you have to be the right partner. As you gain a more realistic view of love relationships, you realize that a good marriage requires commitment, discipline, and the courage to grow and change; marriage is hard work.

Let's take a closer look at number ten, the need to accept the difficulty involved in creating a good marriage, because none of the other nine ideas will come to fruition unless you first cultivate your willingness to grow and change.

BECOMING A LOVER

WE ALL HAVE AN UNDERSTANDABLE DESIRE to live life as children. We don't want to go to the trouble of raising a cow and milking it; we want to sit down at the table and have someone hand us a cool glass of milk. We don't want to plant seeds and tend a grapevine; we want to walk out the back door and pluck a handful of grapes. This wishful thinking finds its ultimate expression in marriage. We don't want to accept responsibility for getting our needs met; we want to "fall in love" with a superhuman mate and live happily ever after. The psychological term for this tendency to put the source of our frustrations and the solutions to our problems outside ourselves is "externalization," and it is the cause of much of the world's unhappiness.

I remember the day when a client whom I will call Walter came in for his appointment with slumped shoulders and a sad expression.

"What's the matter?" I asked Walter. "You look very unhappy today."

"Harville," he said to me as he slumped into the chair, "I feel really terrible. I just don't have any friends."

I was sympathetic with him. "You must be very sad. It's lonely not having any friends."

"Yeah. I can't seem to . . . I don't know. There are just no friends in my life. I keep looking and looking, and I can't find any."

He continued in a morose, complaining voice for some time, and I had to suppress a growing annoyance with his regressed, childlike state. He was locked into a view of the world that went something like this: wandering around the world were people on whose foreheads were stamped the words "Friend of Walter," and his job was merely to search until he found them.

"Walter," I said with a sigh, "do you understand why you don't have any friends?"

He perked up. "No. Tell me!"

"The reason you don't have any friends is that there aren't any friends out there."

His shoulders slumped.

I was relentless. "That's right," I told him. "There are no

friends out there. What you want does not exist." I let him stew in this sad state of affairs for a few seconds. Then I leaned forward in my chair and said, "Walter—listen to me! All people in the world are *strangers*. If you want a friend, you're going to have to go out and make one!"

Walter was resisting the idea that creating a lasting friendship takes time and energy. Even though he was responsible and energetic in his job, he retained the childlike notion that all he had to do to establish intimacy was to bump up against the right person. Because he hadn't acknowledged that a friendship evolves slowly over time and requires thoughtfulness, sensitivity, and patience, he had been living a lonely life.

The passive attitude Walter brought to his friendships was even more pronounced in his love life: he couldn't seem to find the ideal woman. Recovering from a painful divorce (in a bitter legal battle, his wife had gotten custody of their son), he was desperately trying to find a new lover.

The specific problem that had plagued Walter in his marriage was that he was caught up in concepts and ideas, not feelings. He hid his vulnerability behind his formidable intellect, which prevented any genuine intimacy. He had been coming to group-therapy sessions for about six months, and at each session he would hear from the group the same message that he had been hearing from his wife—that he wasn't sharing his feelings, that he was emotionally distant. One evening a member of the group finally broke through to him. "When you talk about your pain," she said, "I can't see any suffering. When you hug me, I can't feel your hugs." Walter finally realized that there was some basis to his ex-wife's complaints. "I thought she was just being bitchy and critical," he confessed. "It never occurred to me that maybe she was right. That I could learn something about myself from listening to her."

When Walter had time to absorb this awareness, he developed more enthusiasm for the therapeutic process and was able to work on dismantling his emotional barriers. As he became more alive emotionally, he was finally able to have a satisfying relationship with a new woman friend. During his last session with me, he shared his feelings about therapy. "You know," he said, "it took me two years to learn one simple fact: that, in order to have a good relationship, you have to be willing to grow and change. If I had known this ten years ago, I would still be living with my wife and son."

Walter can't be blamed for wanting to believe that marriage should be easy and "natural." It's human nature to want a life without effort. When we were infants, the world withheld and we were frustrated; the world gave and we were satisfied. Out of thousands of these early transactions, we fashioned a model of the world, and we cling to this outdated model even at the expense of our marriages. We are slow to comprehend that, in order to be loved, we must first become lovers. And I don't mean this in sentimental terms. I don't mean sending flowers, writing love notes, or learning new lovemaking techniques—although any one of these activities might be a welcome part of a loving relationship. To become a lover, we must first abandon the self-defeating tactics and beliefs that I've discussed in the first five chapters and replace them with more constructive ones. We must change our ideas about marriage, about our partners, and, ultimately, about ourselves.

THE FEAR OF CHANGE

STANDING IN THE WAY of the changes we need to make in order to have a more satisfying relationship is our fear of change. A fear of change is also basic to human nature. We can feel anxious even when we're undergoing a positive change, such as getting promoted, moving into a new home, or going on vacation. Anything that breaks us out of our comfortable or not-so-comfortable routines sets off an alarm in our old brain. The old brain is alerting us to the fact that we are entering territory that has not been mapped or surveyed, and that danger may lurk around every corner.

I see a wish to cling to well-worn paths even in young children. When our daughter, Leah, was two and a half years old, her younger brother, Hunter, had outgrown the bassinet, and Helen and I decided it was time to move her into a youth bed so that the baby could have the crib. The youth bed had a six-inch rail going halfway down the bed to keep her from rolling off in the middle of the night. The bottom half had no rail. The first morning that Leah awoke in her new bed, I heard her familiar wake-up cry: "Daddy! Daddy!" I went into her room, and there she was, on her knees, with her hands on the little rail, saying, "Daddy, pick me up!"—just as she had done in her old crib with the two-foot sides. I was taken aback by her helplessness. She could easily have climbed over the bar or scooted down a few feet to the part of the bed that had no railing at all. "Leah," I said with enthusiasm, "you can get out of your new bed all by yourself!"

"I can't," she said, sticking out her lower lip. "I'm stuck." "Leah, look down here," I implored, patting the part of the bed without rails. "You can climb down right here!" She knelt frozen in place. Finally I had to get up on the bed with her and show her how to do it. With my encouragement, she was able to follow close behind me, overcome her resistance to change, and get out of bed.

I saw a more dramatic demonstration of paralysis in the face of change the other evening while watching the news. A local TV station carried a story about a little boy who was born in 1982 with severe immune deficiency, and from the moment of birth had to spend his life encased in a plastic bubble, sealed off from life-threatening germs. His devoted mother and father were by his side every day of his life, but they were separated from him by the plastic, and the only way they could touch him was by putting on long sterile gloves that were permanently inserted into the bubble.

Shortly after the boy's fifth birthday, he was given a successful bone-marrow transplant, and after elaborate testing, the doctors decided that his immune system was sufficiently developed to allow him to leave his sterile world. On the day he was scheduled to come out, the bubble was slit open, and his overjoyed mother and father held out their arms to him. This was the first time in their lives that they would be able to kiss and hug their son. But, to everyone's surprise, the boy cowered in the back of the bubble. His parents called to him, but he wouldn't budge. Finally his father had to crawl inside and carry him out. As the little boy looked around the room, he started to cry. Since he had lived all his life in a ten-by-eight-foot enclosure, the room must have looked enormous to him. His parents hugged him and kissed him to reassure him, but he wasn't used to any physical contact, and he arched backward to escape their embraces.

The closing segment of the story, filmed a few days later, showed that the child was growing more comfortable with life outside the bubble. But on the day of his emancipation it was clear that his fear of confronting the unfamiliar was stronger than his desire to explore the world.

That little boy lived for five years inside his bubble. The couples that come to me have been living for two, ten, twenty—as many as forty years inside a restrictive, growth-inhibiting relationship. With so many years invested in habituated behaviors, it's only natural that they should experience a great reluctance to change. After all, I am asking them not only to risk the anxiety of learning a new style of relating, but also to confront the pain and fear that have been bottled up inside them for decades—the reason for their dysfunctional behavior in the first place.

THE PROMISED LAND

TO GIVE YOU SOME INSIGHT into the difficulties of creating a conscious marriage, I want to recount my highly abridged version of the story of Moses and the Promised Land, which I view as a parable of the human psyche.[2] It goes like this:

Many centuries ago, the Israelites were a great tribe of people living in a country near the Mediterranean Sea. There came a drought to their land, and, in order to survive, the Israelites migrated south to Egypt, where the bins were full of grain. But in exchange for the grain they were forced to become slaves to the Egyptians and were subjected to cruel treatment and the dreary labor of making bricks without straw. After more than four hundred years of this meager existence, along came a man named Moses, who said to the Israelites, "Good grief. You're going through painful, repetitive behavior that is getting you nowhere. You've forgotten your heritage. You're not slaves of the house of Egypt, you are the children of the great God Yahweh! The God of all gods is your creator, and you are his special people."

Moses' words stirred a sense of recognition in the Israelites, and they became aware of their mental imprisonment. This made them restless and unhappy—not unlike many of the couples that come to me for counseling.

Lured by a vision of the Promised Land, the Israelites followed Moses. But the Israelites were not prepared for the hardships of the journey, and they had little faith in God's protection. When they came to the first obstacle, the Red Sea, they complained bitterly to Moses: "You got us out of our comfortable huts with a promise of a better way of life. Now our way is blocked by an enormous sea! Was it because there were no graves in Egypt that you brought us to the desert to die? What are we to do?"

Moses himself wasn't sure what to do, but he believed that if he had faith a way would appear. While he was pondering their fate, a huge dust cloud appeared on the horizon. To the Israelites' horror, they realized it was a cloud kicked up by thousands of rapidly approaching Egyptian soldiers coming to capture them and return them to their chains.

At this moment Moses lifted his hand and a strong east wind miraculously parted the Red Sea. Awed by this great miracle, the Israelites summoned their courage, took one last look back at Egypt—the only home they had known—and followed Moses fearfully into the watery chasm. There were walls of water to their right and to their left. When they were safely across the sea, Moses raised his hand once more, and the great sea walls collapsed, drowning all the Egyptians in a rushing torrent of water.

The Israelites had only moments to celebrate their safe passage. As they looked at the new land, they were dismayed to learn that they had arrived on the edge of a barren, trackless desert. Once again they cried out in anguish. "You disrupted our secure lives. You urged us to follow you on a long journey. We were almost captured by the Egyptians. We were nearly drowned in the Red Sea. And now we are lost in a barren land with no food or water!"

Despite their fears, the Israelites had no choice but to continue. They wandered for many months in the foreign land, guided by a pillar of cloud by day and by a pillar of fire by night. They encountered great hardships, but God was merciful and made their burden lighter by performing miracles. Finally the Israelites arrived at the end of the desert. Just over the ridge, said Moses, was the Promised Land. Scouts were sent ahead to survey the territory. But when the scouts returned, they brought more bad news: "The Promised Land really does flow with milk and honey, but it is already occupied! This is the home of the Canaanites, gigantic creatures seven feet tall!" The listening crowd cried out in terror and once again yearned for the safety and security of their life in Egypt.

At this point God spoke to them: "Because you have no faith, and because you keep remembering Egypt, you have to wander in the desert for forty years, until a new generation arises that does not remember the old ways. Only then can you go into the Promised Land." So for forty more years the Israelites camped out in the desert. Children were born, and old people died. Finally a new leader arose to take them into Israel to begin the hard work of wresting the land from the Canaanites.

What can we learn from this familiar story that will help us in our exploration of marriage? One of the first truths we can learn is the fact that most of us go through married life as if we were asleep, engaging in routine interactions that give us little pleasure. Like the Israelites in their four hundred years of servitude to the Egyptians, we have forgotten who we are. In the words of Wordsworth, we come into the world "trailing clouds of glory," but the fire is soon extinguished, and we lose sight of the fact that we are whole, spiritual beings. We live impoverished, repetitious, unrewarding lives and blame our partners for our unhappiness.

The story also teaches us that we are prisoners of the fear of change. When I ask couples to risk new behaviors, they become angry with me. There is a part of them that would rather divorce, break up the family, and divide up all their possessions than acquire a new style of relating. Like the Israelites, they tremble in front of the Red Sea, even though the way lies open to them. Later, when they are in a difficult stretch of the journey, their emotional difficulties seem like hordes of pursuing Egyptians and seven-foot-tall monsters. But, unlike the case of the Israelites, the enemy is within; it's the denied and repressed parts of their being threatening to come to awareness.

The final truth in the story of Moses is that we expect life's rewards to come to us easily and without sacrifice. Just as the Israelites wanted the Promised Land to be the Garden of Eden, God's ready-made gift to Adam and Eve, we want the simple act of getting married to cure all our ills. We want to live in a fairy tale where the beautiful princess meets the handsome prince and they live happily ever after. But it was only when the Israelites saw the Promised Land as an opportunity, as a chance to create a new reality, that they were allowed to enter. And it is only when we see marriage as a vehicle for change and self-growth that we can begin to satisfy our unconscious yearnings.

WHAT LIES AHEAD

THIS CHAPTER MARKS a turning point in the book. Up until now, I've been describing the unconscious marriage, a marriage characterized by old-brain reactivity. In the rest of the book, I will explain how to transform your marriage into a more conscious, growth-producing relationship. Here's an overview of what lies ahead. Chapter 7 explores an old-fashioned idea, commitment, and explains why it is a necessary precondition for emotional growth. Chapter 8 shows you how to turn your marriage into a zone of safety—a safe and secure environment that rekindles the intimacy of romantic love. Chapter 9 gives you some techniques for gathering more information about yourself and your spouse. Chapter 10 explores the paradoxical idea that the only way to satisfy your childhood needs is to commit yourself wholeheartedly to the satisfaction of your partner's needs. Chapter 11 talks about ways you can contain your anger so that it can be safely expressed within your relationship. Chapter 12 is an interview with two couples who are well on the way to creating a conscious marriage. Part III contains a series of exercises that will help you translate these insights into practical, growth-producing behaviors. (It is important that you finish Parts I and II before you do the exercises. They will be more meaningful to you once you read the text and understand the theories behind them.)

CLOSING YOUR EXITS

A life allied with mine, for the rest of our lives—
that is the miracle of marriage.

—DENIS DE ROUGEMONT

WHEN A COUPLE WALKS into my office for their first counseling session, I know little or nothing about them. All I know
with any certainty is that they are mired somewhere in the
power struggle. They might be anywhere along that tortuous
path. They might be newlyweds reeling from the shock of discovering that they have married the wrong person. They might
be a middle-aged couple trying to cope with the stress of having
two careers, teenage children, and a relationship that has degenerated into a series of ongoing battles. They might be an older
couple who have lost all feeling for each other and are contemplating a "friendly" divorce. But, whatever their circumstances,
I can rightly assume that they have journeyed past the romantic
stage of marriage and become embroiled in conflict.

Years ago my approach, and the approach of many of my colleagues, was immediately to wade into the details of the power

struggle. In the first few sessions I would determine whether a couple's main problems seemed to be with communication, sex, money, parenting, role expectations, alcohol or drug dependency, and so on. Over the course of the next few months, I would help them gain insight into these problems. An important part of the therapeutic process was teaching them to communicate their feelings more directly: "How did you feel when Mary said that?" Or "How did you feel when George acted that way?" At the end of each session, I would help them negotiate a contract that would specify a course of action. George, for example, would agree to give Mary one compliment a day, and Mary would agree to express her anger directly to George instead of withdrawing in silence. This was all fairly standard problem-oriented, contractual marriage counseling.

The couples learned a lot about each other in the time that we spent together, and they became more skilled at communication. But, to my dismay, few of them seemed able to transcend the power struggle. Instead of arguing about their "presenting" issues, the problems that brought them into therapy, they were now arguing about who had violated which contract first. At times it seemed as though my function as a therapist was merely to quantify and formalize their conflicts.

In those early days, my work was being supervised, and I would share my frustration with my adviser. What was I doing wrong? Why were my couples making such slow progress? All I seemed to be doing was giving people something new to fight over. My adviser would smile knowingly and then chide me for having a vested interest in whether or not my clients were willing to change. If they wanted to change, he assured me, they would. Perhaps I was confusing my agenda with theirs. My role, he reminded me, was to help people gain insight into their problems, teach them certain relationship skills, and let them go on their way.

It was several years before I discovered that, in order to be effective, marriage therapy can't dwell on surface issues like money and roles and sexual incompatibility. Underneath these superficial problems are unresolved childhood needs, and communication skills and behavioral contracts are not going to address these deeper issues. In order to be effective, marital therapy has to address fundamental conflicts. Armed with this knowledge, I began to work with couples more intensively, searching beneath surface phenomena for more primitive issues.

The Need for Commitment

BECAUSE EVERY MARRIAGE is unique, my approach to each couple is a blend of formula and invention. Sometimes a couple's therapy follows a predetermined course, but more often than not I have to tailor my methods to meet their individual needs. If a couple comes to me because of a crisis—let's say, arising from a recently discovered affair—I do some triage and immediately attend to their shock and pain. If, on the other hand, a husband and wife walk in for their first appointment totally numb to their pain, I sometimes find it necessary to stimulate conflict. Unless they are aware of the nature of their problems, it's difficult for them to resolve them.

However, somewhere in the first few sessions, I make it a point to establish some basic ground rules for therapy. With slight variations, these will also be ground rules for doing the exercise section of this book. One of the first rules is that couples have to agree to come to me for at least twelve consecutive sessions. Barring genuine emergencies, they are to orchestrate their lives so that they can come to each and every appointment. The reason I ask for this commitment is that I know from my own experience, and from statistical surveys, that a majority of couples quit therapy somewhere between the third and the fifth appointments, which is about the time it takes for unconscious issues to begin to emerge and for people to begin to experience some anxiety. As we all know, a tried and true method for reducing anxiety is avoidance. Some couples claim that therapy is making matters worse and fire the therapist. Others can't find time to keep their appointments. It is because this avoidance behavior is so common that I insist couples make a twelve-session commitment. In many cases it is productive for couples to continue therapy for longer than three months, but at the very least I have the assurance that they will stay long enough to work through their initial resistance.

When you are working on the exercise section of this book, you may experience the same reluctance to complete the process. Some exercises will be easy for you—even fun. But others will give you new information about yourself and challenge you to grow and change. As you do the more demanding exercises, the temptation will be to put the book aside or alter the instructions. It is precisely at these moments that you need to commit yourself wholeheartedly to the process. You will discover that if, before you begin, you make a strong commitment to finish all of the exercises and do them exactly as prescribed, it will be easier to overcome your resistance.

My second order of business with couples is to help them define their relationship vision. Before I hear all the things they don't like about their marriage, I want to hear how they would like it to be. Defining the vision turns their energy away from past and present disappointments toward a more hopeful future. Achieving their vision is the goal of therapy.

It is surprisingly easy for couples to create this vision—even couples who are in a great deal of turmoil. To get them started, I ask them to list a series of positive statements beginning with the word "we" that describe the kind of relationship they would like to have. They are to frame these statements in the present tense, as if the future were already here. Here are some examples: "We enjoy each other's company," "We are financially secure," "We spend time together doing things we both enjoy." In just one work session, they are able to define their separate visions, isolate the common elements, and combine these elements into a shared goal.

Once the vision is defined, I ask couples to read it daily as a form of meditation. Gradually, through the principle of repetition, the vision becomes imbedded in the unconscious.

THE NO-EXIT DECISION

AS SOON AS THE WORK on the vision is completed, which is usually about the second or third session, I ask couples to make a second commitment, and that is to stay together for the initial twelve weeks of therapy. The reason for this is obvious: marriage therapy isn't possible if there is no marriage to work on. For three months they are not to separate or to end the relationship in a more catastrophic way, by suicide, murder, or insanity. (Although separation and divorce are by far the most common ways my clients contemplate terminating their marriages, a significant minority have a feeling that they might go crazy, and there are numerous couples who fantasize more violent options.) I call the decision to close all four of these escape routes the "no-exit" decision. When you turn to Part III, you will see that the no-exit decision is one of the first exercises you will be asked to do.[1]

FUSER-ISOLATER DYNAMICS

A HUSBAND AND WIFE often react to the no-exit decision in opposite ways. Typically, one partner feels relieved; the other feels threatened. The one who feels relieved is usually the "fuser" in the relationship, the one who grew up with an unsatisfied need for attachment. The one who feels threatened is the "isolater," the one who has an unsatisfied need for autonomy. The reason the fuser is relieved by the commitment is that the guarantee of a stable relationship—if only for three months—reduces the unconscious fear of abandonment. (For the fuser this fear always lurks beneath the surface, but it is more acute in a troubled relationship.) The reason the no-exit decision makes the isolater feel apprehensive is that this agreement closes an important escape hatch, triggering the isolater's archaic fear of absorption. Thus the no-exit decision tends to alleviate fear in one partner and exacerbate it in the other.

During the period of this agreement, I try to ease the anxiety of the client who feels trapped. I remind the client that the commitment is only for three months, and at the end of that time he or she is free to leave. Because this is a finite amount of time, most people find they can cope. Furthermore, I explain that the no-exit decision tends to make the partner less invasive. "One of the reasons your partner is so needy of your attention," I explain to the isolater, "is that you're not emotionally available. When you make a decision to stay together and work on your marriage, your partner will feel less obligated to chase after you." Ironically, by making an agreement to stay within the relationship for three months, the isolater often ends up with more psychic space than before.

A couple's response to the no-exit decision is a fascinating glimpse of more complex fuser-isolater dynamics. Every day of their married lives, husbands and wives push against an invisible relationship boundary in an attempt to satisfy their dual needs for autonomy and attachment. Most of the time, each individual fixates on one of those needs: one person habitually advances, in an effort to satisfy unmet needs for attachment; the other habitually retreats, in an effort to satisfy unmet needs for autonomy. Some couples stay locked in this particular dance step for the duration of their relationship. Others experience a startling reversal. For a variety of reasons, the person who typically advances begins to retreat. The partner who habitually retreats turns around in amazement: where's the pursuer? To everyone's surprise, the isolater suddenly discovers an unmet need for closeness. The pattern is reversed, like the flip-flop of magnetic poles, and now the isolater does the pursuing. It's as if all couples collude to maintain a set distance between them. If one person starts encroaching on this sacred territory, the other has to back away. If one person starts vacating the territory, the other has to pursue. As with a pair of magnets with like charges lined up facing each other, there's an invisible force field keeping husbands and wives a critical distance apart.

Noncatastrophic Exits

ONE COUPLE I WORKED WITH had mastered this game of push and pull. A good indication of their success at avoiding intimacy was that they hadn't had sex in over three years. As an assignment, I asked them to spend just one day together doing something they both enjoyed. The very next day, which happened to be a Saturday, they agreed to go for a hike in the country and then go out to dinner.

The next morning, just as they were about to leave the house, the wife suggested that they invite a mutual friend along on the hike. It had been a long time since they had seen this friend, the woman reasoned, and, besides, the friend always liked to get out of the city. Her husband said that sounded like a bad idea. The whole purpose of the day was to spend time together. Why did she always want to louse things up? They argued heatedly for a good hour; then the husband gave in. The wife called the friend, who was happy to come along. As they waited for him to show up, the wife read the paper and straightened the house, while the husband disappeared into the den to work his way through a stack of bills.

The friend arrived and the three of them got in the car and drove out to the country. On the drive, the two men sat in the front seat of the car—ostensibly because they had longer legs and needed the legroom—while the woman sat in the backseat, reading a book. During the actual hike, either the wife or the husband was engaged in a conversation with the friend, while the partner tagged along behind.

When they got back to the city, the friend went home and the couple made plans to go out to dinner. They decided to go to a restaurant that featured live entertainment. At the restaurant the husband suggested they choose a table right in front of the musicians so they could pay more attention to the music. They had dinner and tried to carry on a conversation, but gave up because the music was so loud they couldn't hear each other. They left the restaurant at precisely a quarter to nine so they could be home in time for a favorite TV show. As soon as they entered the house, they automatically poured themselves a couple of drinks and stationed themselves in front of the television. The wife went to bed at eleven o'clock (after ritually urging her husband not to drink too much), and the husband stayed up until one in the morning, happily nursing his Scotch and watching TV. With consummate skill, they managed to spend the whole day together without a moment of intimacy. Although they didn't realize it, they were living an invisible divorce.

THE INVISIBLE DIVORCE

TO ONE DEGREE OR ANOTHER, most couples who are involved in a power struggle follow a similar pattern: they structure their lives in such a way that true intimacy is virtually impossible. The way that they do this is often ingenious. By asking my clients a simple question, "What does your spouse do to avoid you?" I have come up with a list of over three hundred different answers. Here's a fragment of that list. According to my informants, their mates were: "reading romance novels," "disappearing into the garage," "camping out on the phone," "worshiping the car," "spending too much time with the kids," "volunteering for every committee at church," "spending too much time with the boat," "spending time at her mom's," "having an affair," "avoiding eye contact," "memorizing every word of *The New York Times*," "falling asleep on the couch," "being a sports junkie," "coming home late for dinner," "fantasizing while making love," "being sick and tired all the time," "not wanting to be touched," "four Scotches a night," "spending too many evenings at the Rotary," "lying," "refusing to make love," "having sex but not making love," "living on the tennis court," "bulimia," "jogging ten miles a day," "going on weekend fishing trips," "going shopping," "having his own apartment," "daydreaming," "refusing to talk," "smoking marijuana," "working on the house all the time," "masturbating," "playing his guitar," "keeping separate bank accounts," "picking fights," "reading magazines," "doing crossword puzzles," "refusing to get married," and "going to taverns."

The fact that so many couples perforate their relationships with exits raises an obvious question: why do men and women spend so much time avoiding intimacy? There are two very good reasons: anger and fear. Why the anger? In the romantic stage of a relationship, people find it relatively easy to be intimate, because they are filled with the anticipation of wish fulfillment. Their partners seem to be Mommy and Daddy and doctor and therapist all rolled into one. Months or years later, when they come to the realization that their partners are committed to their own salvation, not theirs, they feel angry and betrayed. A tacit agreement has been broken. In retaliation they erect an emotional barricade. In effect, they are saying, "I am angry at you for not meeting my needs." Then they begin systematically to seek pleasure and satisfaction of their needs outside the relationship. Like a hungry cow stretching its neck over a fence to munch on green grass, they look elsewhere for gratification. The husband who stays late at the office even when he has finished the day's work, the wife who spends the entire evening reading to the children while her husband watches TV—both of these individuals are trying to find pleasure that is missing from their relationships.

The other reason couples avoid intimacy is fear, specifically the fear of pain. On an unconscious level, many people react to their partners as if they were enemies. Any person—whether parent or partner or next-door neighbor—who is perceived by the old brain to be a source of need gratification and then appears to be withholding that gratification is cataloged by the old brain as a source of pain, and that raises the specter of death. If your partner does not nurture you and attend to your fundamental needs, a part of you fears that you will die, and it believes that your partner is the one who is allowing this to happen. When a basic lack of nurturing is coupled with an onslaught of verbal and in some cases actual physical abuse, the partner becomes an even more potent enemy. The unconscious reason some people avoid their partners, therefore, is not that they're scouting for greener pastures, but that they are fleeing death. The appropriate image in this case is not the bucolic scene of a cow foraging for food, but that of a terrified lamb running away from a lion.

In most cases the fear of the partner is unconscious. All that couples are aware of is a mild feeling of anxiety around each other and a desire to be with other people or to be involved in other activities. Occasionally the fear is closer to the surface. One client told me that the only time she felt truly safe around her husband was when the two of them were in my office. He had never physically abused her, but their relationship was so filled with conflict that she was convinced that her life was in danger.

CLOSING THE EXITS

TO UNDERSTAND WHY I ASK couples to close their exits, it may be helpful to understand what I mean by an "exit" and why it is important to close them. An exit is acting out one's feelings rather than putting them into language. (Acting out means expressing a conscious or unconscious feeling in behavior rather than words.) Whether an exit is catastrophic, like an affair or attempted suicide, or noncatastrophic, such as watching TV or fantasizing about someone else while making love, it withdraws energy and involvement from the relationship that belongs in the relationship.

No matter how valid the reasons are for the avoidance behavior, however, it is important in the initial stages of the healing process that couples gradually draw their energy back into the relationship. Until they close some of their numerous exits, they will always be seeking pleasure in inappropriate places. And when their relationship needs are diverted to their children or to their jobs or to substitute addictions, it's not always apparent what is wrong with the marriage. Their basic problem areas need to be defined before they can be resolved.

Surprisingly, it is harder for many couples to close the dozens of small exits in their relationships than it is for them to close the catastrophic exits; in other words, it may be harder for them to cut down on TV viewing for three months than to agree to give up the option of divorce. Part of the reason is that closing the smaller exits deprives them of pleasure. And as long as their partners are not giving them what they want, they are reluctant to let go of established sources of need gratification. Another reason for the resistance is that, as couples become more focused on each other, they often have to come face to face with their repressed disappointment, anger, and fear. They have minimized their degree of unhappiness by distracting themselves with outside activities. They hadn't poked holes in their relationships casually or maliciously—they did it for the important reasons of need gratification and safety.

To help couples overcome their resistance to becoming more intimate with each other, I rely on the principle known as "graduated change."[2] The idea behind this concept is that it's easier to tackle a difficult task if it is divided into manageable units. The units are then ranked according to difficulty, and the easiest units are tackled first; the project becomes even more manageable.

When you come to Part III, you will find complete instructions for closing your exits. For now, here is an overview of how this process works. Let's imagine two people who are trapped in an unsatisfying relationship. To make up for the emptiness of their marriage, they have filled their lives with substitute pleasures. Let's focus on the woman's exits. In addition to the responsibilities involved in having a career and raising two children, she has an active social life, a position on the community board, a passion for physical fitness, two music lessons a week, and an addiction to science-fiction novels. These activities help reduce her underlying feeling of despair, but they drain vital energy away from the relationship.

If this woman were to decide to cut back on some of her activities, she would first have to determine which of her numerous involvements could properly be termed an "exit." Like many people, she would probably find a degree of validity in virtually everything she did. When you do the no-exit exercise in Part III, you may have this same initial confusion: what is an exit and what is an essential activity or a valid form of recreation? The way to find out is to ask yourself the following question: "Is one of the reasons I'm doing this activity to avoid spending time with my spouse?" Most people know whether or not this is the case.

Let's suppose that this woman has asked herself this question and identified activities that she would be willing to curtail or eliminate. Next she would rank them according to difficulty and choose the ones that would be easiest for her to give up. For example, she might decide it would be relatively easy to make two changes: jog three days a week instead of five, and read her novels on her lunch hour, not in the evenings, when she could be spending time with her husband. She might also decide that it would be difficult but not impossible for her to find someone to take over her position on the community board. Other changes would be more difficult. If she were to go ahead and make the two easy changes, however, she would liberate several additional hours a week to devote to her relationship. This would be a good place to start. Other changes, if necessary, could come later.

At the same time that this woman would be eliminating her exits, her husband would be going through a similar process. He, too, would be examining his activities, identifying his exits, and beginning a systematic program of reduction. As a result of this exercise, the husband and wife would be spending significantly more time together.

As you can see, closing an exit is not a specific event that occurs at a particular moment. It is a process that may take time, sometimes as much as several months. The reason for this is that the exit is trying to get a need met that has been frustrated in the relationship. Rather than criticizing one's partner, it is essential that one claim their own exits. To do this requires much soul searching and honesty and the courage to put into words the feelings that have been expressed as a behavior. Paradoxically, that begins to close the exit, because it restores connection. One way couples can do this is for the partner who is acting out to ask for a dialogue (see the "Couples Dialogue" on p. 261). They could start by saying: "One way I act out in our relationship (rather than put my feelings into language) is (thinking about suicide a lot, or fantasizing while we are making love) . . ." "The reason I do this is because (I feel I will never get your attention or you are passive when we are making love). . . ." And then continue to talk until all the feelings are expressed. Then the other partner does the same until both have put all their unexpressed feelings into words and asked for appropriate changes in behavior. When this is done on a regular basis the need to act out diminishes and is replaced with deeper feelings of connection.

The reaction to this heightened interaction varies from couple to couple. Some couples enjoy the additional contact. Others find that closing their exits leaves them fewer avenues of escape from a painful situation. Although this is not a pleasant outcome, they get something from the exercise nonetheless, and that is a clearer delineation of their areas of conflict: they know exactly why it is that they have been avoiding each other, and this is an important first step in therapy.

TILL DEATH DO US PART

WHEN I LEAD COUPLES THROUGH these series of commitments—an agreement to: (1) come to a minimum of twelve therapy sessions, (2) define a relationship vision, (3) stay together for a specified period of time, and (4) gradually close their exits—I let them know that all of these separate agreements ideally lead to a larger commitment: a decision to join together in a journey that will last the rest of their lives. Although this decision cannot be made at the beginning of therapy, I want couples to know that, in order to obtain maximum psychological and spiritual growth, they need to stay together not for three months or three years or even three decades, but for all of their remaining years. Childhood issues do not present themselves to be resolved in one tidy package. They come to the surface slowly, usually the more superficial ones first. Sometimes a problem has to present itself a number of times before it is even identified as a significant issue. And sometimes a psychological need is so deeply buried that it is only triggered by a crisis or the demands of a particular stage of life. Ultimately it takes a lifetime together for a couple to identify and heal the majority of their childhood wounds.

In a culture where serial monogamy is a way of life, the idea of a permanent commitment to one partner has a quaint, old-fashioned ring to it. The prevalent question of the 1950s—"Can this marriage be saved?"—has now become "*Should* this marriage be saved?" And millions of people decide that the answer is no. In fact, ironically, many of them have come to view divorce as an opportunity for personal growth. It's not *within* marriage that people grow and change, according to this increasingly popular view, it's when the marriage falls apart. People believe that this opens their eyes to their self-defeating behaviors and gives them an opportunity to resolve those problems with a new partner. But unless they understand the unconscious desires that motivated their dysfunctional behavior in the first marriage, and learn how to satisfy those desires with the new partner, the second marriage is destined to run aground on the same submerged rocks. The feeling of growth and change between marriages is an illusion: it is merely the pain that comes from exchanging one set of habituated behaviors for another.

Ironically, the more I have become involved in a psychological study of love relationships, the more I find myself siding with the more conservative proponents of marriage. I have come to believe that couples should make every effort to honor their wedding vows to stay together "till death do us part"—not for moral reasons, but for psychological ones: fidelity and commitment appear to be conditions dictated by the unconscious mind.

In Part III, you will have an opportunity to deepen your commitment to each other and begin a process of growth and change. The suggested time period for completing all sixteen exercises is ten weeks. Dedicating two and a half months of your time to improving your marriage may be all that you need to begin realizing your relationship vision.

CREATING A ZONE OF SAFETY

Perfect love means to love the one through whom one became unhappy.

—SØREN KIERKEGAARD

ONCE A COUPLE HAS MADE a commitment to stay together and to take part in a program of marital therapy, the next logical step is to help them become allies, not enemies. It's fruitless to take two people who are angry with each other and try to lead them along a path of spiritual and psychological growth—they spend too much time trying to knock each other off the road. In order to make the surest and fastest progress toward their relationship vision, they need to become friends and helpmates.

But how is this going to happen? How can couples put an end to their power struggle when they haven't had the opportunity to resolve their fundamental differences? Love and compassion are supposed to come at the end of the therapeutic process, not at the beginning.

I found a solution to this dilemma in my studies of the behavioral sciences. I learned that I could influence the way a couple feels about each other by helping them artificially reconstruct the conditions of romantic love. When two people treat each other the way they did in happier times, they begin to identify each other as a source of pleasure once again, and this makes them more willing to take part in intensive therapy.

INSIGHT AND BEHAVIORAL CHANGE

YEARS AGO I was resistant to the idea of such a direct approach to the alteration of my clients' behavior. Coming from a psychoanalytic tradition, I was taught that the goal of a therapist was to help clients remove their emotional blocks. Once they had correctly linked feelings they had about their partners with needs and desires left over from childhood, they were supposed automatically to evolve a more rational, adult style of relating.

This assumption was based on the medical model that, once a physician cures a disease, the patient automatically returns to full health. Since most forms of psychotherapy come from psychoanalysis, which, in turn, has its roots in nineteenth-century medicine, the fact that they rest on a common biological assumption is not surprising. But years of experience with couples convinced me that a medical model is not a useful one for marital therapy. When a physician cures a disease, the body recovers spontaneously because it relies on genetic programming. Each cell of the body, unless it is damaged or diseased, contains all the information it needs to function normally. But there is no genetic code that governs marriage. Marriage is a cultural creation *imposed* on biology. Because people lack a built-in set of social instructions, they can be trapped in unhappy relationships after months or even years of productive therapy. Their emotional blocks may be removed, and they may have insight into the cause of their difficulties, but they still cling to habituated behaviors.

Like many marital therapists, I came to the conclusion that I would have to play an active role in helping couples redesign their relationships. Insight into childhood wounds is a critical element in therapy, but it isn't enough. People also need to learn how to let go of counterproductive behaviors and replace them with more effective ones.

CARING BEHAVIORS

THE PLACE WHERE a behavioral approach proved especially useful was in solving the problem I mentioned at the beginning of the chapter, that of quickly restoring a couple's sense of love and goodwill. In his book, *Helping Couples Change: A Social Learning Approach to Marital Therapy,* psychologist Richard Stuart presents an exercise for couples that helps them feel more loving toward each other simply by engaging in more loving behaviors. Called "Caring Days," the exercise instructs husbands and wives to write down a list of positive, specific ways their partners can please them. For example, a man might write down: "I would like you to massage my shoulders for fifteen minutes while we watch television." Or "I would like you to bring me breakfast in bed on Sunday morning." The husbands and wives are to grant each other a certain number of these caring behaviors a day, no matter how they feel about each other. Stuart discovered that, when the exercise was successful, it generated "significant changes in the details of the couple's daily interaction during the first seven days of therapy, a very firm foundation upon which to build subsequent suggestions for change."[1]

To see whether or not this behavioral approach actually worked, I decided to try it out on Harriet and Dennis Johnson. I chose the Johnsons because they were as unhappy with each other as any couple in my practice. One of Harriet's main anxieties was that Dennis was going to leave her. In a desperate effort to hold his interest, she flirted conspicuously with other men. To her dismay, Dennis responded to her flirtatious behavior the same way he responded to just about everything else she did—with stoic reserve. During one session, he mentioned that he was even trying to adjust to the fact that Harriet might one day have an affair. His quiet heroics exasperated his wife, who was trying everything within her power to penetrate his defenses and get him to be more interested in her. Those rare times when she managed to get him riled up, he would behave in typical isolater fashion and flee the house. Most of their fights ended with Dennis's zooming off to safety in his Audi sedan.

To lay the groundwork for the exercise, I asked Dennis and Harriet to tell me how they had treated each other when they were first in love. As I listened to them, I had the strange feeling that they were talking about two different people. I couldn't imagine Dennis and Harriet going on long Sunday bike rides together, leaving work to meet each other at the movies, and calling each other on the phone two or three times a day.

"What would happen," I asked them when I recovered from my amazement, "if you were to go home today and start doing all those things again? What if you were to treat each other the same way you did when you were courting?" They looked at me with puzzled expressions.

"I think I would feel very uncomfortable," Dennis said after a moment's reflection. "I don't like the idea of acting differently from the way I feel. I would feel . . . dishonest. I don't have the same feelings toward Harriet that I used to, so why should I treat her as if I did?"

Harriet agreed. "It would feel like we were playacting," she said. "We may not be happy, but at least we try to be honest with each other."

When I explained that taking part in the experiment might help them over their impasse, they agreed to give it a try, despite their initial objections. I carefully explained the exercise to them. They were to go home, make their lists, and volunteer to give each other three to five of those behaviors a day. The behaviors were to be gifts. They were to view them as an opportunity to pleasure each other, not as a bartering tool. And, most important of all, they weren't to keep score. They were to focus only on the giving end of the equation. They left the office promising to give the exercise an honest effort.

At the beginning of their next appointment, Dennis reported on the results of the experiment. "I think you're really on to something, Harville," he said. "We did what you asked us to do, and today I feel a lot more hopeful about our marriage."

I asked him to tell me more.

"Well, the day after our appointment, I found myself driving around town in a black mood," Dennis volunteered. "I can't even remember what made me feel so down. Anyway, I decided that it was as good a time as any to do what you asked, so I stopped off at a variety store and bought Harriet some flowers. That was one of the requests on her list. So I gritted my teeth and picked out some daisies, because I remembered she always liked daisies. The clerk asked me if I wanted a note card and I said, 'Why not?' I remember saying to myself, 'We're paying Dr. Hendrix a lot of money to make things better, so I'd better do this all the way.' When I came home, I signed the card 'I love you.'" He paused for a moment. "The thing that surprised me, Harville, was that, as I handed Harriet the flowers, I really did care for her."

"And when I read the card," Harriet added, "tears came to my eyes. It's been so long since he's told me he loved me." They went on to describe all the other things that they had done to please each other. She had cooked him pot roast and potato pancakes, his favorite dinner. He had agreed to curl up together in bed as they fell asleep instead of turning his back to her. She had gotten out her yarn and needles and started knitting him a sweater vest. As they were recounting these events, there seemed to be remarkably little tension between them. When they left the office, I noticed that as Dennis helped Harriet on with her coat she smiled and said, "Thank you, honey." It was a little thing, but it was the kind of pleasurable give-and-take that had been so absent in their relationship.

I asked Dennis and Harriet to continue to give each other caring behaviors, and at each session they reported a gradual improvement in their relationship. They not only were treating each other more kindly, but were also more willing to explore the issues that underlay their discontent. They spent less of their time in my office complaining about each other and more time exploring the childhood issues that were the reasons for their unhappiness in the first place.

Because Stuart's exercise proved so helpful for Dennis and Harriet, I used it as a model for an expanded exercise that I labeled "Reromanticizing" because it effectively restored the conflict-free interactions of romantic love.[2] I introduced the Reromanticizing exercise to my other clients, and, almost without exception, when couples began artificially to increase the number of times a day that they *acted* lovingly toward each other, they began to feel safer and more loving. This intensified the emotional bond between them, and as a result they made more rapid progress in their therapy.

I will explain the details of the Reromanticizing exercise more fully in Part III. When you carefully follow the directions, you, too, will experience an immediate improvement in the climate of your relationship. The exercise is not designed to resolve your deep-seated conflicts, but it will re-establish feelings of safety and pleasure and set the stage for increased intimacy.

WHY DOES IT WORK?

WHY IS THIS SIMPLE EXERCISE so effective? The obvious reason is that, through daily repetitions of positive behaviors, the old brain begins to perceive the partner as "someone who nurtures me." Painful injuries are overlaid with positive transactions, and the partner is no longer categorized as a bringer of death but as a wellspring of life. This opens the way for intimacy, which is only possible in a context of pleasure and safety.

But there are other, subtler reasons the exercise works so well. One is that it helps people erode the infantile belief that their partners can read their minds. During romantic love, people operate out of the erroneous belief that their partners know exactly what it is that they want. When their spouses fail to satisfy their secret desires, they assume that the spouses are deliberately depriving them of pleasure. This makes them want to deprive their partners of pleasure. The Reromanticizing exercise prevents this downward spiral by requiring couples to tell each other exactly what pleases them, decreasing their reliance on mental telepathy.

Another consequence of the exercise is that it defeats the tit-for-tat mentality of the power struggle. When couples take part in the Reromanticizing exercise, they are instructed to pleasure each other on an independent schedule; they mete out a prescribed number of caring behaviors a day, regardless of the behavior of their partners. This replaces the natural tendency to hand out favors on a quid pro quo basis: You do this nice thing for me, and I'll do that nice thing for you. Most marriages are run like a commodities market, with loving behaviors the coin in trade. But this kind of "love" does not sit well with the old brain. If John rubs Martha's shoulders in the hope that she will let him spend the day going fishing, a built-in sensor in Martha's head goes: "Look out! Price tag attached. There is no reason to

feel good about this gift, because I'll have to pay for it later."
Unconsciously she rejects John's attentions, because she knows
that they were designed for his benefit, not hers. The only kind
of love that her old brain will accept is the kind with no strings
attached: "I will rub your shoulders because I know that you
would like it." The back rub has to come as a "gift."

This need to be "gifted" comes straight out of our childhood.
When we were infants, love came without price tags. At least for
the first few months of our lives, we didn't have to reciprocate
when we were patted or rocked or held or fed. And now, in
adulthood, a time-locked part of us still craves this form of love.
We want to be loved and cared for without having to do anything in return. When our partners grant us caring behaviors independent of our actions, our need for unconditional love
appears to be satisfied.

A third benefit of the exercise is that it helps people see that
what pleases them is the product of their unique makeup and
life experience and can be very different from what pleases their
partners. Often husbands and wives cater to their own needs
and preferences, not each other's. For example, one woman I
worked with went to a great deal of trouble to give her husband
a surprise fortieth-birthday party. She invited all his friends,
cooked his favorite foods, borrowed a stack of his favorite
1960s rock-and-roll records, and organized lively party games.
During the party, her husband acted as if he were enjoying himself, but a few weeks later, in the middle of a counseling session,
he got up the courage to tell his wife that he had been secretly
miserable. "I've never liked having a fuss made about my birthday," he told her. "You know that. And especially not my forti-
eth birthday. What I really wanted to do was spend a quiet
evening at home with you and the kids. Maybe have a home-
made cake and a few presents. *You're* the one who likes big
noisy parties!"

His wife had taken the Golden Rule, "Do unto others as you

would have others do unto you," a little too literally. She had unwittingly given her husband a party that suited her tastes, not his. The Reromanticizing exercise circumvents this problem by training couples to "Do unto others as *they* would have you do unto *them*." This turns their random caring behaviors into "target" behaviors, behaviors that are designed to satisfy their partners' unique desires.

The final benefit of the Reromanticizing exercise is that, when couples regularly give each other these target behaviors, they not only improve the superficial climate of their relationship, but also begin to heal old wounds. I have an example from my personal history. My wife, Helen, and I faithfully perform the same exercises that I assign my clients, and the Reromanticizing exercise is one that we have done so many times it has become integrated into our relationship: it's something we do without thinking. One of the things that I ask Helen to do for me is to turn down the covers before we go to bed. This request comes from an experience I had over forty years ago. After my mother died, I was taken in by my sister, Maize Lee. She was only eighteen at the time and recently married, but she did a wonderful job of caring for me. One of the things that touched me most was that she would always find time to go into my room before bedtime, turn down my covers, and put out a glass of orange juice or milk for me to drink. Today, when Helen turns down the covers for me before I climb into bed, I remember Maize Lee and all that she did for me, and I feel very loved indeed. On a deep level, this simple action is re-creating the vital parent-child bond. I feel secure again, and the injury of my childhood is repaired in an adult relationship that has become a zone of love and safety.

The Surprise List

AFTER INTRODUCING the Reromanticizing exercise to scores of couples, I began to notice a curious phenomenon: the positive value of doing this exercise seemed to flatten out after a few months. The couples were faithfully following the instructions, but they were no longer experiencing the deep pleasure they had had when they began the exercise. It occurred to me that maybe I needed to build into the exercise the concept of random reinforcement. Random reinforcement, one of the principles of behavioral science, is the idea that a pleasurable stimulus loses its effectiveness if it's repeated with predictable regularity. Random rewards, on the other hand, create an air of uncertainty and expectancy, and increase the impact of the reward. This concept was discovered accidentally by a group of scientists who were training laboratory animals by rewarding them with treats. One day the apparatus that dispensed the treats malfunctioned, and the animals were not rewarded for their efforts. The next day the machine was repaired and the regular reward schedule was resumed. To the trainers' surprise, the animals were even more highly motivated to perform than before. An unpredictable schedule of rewards actually improved their performance.

The phenomenon of random reinforcement can easily be observed in daily life. Most husbands and wives give each other presents on special occasions like birthdays and Christmas and anniversaries. These gifts are so customary that they are almost taken for granted. Although the presents may be enjoyed, they don't carry the same emotional impact as a present that is given as a total surprise. A behaviorist would say that the reason routine gifts aren't as exciting is that the "psychoneurological system has become desensitized to predictable, repetitive pleasure." The same principle applies to the Reromanticizing exercise. When couples become locked into a particular kind of caring behavior—for example, when they give each other back rubs every night before bed or a bouquet of flowers every Saturday—they begin to derive less pleasure from them. A curve ball needs to be thrown in now and then to pique their interest.

To add this element of suspense, I created the idea of the Surprise List exercise. These were caring behaviors above and beyond those requested by the spouse. A person generated the list by paying close attention to the partner's wishes and dreams. A woman who causally mentioned to her husband that she liked a dress she saw in a store window might be delighted to find that very dress—in the correct size—hanging in her closet. A man who expressed his interest in Gilbert and Sullivan might open the mail and find a love note from his wife and two tickets to a Gilbert and Sullivan opera. When couples added unanticipated pleasures like these to their daily regimen of caring behaviors, the beneficial effect of the exercise continued on a gentle rise.

THE FUN LIST

AS TIME WENT ON, I made a final addition to the Reromanticizing process. I asked couples not only to give each other caring behaviors and surprises, but also to engage in several high-energy, fun activities a week. These were to be spontaneous, one-on-one activities like wrestling, tickling, massaging, showering together, jumping up and down, or dancing. Competitive sports like tennis qualified only if a couple could play the game without stirring up tension.

The reason I added this additional element was that most of the activities that people wrote down on their caring-behavior lists turned out to be fairly passive, "adult" activities; they had forgotten how to have fun together. As soon as I noted this trend, I surveyed all my clients and found that the average amount of time they spent playing and laughing together was about ten minutes a week. Improving this bleak statistic became a priority to me, because I knew that when couples have exuberant fun together they identify each other as a source of pleasure and safety, which intensifies their emotional bond. When the old brain registers a positive flow of energy, it knows that the activity that triggered it is connected to life and safety, and the partners begin to connect with each other on a deeper unconscious level.

THE FEAR OF PLEASURE

WITH THE ADDITION of the Surprise List and the Fun List, I now had a useful tool to help couples begin therapy on a positive note. But, like any exercise that leads to personal growth, this simple exercise was often met with resistance. A certain degree of resistance is to be expected. When a husband and wife have been treating each other like enemies for five years, it's going to feel strange to start writing love notes again. The exercise is going to feel artificial and contrived (which, of course, it is), and to the old brain anything that is not routine and habituated feels unnatural. The only way to lower this automatic resistance to change is to repeat a new behavior often enough so that it begins to feel familiar and therefore safe.

A deeper source of resistance to the exercise, however, is a paradoxical one—the fear of pleasure. On a conscious level, we go to great lengths to seek happiness. Why should we be afraid of it? To make sense of this reaction, we need to remember that the sensation of being fully alive is deeply pleasurable. When we were young children, our life energy was boundless and we experienced intense joy. But this vitality was limited and redirected in order for us to be social beings. Our pleasure was curtailed so that we could be safe and conform to social norms, and also so that we would not threaten the repressed state of our caretakers. As these limits were imposed on us, sometimes in punitive ways, we began to make the unlikely association of pleasure with pain. If we experienced certain kinds of pleasure or perhaps a high degree of pleasure, we were ignored, reprimanded, or punished. On an unconscious level, this negative stimulus triggered the fear of death. Eventually we limited our own pleasure so that we could reduce our anxiety. We learned that to be fully alive was dangerous.

However, applying the strange logic of children, we didn't blame our parents or society for equating pleasure with pain; it simply appeared to be our lot in life. We told ourselves, "My parents limited my pleasure, so I must not have been worthy of it." It was somehow safer to believe that we were intrinsically undeserving than to believe that our parents were incapable of meeting our needs or had deliberately diminished our happiness. Gradually we developed a built-in prohibition against pleasure.

People who grew up experiencing a great deal of repression tend to have a particularly hard time with the Reromanticizing exercise. They have difficulty coming up with any requests, or they sabotage their partners' efforts to carry them out. For example, one of my clients, a man with low self-esteem, wrote down on his list that he would like his wife to give him one compliment a day. This was easy for his wife to do, because she thought he had a lot of admirable qualities. But when she tried to give him a daily compliment, he would immediately contradict her statement or qualify it to the point where it became meaningless. If she were to say something like "I liked the way you were talking to our son, Robbie, last night," he would nullify it with a self-criticism: "Yeah. Well, I should do that more often. I never spend enough time with him." Hearing anything good about himself was ego-dystonic, incompatible with his self-image. His determination to maintain this negative opinion was so strong that I had to train him to respond mechanically to his wife's kind remarks with a "thank you" and leave it at that.

There was one man in my practice whose resistance to the

Reromanticizing exercise took a different form: he just couldn't seem to understand the instructions. "Dr. Hendrix," he told me after the second session devoted to an explanation of the exercise, "I just don't get the hang of this. Now, what is it that I'm supposed to do?" I went over the instructions once again, making sure they were clearly understood. I knew, however, that his lack of comprehension was a cover-up for his inability to ask for something pleasurable. To help him over his emotional roadblock, I told him that, even though it appeared that asking his wife to do nice things for him was solely for his benefit, it was also a way for his wife to learn how to become a more loving person—which happened to be true. When it was put in this less self-serving context, he quickly understood the exercise. He was able to call a truce with the demon inside of him that told him he was not worthy of love. He took out a pencil and in a matter of minutes came up with a list of twenty-six things he would like her to do for him.

Isolaters often have a difficult time with this exercise. They want to cooperate, but they just can't think of anything their partners can do for them; they don't seem to have any needs or desires. What they are really doing is hiding behind the psychic shield they erected as children to protect themselves from overbearing parents. They discovered early in life that one way to maintain a feeling of autonomy around their intrusive parents was to keep their thoughts and feelings to themselves. When they deprived their parents of this valuable information, their parents were less able to invade their space. After a while, many isolaters do the ultimate disappearing act and hide their feelings from themselves. In the end, it is safest not to know.

It is often the case, as I've mentioned before, that isolaters unwittingly re-create the struggle of their childhood by marrying fusers, people who have an unsatisfied need for intimacy. This way they perpetuate the conflict that consumed them as children—not as an idle replay of the past, or a neurotic addiction to pain, but as an unconscious act aimed at the resolution of fundamental human needs. When a fuser-isolater couple does this exercise, it results in a predictable dichotomy. The isolater painfully ekes out one or two requests, while the fuser furiously scribbles a long list of "I wants." To the casual observer it appears that the isolater is a self-sufficient individual with few needs and the fuser has limitless desires. The fact of the matter is that both individuals have the identical need to be loved and cared for. It's just that one of them happens to be more in touch with those feelings than the other.

Whatever a person's reason for resisting this exercise, my prescription is the same: "Keep doing the exercise exactly as described. Even if it causes you anxiety, keep it up. Do it harder and more aggressively than before. Eventually your anxiety will go away." Given enough time and enough repetitions, the brain can adjust to a different reality. The person with low self-esteem can gradually carve out a more positive identity. The isolater has a chance to discover that sharing secret desires does not compromise his or her independence. The fear of new behaviors gives way to the pleasure they stimulate, and they begin to be associated with safety and life. The caring-behavior exercise becomes a comfortable, reliable tool for personal growth.

INSIGHT AND BEHAVIORAL CHANGE

THIS CARING-BEHAVIOR EXERCISE, and several other exercises like it that you will have a chance to read about in coming chapters, have convinced me that insight and behavioral change make powerful allies. It is not enough for a man and woman to understand the unconscious motivations of marriage; insight alone does not heal childhood wounds. Nor is it sufficient to introduce behavioral changes into a relationship; without understanding the reasons behind the behaviors, couples experience only limited growth. Experience has taught me that the most effective form of therapy is one that combines both schools of thought. As you learn more about your unconscious motivations and transform these insights into supportive behaviors, you can create a more conscious and ultimately more rewarding relationship.

INCREASING YOUR KNOWLEDGE OF
YOURSELF AND YOUR PARTNER

> And ye shall know the truth,
> and the truth shall make you free.
>
> —JOHN 8:32

ALTHOUGH WE ALL AGREE in principle that our partners have their own points of view and their own valid perceptions, at the emotional level we are reluctant to accept this simple truth. We like to believe that the way we see the world is the way the world is. When our partners disagree with us, it is tempting to think that they are ill-informed or have a distorted point of view. How else could they be so wrong?

Some people are particularly entrenched in their private view of the world. This was especially true for a client of mine named Gene. The director of a successful corporation, he was very bright and accustomed to dominating those around him with the sheer force of his intellect. He totally eclipsed his wife, a gentle and good-hearted woman named Judy, who would sit beside him with her chin drawn in and her shoulders hunched forward, looking like a chastened child.

One of my objectives during their initial therapy sessions was to bolster Judy up so that she would have enough courage to express her opinions in front of her imposing husband. (In psychology textbooks, this is called "implementing the therapeutic balance.") Normally, as soon as she would utter a few sentences, Gene would pounce on her and refute whatever she had to say. "That's a lie! That's absolutely not true," he would blurt out. Then he would launch into a defense of his position. His summation was invariably the same: "This is not just my opinion, Dr. Hendrix. It happens to be the literal truth." And I could see that he truly believed that his point of view was the only valid one, that he alone had a grip on reality.

It was pointless for me to try to convince him verbally of the narrowness of his vision; he would have turned our conversation into a forensic debate, and I had no doubt who would win. At the beginning of our eighth session together, however, I had a sudden inspiration. Judy had just ventured an opinion about a recent encounter between Gene and his father. Apparently she and Gene and her father-in-law had gone out to dinner together, and Gene's father had said something to Gene that had wounded his pride. Judy's perception was that Gene's father had been trying to give him some constructive criticism; Gene's perception was that his father had been cruel and spiteful. "You are wrong again, Judy," Gene intoned. "How could you be so blind?"

I interrupted their conversation and told them that I wanted them to put their difference of opinion aside for a moment and spend ten minutes listening to a classical-music tape that I happened to have in the office, a recording of Franck's Violin Sonata in A. I slipped the tape into the cassette player and invited them to listen to the music and pay attention to any images that came to their minds. They both were a little puzzled by my request, and I sensed an impatience in Gene: how was listening to music going to help them resolve their difficulties? But by now Gene had enough confidence in me to allow me to run the therapy sessions; he figured there must be some reason for my unusual suggestion.

The three of us sat back and listened to the music. I stopped the tape after the second movement and, knowing full well that I was walking into a minefield, casually asked Judy and Gene what they thought of the music.

Gene spoke first. "What a lovely piece," he said. "It was so lyrical. I especially enjoyed the violin part in the first movement." He hummed several bars, and I was impressed by his ability to remember the notes and to hum them on key. Among his numerous attributes, he apparently had perfect pitch. "Such a beautiful melody," he continued. "For some reason, the image that came to my mind was of the ocean. There were qualities to the music that reminded me of a Debussy sonata. Even though Franck is less impressionistic, there is the same sensuous texture. It must be the French heritage."

I turned to Judy and asked for her opinion.

"That's funny," she said, in a voice that was so low I had to strain to hear her, "I had a different feeling about the music." She burrowed deeper into the leather armchair, showing no desire to elaborate. How could she measure up to her husband's learned critique?

"Tell me what you saw in it, Judy," I urged. "I'd like to know what you were thinking, too."

"Well," she said, clearing her throat, "I guess the music seemed kind of stormy to me. Especially the piano part. All those chords, I got the image of storm clouds and wind—and a darkening sky."

"Honey, what makes you think it was so dramatic?" Gene asked, in the patronizing tone of voice he reserved for his wife. "I almost fell asleep, it was so soothing. Listen to it more closely, Judy, and you'll see what I mean. It has to be one of the most lyrical pieces of music ever written. Don't you agree, Dr.

Hendrix?" (Like many people, he spent a great deal of time trying to get his therapist to see his side of the story.)

"Yes, I do, Gene," I obliged him. "I sensed a gentleness to the music, a romantic quality that at times was very soothing." Then I turned to Judy and said, "But I also agree with you, Judy. There were parts that seemed to have a real sense of passion and drama. I guess I'm agreeing with both of you." Gene started drumming his fingers on the arm of his chair.

"I have an idea," I said. "Why don't the two of you listen to the tape again, but this time I want you to see if you can find evidence that supports your partner's point of view. Gene, I want you to look for the dramatic tension; Judy, see if you can find the lighter, poetic touches."

I rewound the tape, and they listened to the piece for the second time. Once again I asked for their opinions. This time both Gene and Judy heard qualities in the sonata that had previously eluded them. Gene made an interesting observation. The first time he had listened to the sonata, he said, he had been instinctively drawn to the violin. When he forced himself to pay more attention to the piano, he could see why he and Judy had had such different initial reactions. "There *is* a lot of tension to the music," he conceded, "especially in those piano arpeggios in the beginning of the second movement. That was a beautiful passage that slipped by me the first time through. My mind must have been on something else. I can see how someone might think the music was stormy." Judy, meanwhile, had been able to understand Gene's first impression. The music hadn't seemed so overwhelming to her the second time around. "There are some lovely, quiet parts," she said. "In fact, the whole first movement is really quite subdued."

By listening to the music from each other's point of view, they had learned that the sonata was a richer piece of music than either of them had first perceived. There were serene passages and dramatic passages; it was complex, multifaceted.

"I wonder what would happen if we could talk to the performers and get their impressions," wondered Gene, "and then talk to a music historian? I bet each person could add a great deal to the music. The sonata would acquire more and more depth."

I couldn't have been more pleased with the way this discussion was going; my gamble had paid off. "That's exactly what I hoped you would see," I said to him. "That's the whole point of this exercise. If the two of you would look at everything in the same open-minded way, you would realize two things: first, that each of you has a valid point of view; second, that reality is larger and more complex than either of you will ever know. All you can do is form impressions of the world—take more and more snapshots, each time aiming for a closer approximation of the truth. But one thing is certain. If you respect each other's point of view and see it as a way to enrich your own, you will be able to take clearer, more accurate pictures."

Given their new spirit of cooperation, I guided Gene and Judy back through a discussion of Gene's encounter with his father. Gene was able to entertain the idea that there had been some goodwill behind his father's criticism. Perhaps he had been screening out his father's good intentions, just the way he had screened out the piano part to the Franck sonata. Judy, in turn, gained a greater appreciation for the long-term tension between father and son. When she mentally reviewed the dinner conversation in the context of the troubled history between Gene and his father, she could understand why her husband had been so upset by what had at first seemed to her to be a casual, well-intentioned remark. All of a sudden they had binocular, not monocular, vision.

HIDDEN SOURCES OF KNOWLEDGE

WHEN YOU ACCEPT the limited nature of your own perceptions and become more receptive to the truth of your partner's perceptions, a whole world opens up to you. Instead of seeing your partner's differing views as a source of conflict, you find them a source of knowledge: "What are you seeing that I am not seeing?" "What have you learned that I have yet to learn?" Marriage gives you the opportunity to be continually schooled in your own reality and in the reality of another person. Every one of your interactions contains a grain of truth, a sliver of insight, a glimpse into your hiddenness and your wholeness. As you add to your growing fund of knowledge, you are creating reality love, a love based on the emerging truth of yourself and your partner, not on romantic illusion.

In chapter 6 we discussed a number of specific areas in which you need to increase your knowledge. You need to become more aware of the hidden agenda you bring to marriage, of your disowned character traits, of your partner's inner world, and of the healing potential of your marriage relationship. As you can see from this brief look at Judy and Gene's relationship, acquiring this information depends to a large degree on your willingness to value and learn from each other's perceptions. Once both of you demonstrate a desire to expand your individual conceptions of the world, the details of everyday life become a gold mine of information.

An especially good area to mine for this hidden information is your spoken and unspoken criticisms of your partner: "You never come home on time." "I can never lean on you." "Why don't you think of me for a change?" "You are so selfish." At the time you are making these statements, you believe them to be accurate descriptions of your partner. But the truth of the matter is that they are often descriptions of parts of yourself.

Take a look at this composite example from several couples to see how much information can be gleaned from one chronic, emotional complaint. Let's suppose that a woman routinely criticizes her husband for being disorganized. "You are always disorganized! I can never depend on you!" When her husband demands some specific examples, she retorts, "You are terrible about planning for vacations. You always forget the essentials when we go camping. You never remember the kids' birthdays. And you always leave the kitchen a jumbled mess when you cook!" Not surprisingly, the man's automatic response to this cluster of accusations is a blanket denial followed by a counter-criticism: "That's not true. You're exaggerating. *You're* more disorganized than I am!"

How can this heated argument be turned into useful information? First, the husband would learn something about himself if he assumed that his wife's criticism contained an element of truth; most people are experts at spotting their mates' Achilles' heel. Unfortunately, most people deliver this valuable information in an accusatory manner, immediately arousing the partners' defenses. If this man were able to override his defensive response, he would be able to see that there are indeed many areas of his life in which he is not well organized; the pain of hearing a criticism is largely due to its accuracy. If he could accept the truth in his wife's remarks, he would become more aware of a significant disowned trait. That would eliminate his need to project this trait back onto his wife, and it would also give him the data he needed in order to grow and change.

This observation about the hidden information contained in a criticism can be expressed as a general principle:

Principle 1: Most of your partner's criticisms of you have some basis in reality.

What else could the couple learn from the above interchange? If the woman had an open mind, she might be able to gain some valuable information about her own childhood wounds. She could do this by following a simple procedure. First, she could write her criticism on a piece of paper: "You are always so disorganized!" Then she could answer the following questions:

How do I feel when my partner acts this way?

What thoughts do I have when my partner acts this way?

What deeper feelings might underlie these thoughts and feelings?

Did I ever have these thoughts and feelings when I was a child?

By going through this simple analytical process, she could determine whether or not her husband's behavior brought back any strong memories from her childhood. Let's suppose the exercise helps the woman discover that her parents were always disorganized and had little time or energy to pay attention to her needs. Not surprisingly, when her husband acts in a similar manner, she is filled with the same fears she had as a child. Buried in her criticism of her husband, therefore, is a plaintive cry from childhood: "Why can't someone take care of me?"

This leads us to a second general principle:

Principle 2: Many of your repetitious, emotional criticisms of your partner are disguised statements of your own unmet needs.

There is another piece of information that can be derived from such criticism, one that usually requires a great deal of soul-searching. It is possible that the woman's criticism of her husband is a valid statement about herself. In other words, all the while she is berating her husband for his lack of organization, she may be as disorganized as he is. To find out if this is true, she could ask herself a general question: "In what way is my criticism of my husband also true of me?" She should keep in mind that the way in which she is disorganized may be quite different from her husband's. She may keep an immaculate kitchen, for example, and be a whiz at planning vacations—the areas where he has difficulties—but have a hard time prioritizing her tasks at work or managing the family budget. With this new insight, she would be able to determine whether or not she was attempting to exorcise a disowned, negative part of herself by externalizing it, projecting it onto her partner, and then criticizing it. If she found that to be true, she would have the information she needs to allow herself to separate her own negative traits from her partner's—"I am disorganized in this specific way; my partner is disorganized in that specific way." In psychological terms, she would be "owning" and "withdrawing" her projections. Jesus said it more poetically: "Cast out the log in your own eye so that you can see the mote in your brother's eye."

This leads us to a third observation about criticism:

Principle 3: Some of your repetitive, emotional criticisms of your partner may be an accurate description of a disowned part of yourself.

Often, when a recurring criticism is not a description of a disowned part of the self, it is a description of another unconscious aspect, the lost self. If this woman were to scrutinize her behavior and find herself to be supremely well organized in all aspects of her life, her criticism of her husband might be an unconscious wish to be *less* organized—to be more relaxed, flexible, and spontaneous. When she criticizes her husband for behaving in a carefree manner, she may be secretly resenting his freedom. When partners criticize each other for being too energetic, too sexy, too playful, too dedicated to their work, they are often identifying undeveloped or repressed areas of their own psyches. Now we have our fourth and final principle:

Principle 4: Some of your criticisms of your partner may help you identify your own lost self.

In the next chapter, in an exercise called the Stretching exercise, I will show you how to take the knowledge that you can glean from your mutual criticisms and convert it into an effective, growth-producing process.

UNDERSTANDING YOUR PARTNER'S INNER WORLD

EXAMINING YOUR CRITICISMS of your partner turns out to be an excellent way to gather information about yourself. How can you increase your knowledge of your *partner's* inner world? The answer is, through improved channels of communication. Throughout the course of your relationship, your partner has given you thousands of hours of testimony about his or her thoughts and feelings and wishes, but only a fraction of this information ever registered. In order to deepen your understanding of your partner's subjective reality, you need to train yourself to communicate more effectively.

To do this, it helps to know something about semantics: even though you and your partner speak the same language, each of you dwells in an idiosyncratic world of private meanings. Growing up in different families with different life experiences has given you private lexicons. As a trivial example, let's explore what the simple words "Let's play tennis" might mean in two different families. In family A, the full, unspoken definition of this phrase is: "Let's grab any old racket that happens to be lying around, walk to the local park, and lob the ball back and forth across the net until someone wants to quit. Rules are secondary; it's the exercise that counts." In family B, however, "Let's play tennis" has quite a different meaning. It means: "Let's reserve an indoor court at the private club, get out our two-hundred-dollar rackets, and then play tough, competitive tennis until one player is clearly the winner." Mark, raised in family A, is going to be taken aback by the aggressiveness and determination that his wife, Susan, raised in family B, brings to the game.

A less trivial example would be the associations that Mark

and Susan might bring to the phrase "Let's talk about it." Assume that in Susan's family "Let's talk about it" means: "All the adults sit around the table and calmly and rationally discuss their various points of view until they come up with an agreed-upon plan of action." In Mark's family the same words mean: "This is a topic that we will talk about briefly and then shelve until further notice." Underlying Mark's family's more casual approach is the philosophy that even the most difficult problems work themselves out over time. When Susan proposes to Mark that they "talk about" the fact that their son is getting poor marks at school, and Mark says a few sentences and then switches on the TV, she is going to be irate. Mark, in turn, is going to be stunned when Susan storms out the door and does not return for several hours. What did he do wrong? What he did wrong was assume that he and his wife shared the same language.

DENIAL

BESIDES THE PROBLEM of idiosyncratic language, there are other roadblocks to communication. Perhaps the most common mechanism is denial: you simply refuse to believe what your partner has to say. A recent example comes to mind. Joseph and Amira came to one of my weekend workshops. Joseph is a forty-year-old journalist, Amira a twenty-five-year-old television actress. They are both attractive, accomplished people. On Saturday evening, about midway through the seminar, the key source of their conflict began to emerge. During a discussion period, Joseph volunteered that he desperately wanted to start a family. "I'm going to be old enough to be a grandfather before I'm a father," he lamented. But Amira wanted to wait. Her career was just getting off the ground, and she didn't want to take time off to have a baby until her mid-thirties. She protested that she had told Joseph before they got married that she wasn't interested in starting a family until much later. "I was very clear about it in my own head, and I told him over and over again. But he didn't listen to me. I should have worn a T-shirt with big block letters: *I'm not ready to have children.*" Joseph acknowledged that Amira had indeed made her position clear to him, but he had convinced himself that she didn't mean what she said. "I was sure that she was only kidding herself. How could acting a bit part on a soap opera be more important than being a mother?" Satisfying his urgent need to have children was so important to him that he had discounted his wife's priorities.

We all have a number of these subterranean "hot spots" in our relationships, places where our expectations of our partners collide with reality. When our partners behave in ways that conflict with our self-interest, we have an arsenal of weapons to help us maintain our illusions. We can condemn them: "You are a bad (ungrateful, insensitive, boorish, stupid, spiteful, uninformed, crass, unenlightened, etc.) person for feeling that way." We can "educate" them: "You don't really feel that way. What you really feel is . . ." We can threaten them: "Unless you change your mind, I'm going to . . ." We can ignore them: "Uh-huh. Very interesting. As I was saying . . ." Or we can analyze them: "The reason you have such unacceptable thoughts and feelings is that years ago your mother . . ." In all of these responses, what we are trying to do is diminish our partners' sense of self and replace it with our own, self-serving illusion. Unfortunately, this is exactly what happened to our partners in childhood. In dozens of ways, their caretakers told them: "Only some of your feelings are valid. Only a portion of your feelings and behaviors are permitted." Instead of helping our partners repair this emotional damage, we are adding further injury.

THE COUPLE'S DIALOGUE

THE "COUPLE'S DIALOGUE" is the name of a three-part exercise that serves a number of vital functions in your creation of a conscious marriage. First of all, it focuses your attention on the actual words your partner is saying. Most of us rarely listen to what other people are saying. When we should be listening, we are responding to the impact of what we are hearing. In other words, we are listening to ourselves react. When you manage to focus on the words your partner is saying, you stand more of a chance of getting the meaning behind those words. Second, when you engage in dialogue with your partner and really listen to the words and search for their meaning, you discover that you live with another person whose inner experience is different from yours much of the time. In the thinking of the early twentieth-century Jewish philosopher Martin Buber, you begin to move from an "I-It" relationship to an "I-Thou" relationship. It is essential that you realize that you live with another person who is not an extension of you. Not to recognize this is the major source of conflict between partners. Finally, the regular use of the Couple's Dialogue, especially when you are in conflict, creates a deep emotional connection between you and your partner. When talking together reaches this profound level, it becomes a spiritual experience.

The three parts of the Couple's Dialogue are called mirroring, validation, and empathy. Let's begin with the first step, mirroring, which is a straightforward communication technique commonly used in couples therapy. When one of you has something important to say, you begin by stating that thought or feeling in a short sentence beginning with "I." For example, "I don't enjoy cooking dinner for you when you don't seem to appreciate all the effort involved." Your partner restates the sentence in his or her own words and then asks if the message was received correctly: "Let me see if I got it. You find it hard to put the effort into cooking dinner every night when I don't show my appreciation for all that you've done. Did I get it?" You repeat this process until your partner clearly understands what you mean to say.

Then your partner deepens the communication by asking if

you have anything more to add to the topic, typically by using the words "Is there more?" You then add another piece of the message, which your partner paraphrases and confirms. "It takes me at least an hour to cook dinner, and I do my best to make it attractive and delicious. I feel deflated when you eat without comment." You continue with this process until you feel satisfied that you've conveyed your full message and that your partner has received it accurately. In my work with couples, I have found that this "tell me more" part of the mirroring exercise is one of the keys to its success. When you are encouraged to convey the entirety of a thought or feeling to your partner, your partner is given enough information to begin to comprehend your point of view. Sharing just one sentence or two rarely provides enough data.

Although mirroring is a relatively straightforward process, it is so contrary to the way that couples normally converse that it requires a great deal of practice. Here's an example of the common problems that people have with mirroring. The following conversation took place at an Imago Workshop when I asked a couple to volunteer to come to the front of the group and talk about a sensitive issue, just as they would at home. Greg and Sheila, a young couple who had been living together for only a few months, volunteered. Greg started the conversation.

GREG: Sheila, I'm really bothered by your smoking, and I'd like you to be more considerate when you smoke around me.

Because I had yet to introduce Sheila and Greg to the Mirroring exercise, Sheila followed her natural instincts and responded with an automatic defense.

SHEILA: You knew that I smoked when you asked me to live with you. You accepted that fact in the beginning. Why are you always so critical of me? You should accept me as I am. You know that I'm trying to cut down.

Greg, operating on automatic pilot, returned her remarks with an intensified criticism. The conversation was turning into a tennis match.

GREG: I acknowledge your efforts to smoke less. But I find it interesting that, when we come here and the sign in the dining room says "No Smoking," you follow it. Yet I feel invaded at home with the smell of tobacco smoke all over the place.

SHEILA: Well, this is not my home. And I feel I have a right to smoke in my own home!

Sheila delivered this last message with some force, and there was a smattering of applause from the crowd. The score was love-fifteen. It was time for me to referee.

HENDRIX: OK. Let's start this all over again and see if we can turn it into an exercise in communication, not confrontation. Greg, would you repeat your opening statement?

GREG: I'm really glad that we're making a home together, but, with regard to your smoking, when we joined together I didn't realize how difficult it was going to be for me.

HENDRIX: OK. Now I would like you to simplify that statement so it will be easier to understand.

GREG: Let's see. . . . Your smoking bothers me. I didn't think it would at first, but it does.

HENDRIX: Good. Now, Sheila, I want you to paraphrase Greg, trying to mirror his feelings and thoughts without criticizing him or defending yourself. Then I want you to ask Greg if you have heard him correctly.

SHEILA: I'm truly sorry that my smoking interferes—

HENDRIX: No, I'm not asking you to apologize. Just reflect back to Greg what he was saying, and show your understanding and acceptance of his feelings.

SHEILA: Could he possibly repeat himself?

GREG: Your smoking bothers me. I didn't think it would at first, but it does.

HENDRIX: Now, try to feed that back to him with receptive warmth.

SHEILA: I think I'd rather stop smoking! (Group laughter.)

HENDRIX: Take a deep breath and be aware that he is experiencing some discomfort at one of your behaviors. Rather than hearing it as a criticism of your behavior, hear it with concern for his well-being. Whether it's justified or not, he is feeling uncomfortable, and you care about him. I know this is hard to do in front of a lot of people, and I know that this is an issue you feel strongly about.

SHEILA: What could be done—

HENDRIX: No, don't try to solve it. You just want to paraphrase his message and the emotional content behind it, so that he knows that you understand what he is feeling.

SHEILA: (Takes a deep breath.) OK. I think I get it now. I understand that it *really* bothers you that I smoke. You didn't realize how much it would bother you until we actually started living together. Now you are very troubled by it. Is that what you are saying?

HENDRIX: Excellent. I could hear Greg's concern reflected in your voice. Did that check out with you, Greg? Is she hearing what you have to say?

GREG: Yes! That's just how I feel. What a relief! This is the first time she's ever really bothered to listen to me.

As Greg's reaction shows, there is a tremendous satisfaction in simply being heard, in knowing that your message has been received exactly as you sent it. This is a rare phenomenon in most marriages. After demonstrating this exercise for workshop groups, I send the couples back to their rooms so they can practice sending and receiving simple statements. Invariably they return to the group reporting that it was a novel, exhilarating experience. It is such an unexpected luxury to have your partner's full attention.

VALIDATION

ONCE COUPLES HAVE BECOME ADEPT at mirroring each other, I encourage them to go on to the next step of the Couple's Dialogue, validation. In the validation part of the exercise, they learn how to affirm the internal logic of each other's remarks. In essence, they are telling each other, "What you're saying makes sense to me. I can see why you would think that way."

I had my first and most indelible experience with the power of validation when I was a young man. It was 1960, and I had been sent to Louisville, Kentucky, to be a chaplain in a mental hospital where I was assigned to a ward for schizophrenic patients. I was given very little training in the beginning. Basically I was told, "Go in there and relate the best you can." As time went on, I would be given more supervision, but in the first few weeks it was sink or swim. One of the first patients I tried to get to know was a gaunt man in his fifties whom I will call Leonard. One thing I remember about Leonard is that he was a nonstop smoker. I always saw him through a veil of smoke. But the reason he has stayed in my mind all these years is that he was convinced he was Jesus.

"Hello, Leonard," I said to him when we were first introduced. "My name is Harville."

"I'm Jesus," he replied calmly, drawing on his cigarette, "not Leonard."

I was taken aback, but I covered up my reaction. "Oh," I said,

"I'm a theological student, so I have a different concept of Jesus. But I'm pleased to meet you."

As the days went on, I found myself drawn to Leonard, primarily because I was so fascinated by his unshakable conviction that he was Jesus. I didn't try to convince him otherwise because I could see that that would have been pointless. I just studied his internal logic. Eventually, Leonard began to feel safe enough with me that he started to share some of the voices inside his head. When I found out exactly what the voices were saying to him and that those voices were as real to him as the words coming out of my mouth, Leonard's view of himself as Jesus began to make complete sense to me. I hasten to add that *I* didn't think he was Jesus, but I could see why *he* thought that he was. It made all the sense in his world.

The day came when I decided to address Leonard as Jesus. This didn't seem blasphemous to me. Indeed, it seemed a form of respect. Why add yet more conflict to his life when his head was already a battleground? If *he* thought he was Jesus, I was going to go along with it. I walked up to him that morning and said, "Hello, Jesus." To my surprise, he said, "I'm not Jesus. I'm Leonard." I sputtered for a moment and said, "But you've been telling me for weeks that you're Jesus!"

"Yes," he said, "but my voices are now telling me that I don't have to be Jesus with you."

Validation had moved him one step closer to sanity.

ADDING VALIDATION TO MIRRORING

WHEN I FIRST WORKED with couples, the communication exercise stopped with mirroring. I didn't require them to go on and validate the internal logic of each other's messages. As I gained more experience, I began to see that validation is a vital step in the process. I remember the first time I asked a couple to add validation to mirroring. It was many years ago, so some of the details are hazy. If I recall, the two people, I'll call them Rita and Doug, were in their forties. Rita was a schoolteacher, and I think Doug was an insurance salesman. Their central problem was their inability to connect emotionally. When Rita tried to talk with her husband about something important, Doug would answer halfheartedly and then emotionally withdraw. Over time, I learned that one reason he withdrew was that he often felt critical of her, and he was trying to keep from being her constant critic. In his own way, he was trying to improve the relationship. But, understandably, his unwillingness to respond to Rita infuriated her. To get the sense of connection she was longing for, she would raise her voice and exaggerate her statements until he would finally respond. As I write this, I can almost see Doug react to one of Rita's outbursts. He would start breathing very shallowly. His face would flush. Then he would cross his arms and lean his body away from her. If Rita persisted long enough, Doug would finally react. Unfortunately, his response, once it came, was cold and accusatory and served only to throw gasoline on her fire.

To help them break out of this destructive pattern, I taught them the mirroring exercise. It helped a great deal because Rita had to slow down her torrent of words, and Doug had to stay in contact. But the exercise did not produce the kind of results I was used to seeing. Their communication improved dramatically, but there was little enhanced sense of connection. At a loss, I remember turning to Rita one day and asking her, "What do you want from Doug that you're not getting?" Her response was immediate. "I want him to tell me that I make sense. That I'm not crazy!" A light went on in my head. Rita wanted more than to be heard. She wanted her thought processes to be validated. She wanted her husband to tell her that her worldview made sense. I turned to Doug and asked him if he would be willing to add another step to the mirroring exercise. As soon as he had paraphrased Rita correctly, would he tell her that what she was saying made sense to him? Doug thought for a long moment and then said, "But what if she *doesn't* make sense to me?" I told him that he didn't have to agree with Rita or give up his own point of view in order to validate hers, he just needed to suspend his view of the world for a moment and make an honest effort to see hers. Doug thought it over and said he would try.

Rita made a statement—I no longer remember what it was— and Doug paraphrased it back to her. Instead of waiting for me to structure the next part of the exercise, however, Rita blurted out, "Well, do you agree, Doug?"

For once, Doug was equally quick on the draw. "No," he said belligerently, "I do *not* agree."

Rita persisted, "But do I make *sense* to you? Does what I say make sense? Do you think I'm crazy?"

"No, I don't think you are crazy," Doug said, "but I certainly don't agree with you."

Rita got out of her chair and grabbed Doug's forearms. "So, what I say makes *sense* to you?"

"Yes," Doug acknowledged, "when I see it from your point of view, yes, you do make sense. I just see things differently."

I'll never forget how Rita responded. She sunk to her knees in front of Doug and began crying. "That's all that I wanted to hear!" she said. "I haven't heard that before, from you or from anybody! I'm not crazy! I make sense!"

Finally, someone was affirming her truth.

Even today, I am impressed by how aggressively each of us defends our separate reality. It must be connected to our fear of the loss of self. If I see it your way, I will have to surrender my way. If I feel your experience, I will have to invalidate mine. If what I say is true, then what you say *must* be false. There can be only one center of the universe and that center has got to be me. But if I muster the courage to suspend my own view of the universe for a moment and manage to see a fraction of your reality, something miraculous happens. First of all, a feeling of safety comes over you. Because the way you see the world is no longer being challenged, you begin to lower your defenses. At the same time, you become more willing to acknowledge a portion of *my* reality. Because I have been willing to abandon my centrist position, you are more willing to let go of yours. To our mutual surprise, a drawbridge begins to descend on its rusty hinges, and you and I have our first experience with connection.

EMPATHY

THE THIRD STEP in the Couple's Dialogue is empathy. It is only natural that empathy would follow on the heels of validation. If you listen carefully to your partner, understand the totality of what he or she is saying, and then succeed in stretching out of your own worldview to affirm the logic behind your partner's words, you are poised to go one step farther and become empathic. "Given the fact that you see things the way that you do, it makes sense to me that you would feel hurt." For some people, validation of their thought processes is more important to them than validation of their feelings. But for others, empathy is the key to their healing. Once someone affirms their raw emotions, they begin to feel loved and whole.

I hate to say it because it matches our gender stereotypes, but, in my experience, women tend to value empathy more than men. At least at first. If you stop and think about it, this makes sense. In our culture, indeed in most cultures, women are allowed to be freer with their emotions than men. Although this is beginning to change, many men still believe it is unmanly to disclose their emotions, especially their tender feelings or feelings of fear and weakness. So if we men feel uncomfortable showing our feelings to others in the first place, you can hardly expect us to want our partners to empathize with us should we happen to let a feeling slip out! We'd just as soon that they overlook the momentary lapse and focus on our steely logic instead!

Many women, on the other hand, have had the opposite experience. The culture has allowed them to keep more of their emotional wholeness, but they've had to live with men who are relatively devoid of feeling. Their partners not only fail to empathize with them, they'd just as soon ignore the fact that they have feelings altogether. "Why can't you be more rational!"

When couples master the three-step process of mirroring, validation, and empathy, these gender differences begin to diminish. A man who was relatively repressed in the beginning starts to value empathy as much as his female partner. The reason this occurs is that seeing and acknowledging feelings in the other makes them less foreign in the self. Meanwhile, a woman who was emotionally volatile becomes less so. Because she no longer needs to amplify her feelings in order to have her stoic partner acknowledge them, she can express them with less force. This is especially true for anger. It is always surprising to me to see how quickly anger will dissipate once it's been received and fully acknowledged.

As you might imagine, the ease with which you can empathize with your partner depends a great deal on the situation. It's very easy to be empathic when the two of you share the same experience and react similarly to that event. Let's suppose you and I have just been through a major earthquake. We survived the quake without any injuries, and we are relieved to see that the house still stands on its foundation. But there were several frightening minutes when we both thought we were going to die. "I was so terrified!" your partner exclaims. You respond immediately, "I can see that you were! I was, too!" Because you've had the same response to the same situation, there is no stretching involved. What you feel, I feel. We are one and the same.

Now let's make it a little more difficult. Let's assume that your partner was in the earthquake but you were gone on business 500 miles away. Your partner reaches you on the phone, describes the horrific event, and then cries out to you, "I was so terrified!" Although you didn't experience the earthquake yourself, it's not too much of a stretch to imagine that you might have been terrified as well. "I can imagine you were," you reply with only a moment's hesitation.

Problems tend to arise when two people react quite differently to similar events. For example, your partner might be terrified of flying but you can fall asleep during takeoff or landing. You're going to have a hard time empathizing with your partner's fear because you've never experienced it. "Just breathe deeply," you tell your partner. "Think about something else, and the feelings will go away." And, quite frankly, you wish that they would. They seem so irrational.

The most difficult situation of all, however, may be those times when your partner has strong, negative emotions, and you, poor soul, seem to have triggered them. "I am so angry at you that you told Janice she could go to the movies when you know I already told her she has to stay home and clean her room! You always do this!" Or "I felt so humiliated when I saw you flirting with Pat in front of all of our friends. You know how jealous that makes me!" Your instinctual response is to defend yourself and then counterattack. But the more stressful the situation and the harder it is to comply with the exercise, the more profound the rewards. If you manage to block your reactionary response and succeed in mirroring, validating, and empathizing in the heat of battle, you will be a living example of a conscious marriage.

Isn't Dialoguing with Your Partner Tedious?

AS HELPFUL AS the Couple's Dialogue may be, people have an almost universal reaction to it: "Do we really have to go through all those steps in order to communicate something meaningful?" The answer to this specific question is no. If all you're seeking is effective communication, then mirroring alone may be sufficient. But if you want to move beyond communication to *communion*, then you need to include all three steps. That said, I don't want to diminish how time-consuming and artificial the Couple's Dialogue can seem. There are times when you will rebel at the structure and want to revert to old habits. I am reminded of a seventeen-year-old son of a friend of mine who is a superb baseball player. He is so good, in fact, that he's been singled out by a ball club for special instruction even before leaving high school. To the boy's dismay, however, his new coach wants him to change virtually everything about the way that he pitches and hits the ball. He's been given a series of exercises to help him build up certain muscles and stretch out others, and he is required to hit a hundred balls a day using an alien-feeling stance and grip. At times, he has been close to tears because he feels as though he's had to abandon everything he knows about baseball.

So it is with the Couple's Dialogue. It requires you to abandon some deeply ingrained habits and adopt a formulaic way of relating. Much of the time, it's going to feel forced. But as you begin to experience some of its benefits, you will become less resistant. Eventually—and it may take years—you will have transformed your relationship to the point that you will be able to abandon the exercise all together. When that day arrives, you will be communing, not just conversing.

The Imago Workshop

ONCE COUPLES HAVE BEEN TAUGHT the Couple's Dialogue, I introduce them to an information gathering tool, a guided imagery technique that helps them become better acquainted with their childhood wounds. When the exercise is completed, I have them share their observations, using the Couple's Dialogue. This is an effective way for couples to begin to see each other as they really are, as wounded beings on a quest for spiritual wholeness.

Before the exercise begins, I ask the couples to close their eyes and relax. I often put on some soothing music to help them shut out distractions. When they are sufficiently relaxed, I ask them to try to remember their childhood home, the earliest one they can recall. When the vision begins to take shape, I tell them to see themselves as very young children wandering through the house searching for their caretakers. The first person they meet is their mother, or whichever female caretaker was most influential in their early years. I tell them that they are suddenly endowed with magical powers and can see these women's positive and negative character traits with crystal clarity. They are to note these characteristics and then imagine themselves telling their mothers what they always wanted from them and never got.

In a similar manner, I have them encounter their fathers, or primary male caretakers, and then any other people who had a profound influence on them in their formative years. When they have gathered all the information they can about these key people, I slowly bring them back to reality and have them open their eyes and write the information down on a piece of paper.

I am often surprised by how much information people can gain from this simple exercise. For example, a young man did the exercise and realized for the first time how lonely and isolated he felt as a child. He had blocked out this crucial piece of information, because it hadn't made any sense to him. How could he feel lonely in a family with four children, a minister for a father, and a devoted homemaker for a mother? In his fantasy, however, he had searched and searched around the house for his father, never to find him. When he encountered his mother, his spontaneous question to her was "Why are you always so busy? Can't you see that I need you?" Having these insights helped him understand his chronic depression. "Until this moment," he said, "my sadness has always been a mystery to me."

Once people have completed the guided-imagery exercise, they have the information they need to construct their imagos, the inner images of the opposite sex that guided them in mate selection. All they need to do is group together the positive and negative traits of all the key people from their childhood, highlighting the traits that affected them the most. These are the traits that they were looking for in a mate.

When this work is completed, I ask couples to share what they have learned. I ask them to listen to each other with full attention, making no effort to interpret each other's remarks, enlarge upon them, compare them with their own, or analyze them. The only allowable comments are mirroring comments that indicate the degree of their understanding. By doing this exercise, husbands and wives begin to see behind each other's neurotic, puzzling, or compulsive behavior to the wounds they are trying to heal. This creates a more compassionate, supportive emotional climate.

The first five exercises in Part III are designed to help you gather information about your past and get a better idea of how your unmet childhood needs influence your relationship. But once you learn to open your eyes, every interaction between you and your partner, whether spoken or unspoken, can become a valuable source of information.

DEFINING YOUR CURRICULUM

One of the deep secrets of life is that all that is
really worth doing is what we do for others.

— LEWIS CARROLL

SO FAR IN THIS BOOK, I've described the initial steps in the
creation of a conscious marriage. I've talked about narrowing
your exits so that more of your energy is available for your relationship. I've talked about increasing the pleasurable interactions between you to set the stage for greater intimacy. And I've
discussed several ways to increase your knowledge of yourself
and your partner. Now is the time to talk about the healing of
deeper childhood wounds. In this chapter I will describe a way
you can turn your chronic frustrations into avenues for growth.
In the next chapter I will talk about how to handle more explosive conflicts.

When a couple have spent several weeks practicing the Reromanticizing exercise described in chapter 8, they experience a
revival of positive feelings, and they begin to bond with each
other much the way they did during the early stages of romantic

love. Just as they grow accustomed to this more intimate, nurturing environment, however, a disheartening event occurs: conflicts begin to emerge, the very ones that brought them into therapy in the first place. Once again they are plagued with the same troublesome issues, the same basic incompatibilities. It seems as though the Reromanticizing exercise has resurrected romantic love only to let it disintegrate once again into a power struggle.

The reason the good feelings don't last is that, through increased pleasurable interactions, the husband and wife have unconsciously identified each other once again as the "one who has it all," the ideal mate who is magically going to restore their wholeness. After the anger and withdrawal of the power struggle, they are once again turning to each other for salvation. And once again they make the unpleasant discovery that neither of them has the necessary skills or the motivation to meet the other's deeper needs. In fact, many people come to the sobering conclusion that what they want most from their partners is what their partners are least able to give.

What can be done to resolve this central dilemma? The question bedeviled me in my early years as a marital therapist. Given these two facts—(1) that we enter our love relationships bearing emotional scars from childhood, and (2) that we unwittingly choose mates who resemble our caretakers, the very people who contributed to our wounding in the first place—it seems that marriage is destined to repeat, not repair, our early misfortunes.

Years ago when I lectured to groups, this pessimistic view came through loud and clear. During one talk I was explaining the self-defeating nature of mate selection, and a woman raised her hand to say, "Dr. Hendrix, maybe the way to avoid reinjuring old wounds is to marry people you *don't* feel attracted to. That way you won't wind up with people who have the same faults as your parents." Everyone laughed, but at the time I could offer no better solution. Marriages arranged by chance or go-betweens or computerized dating services appeared to have a better chance of succeeding than marriages based on an unconscious selection process. Our tendency to select partners who share the positive and negative traits of our caretakers seemed to doom conventional marriages from the start. My only advice to couples was to become more aware of their hidden reasons for marrying each other and to embrace the cold, hard facts of reality. Awareness, insight, understanding, and acceptance— that was the only solace I had to offer.

At the time I was getting the same counsel from my own therapist. "You have to accept the fact that your mother didn't have any energy for you, Harville," he would tell me. "And your wife can't give you what you want, either. She can't make up for those early years. You just have to let go of those longings." In other words, "You didn't get it then, and you're not going to get it now. Grow up and get on with life." I tried to accept what he was telling me, but I was aware that in the core of my being I was unwilling to let go of my unfinished business. A part of me felt that I had an inalienable right to a secure and loving upbringing. As I scrutinized my clients, I could see that they were clinging just as tenaciously to their needs. They might repress them; they might deny them; they might project them onto others. But they couldn't let go of their childhood needs once and for all.

WHY SELF-LOVE DOESN'T WORK

EVENTUALLY I SOUGHT OUT a different therapist, one with a more optimistic view about the possibility of resolving childhood needs. He believed that it was possible for people to make up for what they didn't get in childhood through self-love. One of his techniques to help me overcome my craving for nurturing was to have me imagine the scene in the kitchen with my mother that I talked about earlier. He would guide me through a deep relaxation exercise, then say to me, "Harville, imagine yourself as a little baby wanting your mother's attention. She is standing at the stove with her back to you. Imagine how you want to be hugged. Call out to her. See her come over to you and pick you up with a big smile on her face. She is now holding you close. Put your arms across your chest. See that little boy! He's right there in front of you and wants to be hugged. Hold him and hug him and fill him with love. Now pull the little boy into your chest. Pull that happy little boy inside of you."

It was his belief that, if I succeeded in creating a vivid picture of myself being loved by my mother, I would gradually fill up my need for maternal love. His approach seemed to work for a while; after each session I would feel less alone, more loved. But the feeling gradually disappeared, and I would once again be filled with emptiness.

The reason this approach doesn't work is that it is sabotaged by the old brain. When we were infants, unable to meet our physical and emotional needs, pain and pleasure came magically from the outside world. When the bottle or the breast appeared, our hunger was satisfied. When we were cuddled, we felt soothed. When we were left alone in our cribs to cry, we felt angry and afraid. As we grew older, our old brain remained frozen in this passive worldview: good feelings and bad feelings were created by the actions of other people; we couldn't take care of ourselves; others had to do it for us. The part of me that hurt couldn't accept love from within myself because I had externalized my source of salvation.

THE LIMITS OF FRIENDSHIP

I GRADUALLY RESIGNED MYSELF to the fact that healing love has to come from outside oneself. But did it have to come from a spouse? Couldn't it come from a close friend? At the time when I was musing over this possibility, I was leading several counseling groups and had an opportunity to observe the healing potential of friendships. Close bonds often develop between members of therapy groups, and I encouraged this love and support. In a typical session I might pair Mary, who grew up with a neurotic, unaffectionate mother, with Susan, a strong, earth-mother figure. I asked Susan to hold Mary on her lap and stroke her and let her cry. Mary would feel soothed by the exercise, but she wouldn't be healed. "I enjoyed the hugging," she said, "but Susan's not the right person. It's not Susan I need hugs from. It's someone else."

After numerous experiments like this, I concluded that the love we are seeking has to come not just from another person within the context of a safe, intimate relationship, but from an *imago match*—someone so similar to our parents that our unconscious mind has them fused. This appears to be the only way to erase the pains of childhood. We may enjoy the hugs and attentions of other people, but the effects are transitory. It's like the difference between sugar and Nutrasweet. Our taste buds may be deceived by the taste of artificial sweeteners, but our bodies derive no nourishment from them. In just such a way, we hunger for love from our original caretakers *or from people who are so similar to them that on an unconscious level we have them merged*.

But this brought me back full-circle to the original dilemma: *How can our partners heal us if they have some of the same negative traits as our caretakers?* Aren't they the least likely candidates to soothe our emotional injuries? If the daughter of a distant, self-absorbed father unconsciously selects a workaholic for a husband, how can her marriage satisfy her need for closeness and intimacy? If the son of a depressed, sexually repressed mother chooses to marry a depressed, frigid wife, how can he recapture his sensuality and joy? If a girl whose father died when she was young moves in with a man who refuses to marry her, how can she feel loved and secure?

An answer began to take shape in my mind. It was the only logical conclusion. If people were going to be healed, I conjectured, *their partners would have to change.* The workaholic husband would have to willingly redirect some of his energy back to his wife. The depressed, frigid wife would have to recover her energy and sensuality. The reluctant lover would have to lower his barriers to intimacy. Then and only then would they be able to give their partners the consistent nurturing they had been looking for all their lives.

It was at this point that I began to see the unconscious selection process in a new light: while it was often true that what one partner needed the most was what the other partner was least able to give, it also happened to be the precise area where that partner needed to grow! For example, if Mary grew up with caretakers who were sparing in their physical affection, she most likely has chosen a husband, George, who is uncomfortable with bodily contact; the unmet childhood need in Mary is invariably matched by George's inability to meet that need. But if George were to overcome his resistance to being affectionate in an effort to satisfy Mary's needs, not only would Mary get the physical reassurance she craved, but George would slowly regain contact with his own sensuality. *In other words, in his efforts to heal his partner he would be recovering an essential part of himself!* The unconscious selection process has brought together two people who can either hurt each other or heal each other, depending upon their willingness to grow and change.

TURNING THE THEORY INTO PRACTICE

I BEGAN TO FOCUS my attention on turning the healing potential of marriage into a workable reality. The unanswered question was: how could people be encouraged to work on overcoming their limitations so they could meet their partners' needs? I decided to develop an exercise with some of the same features as the Reromanticizing exercise. One partner would be asked to come up with a list of requests, which the other partner would be free to honor or not. In this case, however, the requests would be for potentially difficult changes in behavior, not for simple, pleasurable interactions; in fact, virtually every one of the requests would zero in on a point of contention. For instance, people would be asking their partners to become more assertive or more accepting or less manipulative. In essence, they would be asking them to overcome their most prominent negative traits.

As in the Reromanticizing exercise, these general requests would have to be converted into specific, measurable, doable activities. Otherwise the partner wouldn't have enough information to be able to change, and there would be too much room for misinterpretation and evasive maneuvers. Also, like the Reromanticizing exercise, the Stretching exercise would have to rely on the principle of the "gift," not the contract. Otherwise the unconscious mind would reject the change in behaviors. This was very important. If one person made a small change and then waited for the partner to match his or her efforts—"I'll work on becoming less domineering if you will work on becoming more nurturing"—the whole process would quickly degenerate into a power struggle. The old animosities would flare up, and there would be no possibility of healing. People would have to learn how to overcome their limitations and develop their capacity to love, not because they expected love in return but simply because their partners deserved to be loved.

With the general framework of the new exercise in place, I began to fill in the details. How would people determine exactly what behaviors to request of their spouses? Husbands and wives may be quick to complain and criticize each other, but they are rarely able to state in positive, specific terms exactly what it is that they need from each other. How could they come up with this information when it was not readily available to their consciousness? Wouldn't it take months or even years of intensive therapy?

There was an easier solution, fortunately, and that was to examine their criticisms. As we learned in the previous chapter, just by analyzing a couple's chronic complaints of each other it is possible to draw a pretty accurate picture of what they didn't get in childhood. The details aren't there—who did what when—but the raw material is sitting right on the surface, ready to be mined. The months or years that the couple have spent together have worn away their softer, more superficial annoyances and exposed the stony outcrop of their fundamental needs. "You never . . . !" "You always . . . !" "When are you ever going to . . . !" At the heart of these accusations is a disguised plea for the very things they didn't get in childhood—for affection, for affirmation, for protection, for independence, for attachment. To come up with the list of requests for this exercise, therefore, the couples would simply need to isolate the desires hidden in their chronic frustrations. Then they could convert these general desires into specific behaviors that would help satisfy those desires. This list of positive, specific requests would become the ongoing curriculum of their relationship.

DEFINING THE CURRICULUM

HERE'S AN EXAMPLE from a recent couples workshop to show how this exercise works. To begin the demonstration, I asked a volunteer to state a significant gripe about his or her partner. A woman named Melanie, an attractive blonde wearing a bright-print dress, raised her hand. She shared what at first appeared to be a superficial complaint about her husband, Stewart. "Stewart has a terrible memory," she said. "It seems to be getting worse. I'm always nagging at him about his memory. I wish he would take a memory course."

Stewart, a mustached, scholarly looking man, was sitting next to her and, as if on cue, promptly began to defend himself in a weary tone of voice. "Melanie," he said, "I'm a lawyer. I have to remember thousands of pages of legal briefs. I have an excellent memory."

Before Melanie had a chance to restate her criticism, I asked her what bothered her most about Stewart's inability to remember. When did it make her the most upset?

She thought for a moment. "I guess when he forgets to do something that I've asked him to do. Like last week, when he forgot that we had a date to go out to lunch. Another thing that upset me was when we were at a party a few days ago, and he forgot to introduce me to his friends. I stood there feeling like a complete idiot."

"What deeper feelings, like sadness, anger, or fear, might underlie these frustrations?" Basically, I was leading her through the same process I had described early in the workshop, identifying the desire that lies hidden in a criticism.

"Well, when he does those things, I feel unloved. I feel he doesn't care for me. I feel rejected. So I guess what I want is for him to show me that I'm important to him. That he's thinking of me. That I'm as important to him as his work."

At this point I could have asked Melanie to try to figure out what childhood wound Stewart was reinjuring by being so insensitive to her feelings: had her parents treated her in a similar way? But it wasn't necessary for her to dredge up such information to benefit from this particular exercise. All she had to do was identify a chronic criticism, convert it into a desire, and then describe a positive, specific behavior that would satisfy that desire. It was very straightforward.

"Now, Melanie," I continued, "I want you to write down a list of specific behaviors that would help you feel more cared-for. Will you give Stewart some concrete information about how he could become a more positive force in your life?"

She thought for a minute, then said she would.

Next I gave Melanie and Stewart and the rest of the group some detailed instructions on the Stretching exercise and sent them back to their rooms. My instructions were to identify a chronic complaint, isolate the desire that was at the heart of the complaint, and come up with a list of concrete, doable behaviors that would help satisfy that desire. The husbands and wives were then to look at each other's lists and rank each item according to how hard it would be to do. I told them that sharing this information did not obligate them to meet each other's needs. The purpose of the exercise was to educate their partners, so that if their partners wanted to stretch into new behaviors they would have some specific guidelines. Any suggestion of obligation or expectation would reduce the exercise to a bargain, and there was the likelihood that it would end in resentment and failure.

When the group reconvened, Melanie volunteered to share her list. Here are a few of her requests:

"I would like you to set aside one night a week so that we could go out for the evening."

"I would like you to introduce me to your friends when I meet you at the office for lunch next Thursday."

"I would like you to give me a special present on my next birthday that you have bought and wrapped yourself."

"I would like you to call me on the phone once a day just to chat."

"I would like you to remember to pull my chair out for me tonight at dinner."

"I would like you to reduce your hours at the office so that you don't have to work on Saturdays and Sundays."

"I would like you to call me if you're going to be more than fifteen minutes late coming home for dinner."

"I would like you to give up your separate bedroom so that we can sleep together every night."

According to my instructions, Stewart had reviewed Melanie's requests, ranked them according to difficulty, and chosen a request that he could honor with relative ease. In fact, he announced to the group that he would begin the exercise that very evening by remembering to pull Melanie's chair out at dinner. There was a marked contrast between his earlier, antagonistic response to Melanie's complaint about his poor memory and his cheerful response to these specific requests. Because he understood that these behaviors addressed one of Melanie's unmet childhood needs, because he was allowed to rank them according to difficulty, and because he was free to choose whether to do any of them or not, he found it relatively easy to comply.

A sign that Melanie's list contained some growth potential for Stewart, however, was the fact that there were some requests that he found very difficult to do. For example, he thought it would be very hard for him to give up his own bedroom. "I really cherish my time alone," he said. "It would be difficult for me to give that up. I'm not willing to do that now." It came as no surprise to me that that was the thing Melanie wanted most: one partner's greatest desire is often matched by the other partner's greatest resistance. "I don't feel like we're really married unless we sleep in the same bed," she said. "I cried myself to sleep for a week after you moved out. I really hate it!" I reminded Melanie that letting her husband know how much she wanted him to share a bedroom with her was an important piece of information for him, but it in no way obligated him to cooperate. The only legitimate power she had in the relationship was to inform Stewart of her needs and to change her own behavior to meet Stewart's needs.

COMPLEX CHANGE SET IN MOTION

WHEN WE WERE THROUGH WORKING with Melanie's list, Stewart volunteered to share his list. He, too, had identified a chronic complaint, isolated his desire, and composed a list of target activities. His main criticism of Melanie was that she was too judgmental. It seemed to him that she was always criticizing him. This was painful to him, he acknowledged, because he had judgmental parents. "Which," he added with a smile and a sideways glance at me, "given all the information I've gotten at this workshop, is probably one of the reasons I was attracted to her."

One of Stewart's specific requests was that Melanie praise him once a day. Melanie acknowledged that some days it would be hard for her to do that. "I don't think I'm being hypercritical," she said with sincerity, "I think the problem is that Stewart does a lot of irresponsible things. The basic problem is not my attitude—it's his behavior!" The main reason it was going to be difficult for her to praise Stewart was that she was denying the validity of her husband's complaint. She saw herself as a realistic judge of his character, not as a perpetual critic. Stewart had homed in on a disowned negative trait.

One of the benefits of the Stretching exercise, however, was that Melanie didn't have to agree with Stewart's assessment of her in order for the healing process to work. All she had to do was comply with his simple request for one compliment a day. When she did this, she would become more aware of her husband's positive qualities, and eventually she would learn how immersed she had been in the role of judge and critic. Ultimately, both Stewart and Melanie would gain from the exercise. Stewart would be able to bask in some of the approval that he deserved, and Melanie would be able to accept and transform a denied negative trait. In the process of healing her husband, she would be becoming a more whole and loving person herself.

When couples faithfully perform this exercise for several months, they discover another hidden benefit of the exercise: *the love that they are sending out to each other is touching and healing their own wounds*—wounds they didn't even know they had. Stewart and Melanie continued to work with me in private therapy sessions for over a year. About six months after the workshop, Stewart was finally able to overcome his resistance to sharing a bedroom with Melanie. He didn't like the idea, but he saw how important it was to her and decided to give it a one-month trial.

The first week, he had trouble sleeping and resented that he had agreed to the change. In his own bedroom he had been free to open the window and get more fresh air whenever he wanted to, and turn on the light and read when he couldn't sleep. Now he felt trapped.

By the second week, he was able to sleep, but he still felt as though he were compromising himself. By the third week, he found that there was some compensation to sharing a bed. First of all, Melanie was a lot happier. And, second, they were having sex more often: it was much easier to make love when they didn't have to make appointments. By the last week of the experiment, he decided that he could live with the new arrangement. "I've gotten used to having her sleep beside me now," he admitted. "I guess I'm not the hermit I thought I was."

Melanie and Stewart's relationship continued to improve, and during a session several months later, Melanie said that things had gotten so good between them that she no longer needed the reassurance of having Stewart sleep with her. "I know you love your own room," she said. "I'd rather have you stay with me, but I don't think I need it any more." Through the Stretching exercise, he had been able to give her enough reassurance that he cared about her and valued her so that she was able to let go of that particular request. But, to her surprise, Stewart would have no part of it. "I'd be lonely in my own room," he said. "I wouldn't know what to do with myself."

What was going on here? Somehow, in the act of responding to Melanie's need for more intimacy, Stewart was discovering a hidden need of his own. In the conversations I had with Stewart, I learned that his mother and father had not been comfortable with physical or verbal expressions of love. Stewart maintained that this didn't bother him. "I knew that they loved me," he said. "They just showed it in other ways." In other words, his way of adapting to their lack of affection was to decide that he didn't need any. "I remember visiting other kids' homes," he told me, "and their parents were more affectionate to me than my own. One woman would even hug and kiss me. I was really uncomfortable around her. I was much more used to my parents' style of parenting."

When he and Melanie were first married, he was drawn to her because of her affectionate nature, but eventually her need for intimacy seemed excessive to him, and he began to withdraw, just as he had pulled away from the adults who had been physically demonstrative to him when he was a child. But now, with more insight into the nature of his problems and with a desire to be more intentional in his relationship, he had been able to overcome his resistance and respond to Melanie's needs. In the process he had discovered his own repressed need for affection and was able to satisfy a hidden need of his own.

I have witnessed this phenomenon of two-way healing so many times in my work with couples that I can now say with confidence that most husbands and wives have identical needs, but what is openly acknowledged in one is denied in the other. When the partners with the denied need are able to overcome their resistance and satisfy the other partners' overt need, a part of the unconscious mind interprets the caring behavior as self-directed. Love of the self is achieved through the love of the other.

To understand why the psyche works in this peculiar way, we need to recall our earlier discussion about the brain. The old brain doesn't know that the outside world exists; all it responds to are the symbols generated by the cerebral cortex. Lacking a direct connection to the external world, the old brain assumes that all behavior is inner-directed. When you are able to become more generous and loving to your spouse, therefore, your old brain assumes that this activity is intended for yourself.

REWARDS AND RESISTANCE

TO SUMMARIZE, Melanie and Stewart reaped three important benefits from the Stretching exercise:

1. The partner who requested the behavior changes was able to resolve some childhood needs.
2. The partner who made the changes recovered aspects of the lost self.
3. The partner who made the changes satisfied repressed needs that were identical to the partner's.

The result of all this growth was a dramatic increase in positive feelings between them. Both Melanie and Stewart felt better about themselves because they had been able to satisfy each other's fundamental needs. Meanwhile, they felt better about their partners because their partners were helping them satisfy *their* needs. This made them more willing to stretch beyond their resistance into more positive, nurturing behaviors. Through this simple process of defining their needs and converting them into small, positive requests, they had turned their marriage into a self-sustaining vehicle for personal growth.

RESISTANCE

THIS BENEFICIAL CHANGE always involves some resistance. One of Freud's insights was that underneath every wish is a fear of having that wish come true. When your partner starts treating you the way you long to be treated, you experience a strange combination of pleasure and fear. You like what your partner is doing, but a part of you feels that you don't deserve it. In fact, a part of you believes that in accepting the positive behavior you are violating a powerful taboo. I touched on this common reaction before when I talked about the taboo against pleasure, but in the case of the Stretching exercise your resistance will be even stronger.

An example will help clarify the nature of this resistance. Let's suppose that you grew up with parents who were quick to point out your faults. Out of a misguided attempt to help you be more successful, they highlighted every one of your failings. They assumed that making your faults known to you would motivate you to correct them. All they managed to do, however, was erode your self-confidence. When you managed to triumph over their negative influence and act with a degree of self-assertion, you were told to "Stop being so cocky!" You were stung by their reaction, but you were a young child and had little choice but to cooperate with their injunctions. Anything else was dangerous to your survival. When you married, you unwittingly chose someone who perpetuated your parents' destructive behavior, and once again you were under attack.

Let's suppose that for some reason your spouse begins to treat you more kindly. At first you thrive on this turn of events. But gradually an inner voice makes itself heard: "You can't be respected," says the voice. "That's not allowed. If you continue along this path, you will not survive. Your existence is in the hands of others, and they won't let you be whole!" To silence this voice, you find ways to undermine your spouse's behavior. Maybe you deliberately pick fights or become suspicious of your partner's motives. Ironically, you are looking for a way to deny yourself the very love and affirmation you so desperately want.

Resistance to the satisfaction of a deeply held need is more common than most people would believe. Most of my clients who terminate therapy prematurely do so not because they are unable to make positive changes, but because they can't cope with the anxiety that the positive changes bring about.

The way to overcome this fear, once again, is to keep on with the process. I urge my clients to keep on with the Stretching exercise until their anxiety becomes more manageable. Given enough time, they learn that the taboos that have been impeding their growth are ghosts of the past and have no real power in their present-day lives.

I was working with one man who was doing an excellent job of stretching into new behaviors. In response to his wife's requests to be more available to her and their children, he was slowly rearranging his priorities at work. He had stopped bringing work home on weekends and was managing to come home by six o'clock in the evening most days a week. But when his wife asked him to become a more active parent, he ran headlong into his resistance. He came into my office one day and exploded: "Harville, if I have to change one more thing, I'm going to cease to exist! I'm no longer going to be me! It's going to be the death of my personality!"

To change in the way that his partner wanted him to change meant that the "me" that he was familiar with had to go away. The rushed, successful executive was going to have to become more of a relaxed, nurturing parent. On an unconscious level, this change was equated with death. I assured him that, if he were to continue to change his behavior, he would feel anxious from time to time, but he wasn't going to die. *He* was not going to disappear, because *he* was not his behaviors, his values, or his beliefs. He was much bigger than all those things combined. In fact, if he were to change some of his more limiting behaviors and his beliefs, he would become more fully the person he was—the whole, loving, spiritual being he had been as a child. He would be able to develop the tender, nurturing side of his personality, which had been shoved aside in his efforts to excel in the business world. His family would benefit, and at the same time he would become a more complete human being.

So that he could triumph over his fear of death, I advised him to keep on with the activities that stimulated his fear. "At first you'll think you're really going to die," I told him. "A voice from deep inside you is going to say, 'Stop! This is too much! I'm going to die! I'm going to die!' But if you continue to change, eventually your old brain will recycle, and the voice will quiet down. 'I'm going to die. I'm going to die. . . . I'm going to die? But I'm *not* dying!' Ultimately the fear of death will no longer be an inhibiting factor in your campaign for self-growth."

AGAPE

WHEN THE STRETCHING EXERCISE (which is explained in detail on pages 272–274 in Part III) is integrated into your relationship, the healing power of marriage is not just an unconscious expectation, it is a daily fact of life. Marriage can fulfill your hidden drive to be healed and whole. But it can't happen the way you want it to happen—easily, automatically, without defining what it is that you want, without asking, and without reciprocating. You have to moderate your old-brain reactivity with a more intentional, conscious style of interaction. You have to stop expecting the outside world to take care of you and begin to accept responsibility for your own healing. And the way you do this, paradoxically, is by focusing your energy on healing your partner. It is when you direct your energy away from yourself and toward your partner that deep-level psychological and spiritual healing begins to take place.

When the Stretching exercise becomes your standard method for dealing with criticism and conflict, you will have reached a new stage in your journey toward a conscious marriage. You will have moved beyond the power struggle and beyond the stage of awakening into the stage of transformation. Your relationship will now be based on mutual caring and love, the kind of love that can best be described by the Greek word "agape."[1] Agape is a self-transcending love that redirects eros, the life force, away from yourself and toward your partner. As one transaction follows another, the pain of the past is slowly erased, and both of you will experience the reality of your essential wholeness.

11

CONTAINING RAGE

Heaven has no rage like love to hatred turned,
Nor Hell a fury like a woman scorned.

—WILLIAM CONGREVE

SOME COUPLES never fight. "It's really quite pleasant around our house," said Marla, a woman in her late twenties with regular, pleasing features. She was wearing little makeup, and her naturally blonde hair was held back from her face in a loose ponytail. This was the second counseling session for Marla and her husband, Peter, an equally good-looking man. "We don't yell," Marla continued. "We don't criticize each other . . ." She paused for a moment, looked at Peter, and then added with a sad smile, ". . . at least not openly."

In the brief time that I had known them, I had to agree with Marla's assessment. She and Peter did seem to get along quite well. They did a lot of spontaneous touching and smiling and hand-holding, they listened intently to each other, they allowed each other equal time during the session (a rare occurrence), and they struggled to understand each other's point of view. Yet underneath this superficial calm and compassionate behavior was a sea of despair.

They were seeking help because they had reached a stalemate in their relationship. Peter was locked into the role of the bad boy who couldn't do anything right, and Marla was cast as the all-loving, all-giving saint. "I do something dumb," said Peter, "and Marla forgives me. I refuse to take responsibility for something, and she does it for me. We've got it all worked out: I'm difficult; she's wonderful. I hate it."

That one word, "hate," said in a quiet, passionless voice, was as close as either one of them had come to acknowledging the tension between them.

If all couples were plotted on a graph that reflected their degree of expressed anger, Marla and Peter would be on the extreme left side. Moving along the graph would be the couples who criticize each other, yell, and pick fights. Farther along would be those who occasionally hit each other. At the far right side of the graph would be the desperately troubled couples who physically abuse each other. Most of my clients are clustered somewhere in the middle. They have moments of hostility, but they express their anger in words and acts of passive aggression, not in physical violence.

I will return to Marla and Peter's story later in this chapter, but first I want to go into greater detail about the various ways couples express anger.

Physical abuse is rare in my practice, so the few cases I have dealt with stand out in my mind. Nine o'clock one morning, Stephen and Olivia, a couple in their early forties, walked into my office for a hastily arranged appointment. Stephen was unusually subdued, and Olivia looked pale and distraught. I noticed a red-and-blue mark on her cheekbone. They sat down without saying a word to me or to each other. When I asked what had happened, Stephen began describing a devastating fight that had taken place the night before. According to him, Olivia had been the provocateur.

"We were talking about money," Stephen said. "I was trying to explain to Olivia the extreme financial pressure I am under. I wanted her to see that I was slowly crumbling under the weight. I guess I was waving a white flag and asking for help." He looked up at the ceiling, took a deep breath, and began again. "While I was talking, Olivia crossed her arms and sneered at me. She has a way of glaring at me with her eyes half closed that drives me up the wall. Then she said that, if I was so upset, I should get a better-paying job. She was sick and tired of hearing me complain about money. Before I knew what was happening, I was slapping her across the face. Hard. She hit me back, and we got into a clinch. We fell to the floor, and she started pulling my hair and biting me. I kept on hitting her. We were both out of control."

Stephen and Olivia had had numerous verbal battles in the thirteen years of their marriage, but this was the first time they had ever hit each other. They were both in a state of shock from the unexpected violence of the encounter.

For most couples, such explosive episodes are rare. It is much more common for husbands and wives to throttle their rage and let it leak out as corrosive criticism. Such was the case for Elizabeth and Frank, a couple that I saw later on the same day as Stephen and Olivia. By coincidence, they had also fought the day before, but they had limited their confrontation to harsh words. Their argument had been about the new house they were planning to build. On her own, Elizabeth had hired an interior decorator to help with some kitchen details, thinking that it was her province to do so. Her husband was furious that she hadn't consulted him first. Money wasn't the issue—they were quite wealthy. What triggered his rage was that she had acted without his consent.

A comment that Elizabeth made during the session leaped out at me, because it underscored the destructive power of criticism. Describing to me what it was like to bear the brunt of her husband's rage, she said, "His angry words just rained down on me. I felt battered and bruised by the time he was finished." Her husband hadn't touched her, but her psyche felt just as wounded as if he had. He had unleashed his rage not in a slap to the face but in a shotgun burst of criticism and hostility. On an unconscious level, Elizabeth was feeling the same kind of pain and fear as Olivia, the woman with the actual bruises to show.

Rage can be more difficult to detect when it masquerades as depression. For about a year I worked with a couple that I will call Barbara and Allen. Allen was a high school teacher, Barbara a homemaker. Barbara and Allen came to see me because they were concerned about Barbara's chronic depression. In recent years she had been low in energy, had little interest in sex, and seemed to be physically ill more often than not. From the very first session, Allen was candid about the fact that her depression was making him lose interest in her. It wasn't until a few weeks later, however, that he admitted that he was dangerously close to having an affair with another teacher, an attractive, available, outgoing woman. "All it would take is the right opportunity," he confessed.

Barbara and Allen had a breakthrough one day, near the end of a counseling session. When there were only a few minutes left, Barbara looked at her watch and said she had something disturbing that she wanted to talk about. She paused for a moment to gather her courage. She looked at me, avoiding eye contact with Allen. "I had a dream last week that was really awful," she said. "I need to tell it to you. I dreamed that I came in for a session with you by myself, Dr. Hendrix. And in my dream you asked me what was the one thing that I didn't want anyone to know. The one thing I couldn't tell anyone. And what I said to you was that deep in my heart . . . I wanted to kill Allen." She took a short, quick breath, as if someone had punched her in the stomach. "As soon as I dreamed that, I woke up immediately. I was scared and confused. God knows I don't want to kill Allen!

I love him. I'd be devastated without him! Please help me figure out what that dream was about."

Barbara was learning something that I had suspected for some time: she was secretly very angry. She kept her anger hidden from both herself and Allen by turning it inward as depression. But in order to repress her rage, she also had to stifle her sexuality, her appetite for food, her interest in playing the piano, her excitement at new ideas—any stirring of her life energy was threatening to her.

The reason she was so afraid of her anger, I eventually discovered, was that she made an unconscious link between anger and abandonment. As a child she had played the role of the "good daughter," in counterpoint to her older sister, who was hostile and rebellious. Her older sister was punished severely for her behavior, and Barbara feared that, if she were to act out her anger, she, too, would be punished. So she concealed her rage—first from her parents, later from herself. As a consequence, she was living a shadowy half-life. An adaptation that had served a useful purpose in childhood was now draining the life from her marriage.

THE DESTRUCTIVE POWER OF ANGER

THESE STORIES ILLUSTRATE an important point. Anger is destructive to a relationship, no matter what its form. When anger is expressed, the person on the receiving end of the attack feels brutalized, whether or not there has been any physical violence; the old brain does not distinguish between choice of weapons. Furthermore, because of the strange workings of the unconscious, the person who unleashes the anger feels equally assaulted, because on a deep level the old brain perceives all action as inner-directed. Just as the goodwill that we extend to our partner is believed to be intended for us, the animosity that we send out is repackaged for home delivery. When we hurt our partners, we invariably hurt ourselves. In the prophetic words of the Bible, "Whatsoever you do unto others shall be done unto you." With both parties feeling under attack, there is an immediate downturn in the relationship. There is no way the two individuals can relate peaceably except through diplomacy. There can be no intimacy because there is no safety. The old brain will not allow its defenses to be penetrated.

As we have seen, repressed anger can have equally negative repercussions. Whereas overt forms of rage create instantaneous damage, repressed anger often creates an empty marriage. Barbara's depression and lack of energy were forcing her husband to look outside their relationship for the satisfaction of his desires.

I have firsthand experience with the destructive power of repressed anger, because I went through the first thirty-three years of my life subclinically depressed, and my depression was one of the main factors in the dissolution of my first marriage. The reason I was depressed was that I was not in touch with my own pain and anger. In retrospect, it is astonishing to me that I could lose both of my parents by the age of six and not feel much emotional pain. When my mother died suddenly from a stroke, I didn't even cry. I remember my older siblings praising me for being such a "brave boy." Operating out of a childhood logic, I converted this intended compliment into a directive: "You are valued when you are not in touch with your pain." I learned the lesson well: in young adulthood I would look back on these early years and tell myself I was fortunate that my parents had died because it gave me the opportunity to leave the farm and live in town with my sisters, where I got a better education.

This myth had its uses. Its primary function was to allow me to go through my early years pleasantly anesthetized, numb to the pain of abandonment. I pictured myself as a "lucky" person, not a poor orphan boy, and as a consequence I wasted little time bemoaning my fate. But my repressed emotions wreaked havoc with my first marriage. Because I was cut off from an essential part of my being, I was not fully alive. I had little inner warmth or nurturing or tenderness—toward myself or others. Unconsciously, I looked to my wife for what I was missing. I hungered for a great deal of emotional and physical contact, but she was unable to give me enough—partly because of deficiencies from her own childhood and partly because she experienced me as withholding, cold, demanding, needy, never satisfied. It was a vicious cycle. The more I wanted, the more she withheld.

One of the most telling moments in our relationship happened shortly after her father died. We were alone in the bedroom, and her grief over his death was just hitting her, and she cried and cried. I had a very difficult time being supportive. My arms were circled around her shoulders, but my body was rigid and unyielding. The reason I couldn't respond to her was that I was undergoing an internal debate. A part of me knew that it was right for her to feel pain over her father's death, but another part of me said, "What's the big deal?" I had lost both of my parents and had felt no pain. Why was she being so emotional?

A few years later, when I was thirty-three, I saw a therapist for the first time, not because I thought I needed help but because psychoanalysis was a recommended part of my training. In one of the first sessions, the therapist asked me to tell him about my parents. I told him that they had both died when I was very young, but that a lot of good luck had come my way as a result. Because my parents died, I got to live with my sisters, get out of South Georgia, get a good education, and so on and so on.

"Tell me about your mother's death," he said to me, cutting short my edited autobiography.

I started to tell him how she died, but for some strange reason my throat felt dry and constricted.

"Tell me about her funeral," he said.

Once again I tried to talk. Then, to my great surprise, I burst into tears. I cried and cried. There was no stopping me. I was thirty-three years old, and I was crying like a six-year-old boy. After a few minutes, my therapist looked at me kindly and said, "Harville, you are just beginning to grieve over your mother's death."

Once I began to experience my own pain and the inevitable rage that accompanied it, I began to change. I was less anxious. I had more compassion for other people's pain. And, for the first time in my conscious memory, I felt fully alive. I knew who I was and where I had been, and I felt in tune with the beating of my own heart. All of my senses opened up, and I began to make peace with the world.

The idea that one should be in touch with one's own pain and anger goes against some powerful directives. When children cry because of fatigue or frustration, it is all too common for parents to ignore them, spank them, make fun of them, or yell at them to be quiet. An adolescent who slams the bedroom door in a fit of rage is often criticized, forced to apologize, or denied some coveted privilege. The specific punishment for anger varies from family to family—in some families even angry looks are forbidden—but I think it is safe to say that most of us grew up with the message that anger is a bad, destructive, or self-indulgent emotion. Our options were either to flaunt this anger and brave the consequences, or to force it deeper and deeper inside of us, where we hoped it wouldn't do us or anyone else any harm.

But if we chose to dampen our anger, we also dampened our capacity to love, because love and anger are two sides of the same coin. They are not two separate entities, one good, the other evil. They are, in fact, the very same life force expressed in two different guises. The joyful abandon that fills us as children and makes a brief reappearance when we "fall in love" is the same emotional current as the rage that we hurl at our partners in a Friday-night fight. When we feel joyful, it is because our life energy is allowed to flourish. When we become angry, it is because our life energy has been thwarted. We become angry when the promise of life is denied.

The Idea of Containment

THAT RAGE is a vital expression of life energy is readily apparent. If we repress our anger, we become sick or depressed or condemned to a pale, muted existence. But, on the other hand, if we unleash our rage, we inflict physical or emotional damage on others. How can we release our anger and not hurt the people we love? The answer is a process called "containment."

To understand what I mean by containment, think for a moment about the destructive potential of gasoline. Pour a pool of gasoline on the ground and drop a lighted match into it. Instantly there is a raging fire. Now take this same gasoline and squirt it in measured jets into an internal-combustion engine. Apply a spark of electricity at exactly the right moment and the engine will spring to life. Power is generated that can be used to drive a car, run a tractor, or fly a plane. Through the process of containment, a potentially destructive fuel has been converted to a useful form of energy. The same process needs to happen to archaic rage. Your anger needs to be released in measured doses, ignited in a safe environment, and converted back into eros, its original, life-giving form.

Exercises designed to reduce rage are a fairly new arrival to the field of psychotherapy. Traditionally, an orthodox psychoanalyst alleviates fear and anger simply by bringing them into the client's consciousness. The client is encouraged to free-associate and talk about whatever comes to mind. The psychoanalyst responds at pregnant moments with an interpretive comment designed to bring together seemingly disconnected ideas. Ideally, these carefully timed remarks are followed by insight. If the client happens to be writhing on the couch in rage, reliving some painful event, the therapist responds in the same controlled manner. There is no attempt on the therapist's part to call forth a greater or lesser emotional response.

A Gestalt therapist—following the lead of Gestalt therapy's founder, Fritz Perls—would respond more directly. Such a therapist might take advantage of the client's show of anger by initiating what is called a "two-chair dialogue." The client would be asked to sit and face an empty chair and imagine that the person who provoked his angry or sad feelings is sitting in the chair. He would then be encouraged to magnify his rage or break through his hurt feelings into his anger by pummeling a pillow or brandishing a baton at the invisible protagonist. Sometimes the therapist would put other imaginary people in the chair to help the client discover a deeper source of the anger. By these evocative techniques, the client's angry or sad thoughts would be translated into a physical and emotional catharsis and directed at primary targets. In theory, there would be a net reduction in the client's "unfinished business."

A therapist specializing in psychodrama might use a somewhat different approach. In this case the therapist might become the director of a drama, instructing the client to create an entire cast of characters. The client would then go around the room and play the various characters. He might pretend to be his own mother, brother, or employer, for example, then merge back into his own role and respond to these imaginary people. As in the Gestalt two-chair dialogue, the intent of the exercise would be to provide both emotional release and insight into the true source of the anger.

THE CONTAINER TRANSACTION

THE "CONTAINER TRANSACTION" is a rage-containment exercise that I have specifically adapted for couples. Its purpose is to allow you to express your angry feelings without having your partner counter them, invalidate them, or deny them.

Instead of arguing about the cause of your anger, your partner is trained to acknowledge its existence: "Yes, I can see that you are very angry." When your partner listens carefully, paraphrases your remarks, and then acknowledges the existence of your intense emotions, your need for attention is satisfied, the environment becomes safe and affirming, and your anger gradually dissipates. The Container Transaction is not designed to eliminate the source of your anger—that can be done at a later date by requesting a specific behavior change. The exercise simply affirms the reality of your emotions.

When your partner is angry and it is your turn to be the containing person, you also benefit from the exercise, because you learn to interfere with your defensive reactions. Acknowledging your partner's anger does not mean that you agree with your partner or that you accept blame. It means that you understand that your partner is angry. All you are doing is affirming the emotional state of your partner.

Essentially, the Container Transaction is a graduate-level version of the Mirroring exercise, described in chapter 9. For this reason, it should not be attempted until the earlier exercise is mastered. The main difference between the two exercises is that in the Container Transaction the person who is sharing the information has more intense emotions. This increased voltage necessitates three ground rules: (1) Neither partner is allowed to leave the room until the exercise is completed. (2) Neither partner can damage any property or touch the other partner in a hostile manner. (3) The angry person must limit all remarks to a description of behavior, not a description of character. In other words, the angry person can say, "I am furious at you for not coming home last night," but not "You are a despicable person for staying out all night." (You will find complete instructions for this exercise in Part III.)

A variation of the container mode that I assign as an option to some of my client couples is the "Container Day" exercise, which was suggested by my wife, Helen. Essentially, the Container Day is the Container Transaction stretched out for a twenty-four-hour period. For one full day, one of you plays the role of container and the other is allowed to express any and all frustrations. The containing partner listens, paraphrases, nurtures, and supports, without becoming defensive, critical, or countering with another frustration. When it's your turn to be the expressive partner, you have an opportunity to become better acquainted with the depth of your emotions. Sometimes feelings emerge that haven't been felt before because there hasn't been the requisite degree of safety. In a sense, the exercise is a license to be a child again, only this time with a supportive, validating parent. This deeper regression in a safe and loving environment can be very healing.

When it's your turn to do the containing, you learn to become more skilled in nonreactivity. You learn that your partner's anger won't harm you. You begin to allow each other fuller expression of your emotions, because you have desensitized yourselves to anger. Eventually you develop a clearer sense of boundaries, learning that you don't have to be entwined in your partner's emotional state.

CORE-SCENE REVISION

A TECHNIQUE that I use with couples who experience the same intense frustrations over and over again is called "core-scene revision." This exercise helps reduce the frequency and intensity of core scenes, painful fights and arguments like the ones I mentioned at the beginning of the chapter between Stephen and Olivia and Elizabeth and Frank, which can be so destructive to the climate of a relationship. Core scenes occur when the childhood adaptations of one partner are pitted against the childhood adaptations of the other, making the encounter doubly wounding. Typically, core scenes end in an impasse, with both individuals in deep emotional pain.

One couple, Jack and Deborah, had recurring fights that they named "three-o'clockers," because they often lasted until three in the morning. These were not explosive fights, but wearing, exhausting, repetitive confrontations that ended without resolution. Following a three-o'clocker they would be depressed for days.

After recounting four or five versions of what was essentially the same fight, Jack and Deborah were able to see what the fights had in common. At first they found it amusing to reduce the fights to their lowest common denominators; there was a lot of laughter as they looked at their pain from afar. But then a sadness crept into the discussion: "This isn't something that I feel very proud of," said Jack. "Why do we fall into the same trap over and over again?"

Their core scene goes something like this:

Act I: It is five o'clock in the evening. Jack comes home from work and is confronted by Deborah, who wants him to do something. It could be anything—help plan a vacation, do some yardwork, sort through the mail. Jack says he would be happy to do it—later. After he has had a chance to jog.

Act II: Jack goes jogging. He comes home. As he enters the door, Deborah confronts him and asks him if he will now do X. Jack says, "Sure. After I take a shower."

Act III: Jack takes a shower. Deborah tracks him down and insists that now is the time to do X. Jack says, "Sure—after I have a drink."

Act IV (the climax of the drama): Jack has several drinks. He begins to relax and enjoy himself. Deborah enters the room, irate. "Why don't you either do it now or tell me you don't want to do it?" Deborah yells. "I hate all this foot-dragging!" "But I want to do it," counters Jack. "Just give me time. I'm tired. I want to relax. Back off." Jack begins to work on a crossword puzzle and ignores his wife. She gets hysterical. "I hate you!" she cries out. "You never do what you say. You never listen to me! I feel like I'm living with a robot! I have no feelings for you!" Jack tries to block out her anger by concentrating even more intently on his puzzle. Then, finding no peace, he gets up and leaves the house.

Act V: Jack comes home, hours later. He's been drinking. Deborah launches into her attack once more. The fight continues, with Deborah delivering devastating criticisms and Jack trying either to placate her or to ignore her. Eventually they both get tired of the melodrama and turn away from each other in despair.

Let's analyze this core scene for a moment. If one were to search for Jack and Deborah in the psychology textbooks, Jack would be described as "passive-aggressive." He is angry at Deborah for organizing his life and intruding on his space, but is afraid to express it directly. Instead he stalls, jogs, showers, drinks, works on the crossword puzzle—in other words, takes full advantage of the numerous exits he has carved into the relationship. Deborah would be labeled as "aggressive-aggressive." "She's a bulldog," says Jack, not without admiration. She is up front with both her demands and her anger. The irreducible element in their core scene is that the more Deborah attacks the more Jack retreats, and the more Jack retreats the more Deborah feels abandoned. Deborah's anger at Jack's passivity is really disguised panic. She is terrified of being left alone, and Jack's inertness makes her feel as if she were dealing with a nonentity, a pale ghost with no real substance.

I explained to Deborah and Jack that, in order to end the impasse, they would need to rewrite their play—not metaphorically, but literally. They would need to go home, take out pencils and paper, and rewrite the drama so that when the curtain goes down after the final act, they would be locked in an embrace, not in conflict. Then they would need to read their new script over and over again so that the new options would be just as available to them as their habituated ones.

I assured them that any change at all would be beneficial. Just their ability to recognize a fight as a core scene would be a marked improvement. They would be able to say, "Here we go again; we are trampling on each other's deepest wounds." Then, even if only one of them was able to introduce a new line, it would be impossible for the old script to proceed, because they wouldn't be feeding each other familiar cues.

Here are a couple of specific ways Jack and Deborah's core scene might be revised. Deborah could become less aggressive, honoring Jack's request to "back off." After asking him once or twice to do a particular chore and getting no response, she could stop making demands. Jack's automatic response to withdraw would no longer be necessary. He might decide to have a couple fewer drinks, or stay at home instead of leaving the house. And eventually he might even decide to cooperate.

Or the script might be rewritten so that Jack became a more forceful character. If he didn't want to do a particular project, he could try saying, "No. I don't want to do that. That's not important to me. I have my own plans." Deborah would probably be startled by this response, but if Jack were to persist in affirming his feelings, she would eventually be relieved. After all, what she really wants is not his weak-kneed compliance: she wants to be married to a vibrant, alive human being.

This practice of defining a core scene and then writing alternative versions can be a highly effective tool. When couples are able to objectify their arguments, identify their key elements, and create flexible options, they have gained some control over one of the most potentially destructive aspects of their relationship. Although neither this exercise nor the Container Transaction exercise is designed to get to the roots of a couple's problems—the Stretching exercise in the previous chapter is better at doing that—both of them reduce the destructive impact of rage.

THE FULL CONTAINER

THE FINAL EXERCISE I want to describe, the "Full Container," helps people get in touch with their rage and connect it to its original childhood source. The Full Container works equally well for people who are depressed and for people who are overtly angry. I must emphasize that this exercise, unlike the others, requires the supervision of a therapist and does not appear in Part III. I am describing it in general terms here, however, because it will help you understand the role that anger plays in your marriage.

The Full Container is based on the Gestalt two-chair exercise that I described earlier. An important difference is that the Full Container has two starring roles. I lead the partner who is experiencing recurring anger or emotional pain through a fairly standard rage-reduction process. I encourage him or her to come to a session with a "triggering" event in mind, some experience that provoked unusually strong feelings. I then help the client escalate those feelings and reconnect them with the childhood experiences that give them their potency. Getting in touch with these primitive emotions helps the client become more whole and unified and connected to core life energy.

The supporting partner, meanwhile, has an important role to play, which is to encourage the active partner to get deeper and deeper into the pain and anger. Instead of succumbing to the old brain's directive to fight back or run away, the supporting partner is encouraged to solicit strong feelings from the spouse. By saying words like "I want to hear more about your anger" and "Go on, I want to know about all of your feelings," the supporting partner facilitates the escalation of rage. To do this, the supporting partner has to don some protective armor. I ask the supporting partner to relax, take three or four deep breaths, and mentally assume the role of a strong and nurturing parent. Later on in the exercise, when the expressive partner has successfully broken through the rage into feelings of pain, I ask the supporting partner to hold and comfort the partner, the way one would comfort a hurting child. By helping to call forth the anger, contain it, and then relieve the pain that underlies the anger, the supportive partner contributes to the spouse's psychological healing.

There are several more steps to this rather complicated exercise. A behavior-change component follows the catharsis and nurturing, so that the couple has an opportunity to minimize the triggering behavior and eliminate future conflicts. The exercise concludes with a period of high-energy fun, to end on a high note and increase the emotional bond between the two individuals.

On the following pages is an edited transcript of an actual Full Container exercise between Marla and Peter, the couple that I introduced in the beginning of the chapter who were living in a world of superficial calm. If you recall, when Peter and Marla encountered a conflict, they had an unspoken agreement to defuse the crisis rapidly in order to preserve the tranquillity of their relationship. The incident that Marla brought to this session to serve as the basis for the Full Container exercise was a typically muted one. There had been no angry words. No lashing out. But the experience created a deep rift between them all the same. To begin the exercise, I asked Marla to describe in a few words exactly what had happened.

MARLA AND PETER'S FULL CONTAINER EXERCISE

MARLA: (Speaking softly, with no trace of anger.) I was lying in bed the other night trying to describe an important dream to Peter, one that had a lot of impact on me. As I was telling it, I was re-experiencing the dream and was feeling very moved. All of a sudden I realized that Peter was just going through the motions of listening to me. He was saying 'uh-huh,' 'uh-huh.' I was so hurt that he wasn't taking me seriously that I rolled over and started crying. I cared about the dream a lot, and he didn't care about it at all.

HARVILLE: OK. Marla, I would like you to talk to Peter directly and simplify what you just said to just one sentence.

MARLA: (Turns to Peter and continues to talk with very little expression.) I was hurt because I was describing a new dream, one that I felt was really important to me, and you weren't listening.

HARVILLE: Good. Peter, now I would like you to mirror that back to Marla, so that she knows that you heard her correctly. (They were both skilled at doing the Mirroring exercise.)

PETER: You were trying to re-experience and tell a dream you had, something that was very important to you, and I didn't listen.

MARLA: Yeah, that's it.

Now that they had defined and agreed upon the triggering event, it was time for Peter to erect a protective shield around himself so that Marla could explore her anger without hurting him.

HARVILLE: Peter, would you put your coffee cup down and do whatever you need to do to get contained and protected. You may want to take a few deep breaths to help you relax. . . . Now imagine that you are in a safe place. Any safe place you want to construct. You can envision a Plexiglas shield in front of you, or a psychic raincoat to ward off the storm, or you can imagine yourself tucked away in a beautiful safe place in the woods. . . . Let us know when you're ready.

Peter took a few minutes to relax. He breathed deeply, settled himself into the armchair, and then sat quietly in a meditative position with his eyes closed and his arms resting on his legs, palms up.

PETER: OK. I'm ready.

HARVILLE: Good. Now tell Marla that you're ready to invite her feelings.

PETER: I'm ready to listen to everything you have to say.

HARVILLE: Marla, I want you to start with what you are thinking and feeling and stay with the feelings. What you want to do is build up your feelings to the peak of their intensity, to break through your sadness and frustration into your pain.

MARLA: (In a quiet, shaky voice.) Oooh. I'm feeling really scared right now, of getting into those feelings.

HARVILLE: So you're feeling that you shouldn't explore these feelings. That your reaction . . .

MARLA: I feel it's not fair to Peter. It's not fair to dump this on Peter. It's not his fault.

PETER: I want you to go ahead, Marla. This is just for you. Don't worry about me. I'm protected. I want to hear all your feelings.

MARLA: I know. (She laughs and breaks her tension.) It's probably an excuse not to do it.

HARVILLE: Take your time and tell the event. You can get into the feelings by going back into the event. Let yourself feel what you were feeling in the experience as you tell it.

MARLA: (Sighs.) I was telling Peter about a dream. (She hesitates.) What I would like to do right now is avoid telling the dream, because I think it would be a lot easier.

PETER: I want to hear about it. I want to hear all about your dream and how you felt about it.

MARLA: (Breathes deeply four or five times and begins again.) The dream was about being attracted to a woman. That's really scary for me. It's scary, but at the same time it was a great dream. It was a positive dream. Which is sort of a first. I felt very good about this other woman. Very attracted to her. (Long pause.) In my dream this was very nice. Very normal. And I was sort of reliving that feeling as I was talking to you, Peter. In the dream, it was OK with you that I liked this woman. (She starts to cry.) And as I was telling it to you . . . it was very embarrassing to tell you about it . . . (sobs) and I wanted you to be accepting me like you accepted me in the dream. And I didn't like it that you weren't paying any attention to me.

HARVILLE: Say that again—"I didn't like it."

MARLA: (Quietly.) I didn't like it. (Cries.)

HARVILLE: Stay with your feelings. Be aware of any frustrations and express those.

MARLA: (Whispers.) Oh, God. There's like this big wall in my head against being angry.

HARVILLE: I want you to look at Peter and own your resistance. Tell him: "I won't tell you about my angry feelings."

MARLA: (Barely audible.) I won't tell you about my angry feelings.

HARVILLE: Stay with it. Say it louder.

MARLA: (Shouts.) I won't tell you about my angry feelings. (She begins to cry.) You never listen anyway. (Cries.)

HARVILLE: Tell Peter again: "You never listen."

MARLA: (To Peter, very softly, trying to hold back her anger and retreat into the safety of her hurt feelings.) I want you to listen to me. I want you to listen to me when I'm really being me, and not trying to be perfect or trying to be those things that frustrate you, too.

HARVILLE: Say: "It hurts me when you don't listen."

MARLA: (Quietly.) It hurts me when you don't listen. (Cries.) I'm so afraid of getting angry at you. (There is the first evidence of passion in her voice.)

HARVILLE: Stay with that feeling.

MARLA: (Whispers.) Oh, God.

HARVILLE: Finish this sentence: "If I get angry . . ."

MARLA: (Sobbing.) If I get angry at you . . . you're going to hate me!

HARVILLE: Good. Go on.

MARLA: (Forcefully.) And I'm afraid you'll think I'm *stupid*. And crazy.

HARVILLE: Say it all. Stay with the fear.

MARLA: (Loudly.) It doesn't make sense! I know I can get angry. I know I have that right. It's just . . .

HARVILLE: Say that again: "I have a right to be angry." (I want her to experience her anger rather than her fear at this point.)

MARLA: I have a right to be angry! (Louder.) I have a right to be angry!

HARVILLE: Say it louder.

MARLA: (Getting out of her chair, clenching both of her fists at her sides.) I have a right to be angry!! (Sits down and breaks down in sobs. Then suddenly she says in a fearful tone of voice:) Oh, Jesus.

HARVILLE: Is there anyone else in your mind that you want to say that to?

MARLA: (Quietly, with a sense of surprise.) Oh, boy.

HARVILLE: Who are you seeing?

MARLA: (In a resigned tone of voice.) It's my dad. . . . Ooh. (Whispers.) I have a right to be angry.

HARVILLE: I didn't hear you.

MARLA: (In a normal speaking voice.) I have a right to be listened to. I have a right to be paid attention to. (Cries.)

HARVILLE: Yes. Say it.

MARLA: (With energy.) I have a right to be who I am! And not try to be somebody else because I'm not good enough!

HARVILLE: Say it all. You have a right to your feelings.

MARLA: God! (Long pause.) Ohhhh. (Sighs.) I just . . .

HARVILLE: See your father again and say: "You never listen to me."

MARLA: Oh, Dad, this is breaking all the rules. (Laughs.)

HARVILLE: And if I break the rules . . .

MARLA: (Cries.) I'll be alone.

HARVILLE: And if I'm alone . . .

MARLA: I won't have anyone to take care of me.

HARVILLE: And then . . .

MARLA: And then . . . I'll die. (Said matter-of-factly:) That's why I'm so afraid of being angry.

HARVILLE: Say this: "If I'm myself, I'll die."

MARLA: (Without emotion.) If I'm myself, I'll die.

HARVILLE: How do you feel about that?

MARLA: I'm not sure.

HARVILLE: Try saying the opposite: "If I'm *not* myself, I'll die."

MARLA: If I'm not myself, I'll die.

HARVILLE: Is that true?

MARLA: I think so. Sort of. It's like I have to be partly myself and partly not myself in order to live. If I'm wholly one or the other . . .

HARVILLE: Say again: "If I'm myself, I'll die."

MARLA: (Reluctantly.) If I'm myself, I'll die.

HARVILLE: Is that true or not?

MARLA: No, it's not true.

HARVILLE: Say that again.

MARLA: It's not true! No. No! No!! NO NO NO!

HARVILLE: Stay with it. What is true?

MARLA: That I deserve to be loved!!

HARVILLE: Yes. Say it again.

MARLA: (Cries and cries. Takes a big breath.) I'm myself. I deserve to be loved. I deserve to live. I deserve to be loved. (She suddenly stops crying and speaks in a tight voice.) I keep seeing my dad in my head. He's saying I don't deserve to be loved.

HARVILLE: Talk to your dad.

MARLA: I deserve it!

HARVILLE: Say it with energy!

MARLA: I deserve it!!!

HARVILLE: Deserve what?

MARLA: (Whispers.) I deserve to be loved.

HARVILLE: Let him hear you. All of it.

MARLA: (Crying.) I deserve to be loved! I'm not an idiot!

HARVILLE: Say it again.

MARLA: I deserve to be loved.

HARVILLE: What are you?

MARLA: (Quietly.) I'm me.

HARVILLE: Louder!

MARLA: I'M ME!

HARVILLE: Louder. Make him hear you. Let him hear it. Shut down his voice in your head.

MARLA: I'M ME! I'M ME! I'M ME!

HARVILLE: Good. Say this: "I'm me and I'm alive."

MARLA: I'm me and I'm alive. I'm me and I'm alive.

HARVILLE: Deeper. Build it up.

MARLA: I'M ME AND I'M ALIVE!

HARVILLE: Will you stay alive?

MARLA: Yes! (She puts her head in her hands and sobs with obvious relief.)

HARVILLE: You're doing great. I want you to do something else. I want you to see your father and tell him that he can't kill you. That you'll stay alive no matter what.

MARLA: (Breathes deeply. Long pause. Whispers.) You can't kill me.

HARVILLE: Say it again with more energy.

MARLA: (Screams.) DAMN YOU! YOU CAN'T KILL ME! (Laughs.) Wow. (Laughs again and breaks out of her intense mood.) What a relief to say that to him. And I didn't even know that I was angry at him. Or that I was afraid.

HARVILLE: Now look at Peter and say: "I can be angry and stay alive."

MARLA: (Quietly, but with some authority.) I can be angry and stay alive.

HARVILLE: Now say: "I'm angry at you."

MARLA: (Laughs.) Do you mean I have to prove that I can be angry? Oh, no. (She laughs and talks with a smile.) Peter, I'm angry at you. When you don't listen to me, I get angry at you.

HARVILLE: Let him see your anger. Try not to smile.

MARLA: (With a strong voice.) I'm angry at you. I want you to listen to me. I want you to hear who I am. . . . (Turning to me.) This is good. It's really good to feel this way. This is going to be just great.

HARVILLE: Tell him: "I'm going to show you my anger when I want to."

MARLA: I am going to show you my anger. I can do that. I deserve that. (Laughs.) That's how much I love you.

At the end of the session, I explained to Marla that it would take numerous encounters of this kind before her fear of being angry would go away. The brain tends to favor messages that were laid down early in life over ones that are added later. Especially in times of stress, it is likely she would retreat to old patterns and withdraw from Peter to cry out of pain and frustration rather than feel her anger. But after going through ten or fifteen exercises around this issue, she would finally be able to integrate the full truth, which is that she could have all her feelings and survive.

• • •

One of the reasons I wanted to share this particular transcript with you is that it demonstrates the complex layering of emotions that is common to all of us. As for many people, Marla's initial response was sadness. She was sad that Peter wouldn't listen to her describe a dream that was very important to her. It was easy for her to feel sad, because that was a feeling that her caretakers allowed her. Without my urging, she probably would have stayed with this familiar and comfortable feeling and never experienced the more archaic emotions about her father that underlay it. Her natural response was to let the sadness evolve into withdrawal and long-term resentment.

By escalating her feelings, however, Marla was able to break through her sadness to her fear of anger. Then she experienced some of her anger, which, as is often the case, was directed not at her partner but at herself, for being unable to experience rage. This was followed by an important discovery. The reason she was not in touch with her rage, she realized, was that she had internalized her father's injunction against anger. When she was a child, her father had made her feel crazy or stupid for being angry. Violating his taboo against anger meant potential abandonment, and if she were abandoned, reasoned her old brain, she would die. This palpable fear of death was amplified by the fact that she was afraid that if she were to reveal her anger, her father would not just leave her, he would kill her. It's no wonder that, when her fear of abandonment was coupled with the even more powerful fear of being murdered, it was extremely difficult for her to be angry at Peter, the person whom she had unconsciously fused with her father.

At the conclusion of her exercise, Marla was clearly relieved to be in touch with her anger, an essential but long-denied part of her being. "This is good," she said, and her laugh was a laugh filled with life and energy. Peter and I were as elated as she was, because we knew that she had just won a momentous psychological victory: she had overpowered her father's tyrannical voice, and, despite her fears, his ghost had not risen out of the ground to strike her dead. She was alive; she was whole; she no longer had to cover up her real feelings to survive. She cried out in the ultimate expression of joy: "I'M ME! I'M ME!"

When she and Peter talked about the experience at the end of the session, Peter said, "My feeling the whole time you were getting into your feelings was that this was important work not only for you but for both of us. Your lack of anger accommodates this whole unhealthy dynamic we have together. It allows me to do anything I want to and know that I won't have to face your anger. I can be the irresponsible kid and know I won't have to face any consequences. If you would break out of the saint role and start getting mad, I would respond to that positively. I have a lot of respect for your anger." Being angry at Peter and then gaining his love and acceptance was what psychologists call a "corrective emotional experience" for Marla. An important lesson she was learning was that Peter was not her father. She had confused her husband with her imago. Now she was gaining a new appreciation for the real Peter. She was discovering that she could be angry at him and not only be safe from danger but gain his love and appreciation as well.

To some degree, Marla's struggle with anger is a struggle familiar to all of us. We all hide intense feelings. Some of us hide our sadness. Some of us hide our fear. Some of us hide our anger. But, to one degree or another, we hide our true feelings from ourselves and from the people around us. Superficially, this is because we fear that we will be laughed at or criticized or punished. On a deeper level, we fear that we will die. Like Marla, we believe that we have to be "partly myself and partly not myself" in order to survive. So we hide behind a mask that we hope will gain us greater protection and safety.

Over the years, I have had the opportunity to witness hundreds of people go through the Full Container exercise and for a moment lay down their masks. At the start of the exercise, many of them appear to be superficial or abrasive or selfish or weak or lifeless—qualities that are in reality childhood adaptations to pain. When they manage to break through this crust of assumed character and connect with their own pain and anger, they become immensely real and lovable. The artifice is gone, and, without exception, their husbands and wives are overcome with love for them.

During my weekend seminars, I demonstrate the Full Container exercise in front of the group. Nothing that I have said or done up to that point can match the power of a man or a woman tapping into archaic pain, fear, and rage. And the men or women courageous enough to reveal these feelings have the support of every person in the room. We want them to feel their repressed anger and pain. We intuitively sense their missing life energy and pray for its recovery.

Yet, when it comes to our own repressed emotions, we cower in fear. We fear that what is inside of us is dark, ugly, and overpowering. But once we gain the courage to wrestle with this fear, we learn an astonishing fact: what is hiding inside us is our own blocked life energy. It is love; it is light; it is the essence of God. And releasing this energy is the ultimate purpose of love relationships.

PORTRAIT OF TWO MARRIAGES

What makes a happy marriage? It is a question which all men and women ask one another. . . . The answer is to be found, I think, in the mutual discovery, by two who marry, of the deepest need of the other's personality, and the satisfaction of that need.

— PEARL BUCK

I STARTED OUT LIFE as a minister, not a therapist. I was introduced to the ministry at a tender age. As a young boy, I was a member of the First Baptist Church in Statesboro, Georgia, and was involved in a youth group called the Baptist Training Union. Once a year our church sponsored what we called "Youth Sunday," a special day devoted to the young people in the community. The year I turned fifteen, I happened to be chosen to deliver the traditional youth address. I remember standing behind the pulpit dressed in a suit and tie, a cold sweat slicking my shirt to my back. I looked out over a church filled with young people and their parents and somehow managed to open my mouth and talk. Despite my anxiety, I must have given a reasonably good sermon, because several people came up to me afterward and said, "You should be a preacher."

Apparently the minister of our church, George Lovell,

thought so, too, because several weeks later he called me to his office. "Harville," he said, "there's a little Baptist church about twenty miles out of town. They just lost their minister. They called me and asked if I knew anyone who could preach for them the next couple of Sundays. Would you like to do that?" Flushed with success from my youthful address, I said that I would.

For the next few days, I studied the Bible with a new sense of responsibility and pored over a book Lovell had given me called *Great Sermons*, a collection of sermons from famous religious leaders. On Sunday my sister and brother-in-law drove me to church, because I was too young to drive. If I recall, the message that I delivered that morning from the depths of my experience went something like this: "Man is a sinner. We have a loving God. In order to be saved, we have to meet God. And you do that through commitment, confession, Baptism, prayer, and trying to lead an exemplary life." I believe I also warned about what Baptists call "backsliding," the tendency of even devout Christians to fall away from a faithful life.

I preached at the little church for the next couple of Sundays, and word got back to George Lovell that I was doing a good job. From that point on, he began to think of me as his "preacher boy," and for the next few years, when other small communities needed a stand-in minister he would send me.

One Sunday he sent me out to a little church in Guyton, Georgia, called the Pine Street Baptist Church. I preached for four consecutive weeks. After the fourth sermon, the church leaders held a meeting and decided to ask me to be their permanent preacher. I was only seventeen at the time—a gangly young man with a cracking voice—but they wanted me anyway. (In the Baptist church, you don't have to have extensive theological training to be ordained; you just need to be called by God and by a congregation. If your home church honors the request of the petitioning congregation, then you can become a minister.)

As I look back on that period of my life, I realize that being called to preach at the Pine Street Baptist Church was one of the real gifts of my life. The Pine Street congregation was a very loving congregation, and they ministered to my hidden depression and loneliness. Their love for me gave me increased self-confidence, and in a few years I managed to increase the active church community from thirty to a little over two hundred people. I preached there every Sunday for two and a half years. Between the ages of seventeen and nineteen and a half, I baptized over fifty people and buried eighteen.

In the summers I began to be called upon by various churches to lead youth revivals, and as a result of all this experience, my sermonic style got better and better. During one revival I looked around me and realized that there were over a thousand people straining to hear my every word. At the end of the session, sixty young people came down the aisle and gave their lives to Christ. Twelve of them decided to join the ministry. My reputation as a youth evangelist began to grow outside Georgia.

I wanted to continue as a minister, but to do that I felt the need for a college education. Eventually I saved enough of my weekly fifty-dollar paycheck from the Pine Street Church to buy a car and pay my tuition at Mercer University, a Baptist college about a hundred miles away. I studied hard during the week and drove back to the Pine Street Church each weekend to deliver the sermon.

In my third year of college, I took an excellent course in philosophy, and a whole new world of logical thinking opened up to me. As I became absorbed in the realm of abstract ideas, nothing seemed simple any more, and when I went out to preach, my sermons were filled with probing questions.

I soon discovered that you don't win souls to Jesus by engaging in a linguistic analysis of the Bible. The summer after completing that fateful philosophy class, I was invited to lead a revival at a church in a fairly good-sized town, a church where I had worked wonders the year before. The first night, all the seats in the arena were filled with people eager to hear the new preacher boy. To their surprise, my opening speech was about the concept of "eternal life" and whether the word "eternal" referred to the quality of life or its duration. When I got up to speak the second night, I looked up and noticed that there were some empty seats in the balcony. By the third night, there were empty seats riddling the main floor. At the end of the weeklong revival, only a faithful few had stayed to listen. When it was all over, the minister took me aside to have a heart-to-heart talk. He brought up the fact that the previous year I had convinced 120 people to devote their lives to Christ; this year only eight people had ventured down the aisle. "You've started college, Harville, haven't you?" he said, the disappointment evident in his voice. I nodded. "Well, college has ruined you," he concluded.

My brief career as an evangelist rapidly drew to a close, but my intellectual curiosity about philosophy and religion flourished. In my remaining year of college, I added a third interest— psychology. To me, theology, philosophy, and psychology were three portholes into one central reality, the reality of man's existence, and each one offered a slightly different perspective. If I looked through all three portholes at once, I believed that I saw more of the total picture. When I enrolled in graduate school at the University of Chicago, it was in the new interdisciplinary field of psychology and religion.

From that point on, the events of my life led me deeper and deeper into the study of just one of these disciplines, psychology. When I finally arrived at my destination, I looked up and discovered that I had landed in the rather specialized field of couples therapy. From my beginnings as a preacher boy in South Georgia, I had wound up as a marital therapist in upper Manhattan. But the formative years that I spent preaching and baptizing and bringing souls to Christ were not left behind me. To this day they continue to be very much a part of the way I view the world. To me, man's spiritual wholeness is inextricably linked with his psychological wholeness, and the work that I am now doing as a therapist feels just as much a part of God's work as my summer revivals. When I help a man and a woman heal the rift between them and become passionate friends, I believe that I am bringing them closer to God.

What leads me to believe that marriage therapy is a spiritual process? How can talking to people about mundane things such as "behavior changes" and "caring behaviors" and "rage reduction" have anything to with helping them experience the divine? I had better define my terms. When I use the word "spiritual" I'm not giving the word its most common usage. I'm not talking about going to church or following the doctrines of a particular religion or attaining a rarefied state of mind through meditation, fasting, or prayer. What I'm talking about is a native spirituality, a spirituality that is as much a part of our being as our sexuality, a spirituality that is a gift to us the moment we are conceived, a spirituality that we lose sight of in childhood but that can be experienced once again in adulthood if we learn how to heal old wounds. When we regain awareness of our essential inner unity, we make an amazing discovery: we are no longer cut off from the rest of the world. Because we are in touch with the miracle of our own being, we are free to experience the beauty and complexity of the world. The universe has meaning and purpose, and we experience ourselves as part of a larger whole.

It is my conviction that one of the surest routes to this exalted state of being is the humble path of marriage. When we gather the courage to search for the truth of our being and the truth of our partners' being, we begin a journey of psychological and spiritual healing.

INTEGRATION

THE PREVIOUS CHAPTERS detail various ways in which this healing process takes place. Now let's stand back and get an overview of the entire process. The first step is to become more conscious of our old wounds. We look into the past for evidence of how we were denied adequate nurturing and how we repressed essential parts of our being. We do this through therapy, prayer, and reflection, and by becoming more astute observers of everyday events. As we gather new insights, we share them with our partners, because we no longer assume they can read our minds. When our partners share their thoughts and feelings with us, we listen with understanding and compassion, knowing that this sharing is a sacred trust. Gradually we start to "reimage" our partners, to see them as they really are—wounded children seeking salvation.

Once we have this more accurate image, we begin to redesign our relationships to heal our wounds. To do this, we first build an atmosphere of safety and trust. By closing our exits, renewing our commitment to each other, and deliberately pleasuring each other, we create a safe and nurturing environment. We add to this feeling of safety and validation by learning to communicate openly and effectively. As we overcome our resistance to this new way of relating, we begin to see our partners with even more clarity. We learn that they have fears and weaknesses and desires that they have never shared with us. We listen to their criticisms of us and realize that these illuminate our own darkness. We tell ourselves: "My partner has something to say about me. There is probably a measure of truth in this comment." Gradually we come to accept the fullness, the dark and the light of our own being.

The next step in the healing process is perhaps the most difficult: we make a decision to act on the information we are acquiring about ourselves and our partners and become our partners' healers. We go against our instinct to focus on our own needs and make a conscious choice to focus on theirs. To do this, we must conquer our fear of change. As we respond to our partners' needs, we are surprised to discover that, in healing our partners, we are slowly reclaiming parts of our own lost selves. We are integrating parts of our being that were cut off in childhood. We find ourselves regaining our capacity to think and to feel, to be sexually and spiritually alive, and to express ourselves in creative ways.

As we reflect on all that we are learning, we see that the painful moments in life are in reality opportunities for growth. Instead of blocking the pain, we ask ourselves: "What truth is trying to emerge at this moment? What primal feelings are hiding beneath these feelings of sadness, anxiety, and frustration?" We learn that the underlying feelings are pain and rage and the fear of death, and that these feelings are common to us all. Finally, we find a safe and growth-producing way to express these powerful emotions and no longer allow them to jeopardize our relationships.

One by one, the elements of our marriage that were once unconscious—the fears, the anger, the childhood needs, the archaic pain—are brought to the surface, first to find acceptance, then, ultimately, to be resolved. As our wounds heal and as more hidden parts of ourselves come into our awareness, we have a new sense of our inherent unity and wholeness.[1]

Marriage is a spiritual path, but it is not necessarily an exalted path. For the most part, striving to create a more conscious marriage is a very practical, day-by-day sort of struggle. To give this process greater reality, I want to share with you the story of two couples.

There are obvious differences between these two couples. The first couple, Anne and Greg Martin, are in their forties. They have been married for only five years. Both of them have been married before and have children from their previous marriages. Both of them have full-time careers. The Martins learned about Imago Relationship Therapy early in their relationship and managed to resolve their major conflicts in just three years. Kenneth and Grace Brentano are in their mid-sixties and have been married for thirty-five years. They have four grown children. Kenneth provides most of their income, and Grace is primarily a homemaker. Kenneth and Grace struggled for thirty years before achieving a satisfying relationship. Much of this they did on their own before becoming acquainted with my ideas.

What these couples have in common, however, is more significant than their differences. Both the Martins and the Brentanos have managed to create a marriage that satisfies each individual's need for healing and wholeness—a marriage that makes each individual feel safe and vital and loved.

ANNE AND GREG

ANNE AND GREG MET in Santa Fe, New Mexico, in 1981. Anne, who lived in Dallas, was spending the weekend in Santa Fe with two friends. She had been divorced for three years and had dated several men casually, and was just getting to the stage where she wanted to remarry. "I wasn't interested in casual relationships anymore," she says. "I was looking for something permanent." That weekend, however, Anne was not thinking about meeting men; she was mainly interested in having a good time with her friends Josie and Shelley. On Friday night the three women went out to a lounge. During dinner Josie mentioned that she wasn't very good at meeting men. Anne jokingly agreed to be Josie's coach. "You don't have to do anything seductive," she told Josie. "If you see an interesting man, just look his way when he looks at you and smile. And if anybody asks you to dance, get up and dance. Then the guy will know that you're willing to dance and will have more courage to come over."

Anne was having a fun time giving Josie pointers on how to seduce a man, when she glanced up and happened to see a lone man walk into the room. He was tall and slender, and he was wearing a corduroy jacket. Anne remembers thinking that he looked "rugged yet neat." She also thought he had a presence about him, an aura of self-confidence and intelligence. Anne forgot all about her coaching job. "Now, *that* one's mine," she said to Josie.

Greg has an equally vivid memory of the encounter. He was in town for the weekend, celebrating his imminent divorce from his third wife. In fact, he had filed the divorce papers the day before. He was interested in having a good time but, with three failed marriages behind him, he had no interest whatsoever in establishing a permanent connection. He walked into the Inn at Laredo and glanced around. He noticed Anne, a tall, animated blonde in her mid-thirties, and was immediately attracted to her. After a while he asked her to dance.

"We started talking right away," says Anne. "A lot of guys don't know how to talk to women, but we were going a mile a minute. I liked that about him." Another thing she liked about Greg was the fact that he wasn't daunted by her academic background. (She has a Ph.D. and is an associate professor of counseling at a Southern university.) Several of the men she had dated had been intimidated by her intelligence. To appear less threatening, she had learned to refer to herself as a "teacher." "But I knew right away that I wouldn't have to keep back anything from Greg," she says. "He told me he had a Ph.D. himself—in engineering—and that he admired bright women."

Greg and Anne talked and danced all evening, and Greg walked her back to her motel. The next morning they met for breakfast and went for a walk. The attraction was strong on both sides, but not overpowering. That weekend might have been the beginning and end of their relationship if Anne hadn't impulsively sent Greg a card the next week. When Greg opened the card, he telephoned Anne and asked if he could come to Dallas that weekend to see her. Anne had other plans, but rearranged her schedule so that she could spend time with him.

"That was it," says Anne. "We were off and running. It was

almost as if a drug took over." When Anne reflects on those early days, she is amazed that she plunged so abruptly into the relationship. Greg had a lot of strikes against him. He had not one, not two, but *three* previous marriages, and he had four children from two of those marriages. Anne had written her doctoral dissertation on the difficulties of being a stepparent, so she knew exactly what she was getting into. On top of all this, she and Greg lived 250 miles apart and had well-established careers in their respective cities. "A sane person would have looked at those facts and run in the opposite direction," she says, "but the attraction between us was too strong."

What was the source of this attraction? To find out, we need to know something about their separate childhoods. Anne was an only child. Throughout her early years, her father was in the service, so she saw him only when he was on leave. Her mother joined the navy when Anne was six months old, leaving Anne in the care of her grandfather and stepgrandmother. By the time her mother came back a year later, Anne had become very attached to her grandparents and once again had to sever close bonds.

This early pattern of abandonment was reinforced when Anne was seven years old and her mother and father divorced. Her father left town, and Anne didn't see him again until she was thirteen and managed to locate him by writing to the Red Cross.

Anne has clear memories of her early years with her mother. Her mother was a flighty, social woman who frequently placed her needs above Anne's. There were many times when her mother stayed out all night and didn't come home until late the next day. Anne would wake up, discover that she was alone, and stalwartly go about getting herself ready for school.

When Anne's mother did happen to be around, she was not very nurturing, according to Anne. "I don't remember being held or touched or stroked," she said. But her mother was the source of some vital approval. "She really thought I was neat and was very confident in my ability. She didn't say ugly things to me or criticize me."

Partly because of the need to care for herself and partly because her mother praised her self-reliance, Anne became a responsible, independent child. She turned to her school and to church for the nurturing she missed at home. She denied the pain that came from the lack of security and warmth in her upbringing, because it was too overwhelming. To the outside observer, Anne appeared to be a self-confident, assertive young woman.

Her husband, Greg, the oldest of five children, grew up on a farm in Arkansas. What he remembers most about his childhood is that there was not much affection between his mother and father. "There was a lot of yelling," he says, "mainly on my mother's side. She was a real vocal person. She had a lot of anger. But she was also very loving."

Money was always an issue in Greg's family: "My mother would bitch about money, and my father would ignore her." He describes his father as a kind, intelligent man, though without a lot of drive. "He worked hard, but he wouldn't accomplish much," says Greg. "He always seemed to be living in the future. He would say things like 'If it rains in August, we'll get seventy bushels of corn, and everything will be all right.' Or 'If it rains, the soybeans will make.' He was always saying, 'Next year things will be better.' He sustained himself with a vision that things were going to be OK." One of the things that bothered him about his dad was that he had dreams that he never realized. "He always talked about wanting a plane," says Greg. "It was really important to him. But he never did anything about it. If I wanted a plane, I would make it happen. I would do whatever was necessary to realize that goal. My dad just let life slip by him."

Greg's parents were never abusive to him or his brothers and sisters, but, in his words, "it wasn't a hugging family." Greg played on his own a lot, spending a lot of time roaming around the farm creating vivid fantasies in his head. By and large, Greg remembers his childhood as being a happy period. "I was cheerful. Not much bothered me. But I was usually alone. Kind of aloof. I had friends, but I didn't let them get close. I didn't feel lonely, just apart. I had a sense that I was different from everybody else. Not worse. Not better. Just different."

Greg didn't break out of his isolation until late in life, well into his second marriage, and, surprisingly, it wasn't his second wife who managed to get close to him; it was a male friend. Greg explains how this came about. "This casual friend of mine kept wanting to get closer," he says. "I didn't like the guy at first, but he kept moving in, moving in. He kept asking me to do things with him. When that didn't work, he arranged for a foursome with our wives. I kept saying no, but he persisted. Finally I remember saying to myself, 'I'd better get to know this S.O.B., because he's not going to go away.' He forced his way into my friendship. Kind of plowed his way in. He became my first intimate friend. It kind of broke the ice. But even though I finally learned what it was like to be close to someone, I didn't seek it out. I felt pretty self-sufficient as I was."

Greg's first marriage was to his high school sweetheart. "That one was easy," he recalls. "My first wife was more like a buddy or a friend. There never was a real strong love." The marriage lasted eleven years. Greg felt that they lived on different intellectual planes and that they had little in common, but to him the fact that they were different kinds of people didn't justify ending the marriage. "We had two kids," he says, "and it wasn't considered proper in either of our families to divorce." Eventually Greg got involved with another woman. "I think I was using it as an excuse to end the marriage," he says. "In everybody's eyes, an affair was a good enough reason to call it quits. You have an affair, you get divorced."

The worst mistake in his life, says Greg, was marrying the woman with whom he had been having the affair. "She wasn't a very kind person. She was smart, and I felt a strong physical attraction for her, but she wasn't the kind of person I wanted to marry. We had a lot of problems. We had sexual problems, communication problems, and she was always suspicious of me. She kept accusing me of having other affairs." Their stormy relationship lasted five years. During this time they had a child, and Greg adopted her son by another marriage. (Now he was the father of four children: two by his first marriage, two by this one.) When his second wife threatened divorce for the third or fourth time, Greg told her, "I've had it. I'm leaving and not coming back. Go ahead with the divorce."

Greg was single for four years and then married his third wife, a woman from a wealthy family in Alabama. She was five years older than he and, in contrast to his second wife, a "high-class" woman. He says that he married his third wife largely because he wanted a mother for his ten-year-old daughter, the only one of his children who was living with him. "I thought she could give my daughter a lot of things that I could not, or would not, provide for her." Greg and his third wife were good friends, and he had a lot of respect for her. There was nothing particularly bad about the marriage, according to Greg, but "there wasn't anything really wonderful about it, either. The highs weren't very high. The lows weren't very low. And there was no communication. There was no intimacy. No sharing. She was intimate with me, but my intimacy would only go so far. So that was the end of number three."

Greg's casual approach to divorce and marriage might alarm some people, but in an age where divorce is easy and genuinely helpful information on marriage is scarce, he was choosing one of the few options available to him. All he knew was that none of his three marriages worked for him. There was something missing in all of them—and in his life—that made staying married intolerable.

. . .

Anne's first marriage was similar to Greg's first marriage in that it was fairly serene, traditional, and uneventful. Her husband, Albert, was a high school math teacher in a private school. The first ten years of their marriage were smooth and serene: "Albert was busy with his teaching job, and I was busy raising our two little girls." Because of Anne's unusual childhood, she didn't have a good role model for married life. "I think I got my image of marriage from the television," says Anne, "and from books and watching other people. I didn't have any of the details. No skills. So my first marriage was all on the surface. But it didn't feel superficial; we were doing the best that we could."

Things went along fairly smoothly until Albert went through an emotional crisis in the tenth year of their marriage. It seemed to them that this was totally unrelated to anything that was happening in their lives. His suffering became so acute that he went to his doctor for help. The doctor told him he was suffering from anxiety and prescribed some sedatives to help him sleep. Albert dutifully listened to what the doctor had to say, and went to a pharmacy to fill the prescription, but when he got home his first words to Anne were "What does 'anxiety' mean?" She couldn't explain it to him. "That's how naïve we were," says Anne.

Albert went through the bottle of pills and still felt no better. Eventually he discovered a workable solution, which was to withdraw. He spent a lot of time by himself; when he and Anne were together, he wasn't emotionally available, because he was too busy trying to maintain his own internal equilibrium. Anne was deeply troubled by his withdrawal. Outside of her awareness, it brought back memories of her early abandonment. She struggled to break through to Albert, but nothing seemed to work. In desperation, she began to pull away from *him*. "I went back into my old childhood pattern of taking care of myself, that old coping mechanism of mine of being totally independent."

In addition to the lack of intimacy between them, Anne and Albert began to have other difficulties. "He wanted me to be a good faculty wife," Anne says. "I was friendly and outgoing and very involved, and the people at the school liked me. But there was a part of me that was not happy in this role." She, in turn, was unhappy with Albert's role as a teacher. "I wanted him to go back to school and get a degree in administration. I hoped that he would move into an administrative position at the school, which would spare him some of the pressures of teaching." When Anne reflects on the situation today, she realizes that she had hidden motives for wanting him to change careers. "Consciously I was thinking about what the degree would do for him, but underneath it all I think I was projecting my own unfulfilled ambitions onto him. I was the one who wanted to go back to school. I was taking my own frustrated career drive and putting it onto Albert," she says.

Albert eventually went back to school and got a Ph.D. When their children were old enough, Anne entered a master's program in counseling. She began to acquire a lot of information that helped her understand her own childhood, but she didn't learn much that she could apply to marriage. Furthermore, she observed, "Most of the therapists I knew had relationships that were about the same as or worse than my own. They were getting divorced, having affairs. Why turn to them for advice?"

Meanwhile, the conflict between Albert and Anne intensified. As soon as Albert finished his degree, he decided to go back to teaching. This was devastating to Anne. "I thought all that schooling was going to be a springboard to launch him into a different career. I turned to Albert one day and said, 'What are the next twenty years of our life going to be like?' He said, 'This is it.' And I said, 'No, I don't think I want to do this.' What I was seeing in those twenty years was more of the same. I felt a void in my life. There was something very important that was missing."

By this stage of their marriage, there was little love between them. "We didn't fight much," says Anne, "but we were kind of at odds with each other. I wanted him to be different. He wanted me to be different. I was becoming more independent, and he wanted the sweet and supportive wife that he thought he had married. We were both growing individually, but we weren't integrating it back into our relationship. We didn't know where to get any help, and as I look back at it, I don't think we really wanted any. We were dead. Numb. We wanted something from each other that we weren't getting, but we didn't know what that was. We were both out of touch with our needs. On a scale of one to ten, I would say that our understanding of what was really going on in our marriage was about a three."

Anne and Albert got divorced in February of 1978. Their two children were ten and thirteen. "My older daughter took it very stoically, like her dad," says Anne. "But my younger daughter was very verbal and very clear about her pain. She acted out her anger." Anne and the two girls moved to Berkeley, California, where Anne entered a doctoral program in counseling and guidance. As part of her training, she underwent extensive therapy. Slowly gaps in her self-knowledge started to fill in. She began to see that a lot of her discontent in her first marriage was due to the fact that underneath her confident exterior she was an anxious, fearful person. "For the first time I realized that I was still aching from my earlier abandonment," she says. "I had all this pain and didn't know it. I was removed from it, yet it was affecting everything in my life." At one point her therapist asked her if she had ever experienced an anxiety attack. She said, "Well, no." Later on she realized that she had been fighting off a constant state of anxiety all her life. "It was a constant barrage. If I'd had an anxiety attack, it would have been like a pebble in the ocean. But I wasn't aware of my anxiety. It was second nature to me. That's the way the world was."

Anne eventually moved to Texas, where she became an associate professor of counseling and guidance at a large university. During this time she learned about my views of marriage therapy. For the first time Anne had a more comprehensive understanding of the psychology of marriage. "And, more important," she says, "I had a model of how to make it better. Once someone explains something to me and gives me a model, I can do it. Up until that time, I was really leery about remarrying. I kept asking myself, 'What makes you think that the next one is going to be any different?'"

This was about the time that Anne met Greg. Let's take another look at their initial encounter to see if we can now decipher any of the unconscious sources of attraction. When Anne describes her first impression of Greg, she describes him as an intelligent, resourceful man who possessed that enviable quality of inner contentment. Now that she has a lot more self-knowledge, she can see that he was also sending her clues that he was emotionally unavailable. Like the father who was always gone in the navy and later abandoned her, and like the mother who didn't come home at night, Greg, with his extreme self-reliance and history of three divorces, was not going to let her get too close. His isolation triggered Anne's primary drive, which was to make a person who was distant and unavailable become close and dependable. Meeting Greg crystallized all of her unfinished business.

Why was Greg attracted to Anne? A warm, loving, aggressive, volatile woman, Anne evoked strong memories of his mother. "I sensed that she could be just as loving as my mother," he said, "and just as aggravating. But one thing for sure, I knew she would stir things up. I may say I want peace, but the truth of the matter is, I want life to be challenging." And what he was also wanting, although he didn't know it, was to become involved with a woman who could break through his emotional barriers just as that persistent friend had done years ago. When he met Anne, he sensed that she had the willpower and the determination to do it.

Anne and Greg got married on New Year's Day, 1982, only four months after they met. For the first few weeks of their marriage, intimacy came easily. "I trusted Annie, more than I've trusted any other person," says Greg. But after a while he began to feel that Anne was using intimacy as a weapon. "I felt she was asking me questions to invade my space. She always wanted to know what I was thinking and feeling." Gradually, he began to shut down. Being self-contained was a safe and familiar experience for him; being emotionally vulnerable was not. When Greg withdrew, Anne experienced it as a repetition of the withdrawal of her first husband, Albert. She became angry and demanding and was convinced that Greg was planning to leave her. "She would go really crazy," says Greg. "She would have all kinds of suspicions and want to know what I was planning. Well, I wasn't planning anything. I was just licking my wounds to get ready for the next offensive." The independence that Anne admired in Greg and the aggressiveness that Greg admired in Anne were now developing into a power struggle.

Anne remembers one significant episode. "I was really upset about something. Something had happened at work that was really painful. I was talking about it with Greg, and I started crying. He looked at me and said, 'I don't console people. I'm not good at it, so I don't do it. Don't turn to me for comfort.' And, of course, that's what I wanted from him more than anything else."

Soon there were other difficulties. Having four teenaged children between them, they had a relationship that was fraught with complexity. There were numerous times when they both wanted to call it quits. The only reason she stayed in the relationship, says Anne, is that "I was very aware of the fact that, if I broke up with Greg, I would be bringing the same issues to another relationship. And when I looked at him, I realized that he was someone I wanted to be with. He was worth the effort. The pain we caused each other was intense, but the attraction between us was very strong."

Knowing that they would not be able to deal with their problems without outside help, Anne invited Greg to one of my weekend couples seminars. Although she was well acquainted with my theories, she had been reluctant to introduce them to Greg. "Because I was a therapist myself," she explained, "I was afraid of getting into the position of telling him what he was doing right and wrong. That had gotten me into trouble with earlier relationships. I wanted to have the ideas presented to him by a third person."

Greg had two important insights at the seminar. First of all, he was very moved by the exercise that helped him envision Anne as a hurting child. "I had never understood her pain before," he said. "All of a sudden I understood what she was going through. She used to tell me that, when I wouldn't talk to her, she felt abandoned, but I didn't know what she meant. How can a grown woman feel abandoned? I had never experienced that kind of insecurity before. Suddenly, during this guided-imagery exercise, I began to see her as a hurting four-year-old child. As an eight-year-old waking up to find no one home. Here was this child being formed and I could see that and feel that—get in touch with Annie as a child. It was real touching to me, and it made me more willing to listen to her complaints and to try to change my tendency to withdraw."

The other insight Greg had at the workshop had to do with communication skills. When he saw the Mirroring exercise demonstrated in front of the group, he realized that it would help him cope with his wife's intense emotions. Greg remembers the first time he tried it out. "Annie and I were driving in the car," he says, "and she was really angry. I think it was about my relationship with one of the kids. I remember that she was all fists and fury. I felt that she was throwing these lightning bolts in all directions, and all I could do was dodge them. My instinct was to throw some lightning bolts in *her* direction or just close down—that's what I would have done in the past—but instead I made a conscious choice to mirror her. I didn't react. I didn't accuse. I just listened and repeated back to her what she was saying. As I listened to her, it was as if I absorbed some of her fury. She got smaller and smaller, until finally she was in a contained package. Then we were able to talk calmly and rationally. By not hooking into her anger, I was able to contain her." This experience made Greg feel good about himself and gave him renewed hope for the future of their relationship. "I was able to defend myself without attacking her or crawling inside my shell."

Eventually Greg got so good at the mirroring technique that it became second nature to him. Whenever he felt threatened by Anne's intensity, he would put on his armor, listen, and stay in touch. "The result of all this," says Greg, "is that Anne has stopped getting so angry. She simply won't do it. It doesn't work anymore. We've progressed way beyond that. We can communicate now."

Another tool that Anne and Greg brought home from the workshop was the Stretching exercise. "Instead of fighting, we started asking for what we wanted," says Anne. "It's made all the difference." Initially this exercise was difficult for both of them, though for different reasons. Greg's problem was that he prided himself on being self-sufficient. It was very difficult for him to admit that he needed anything from anybody, but especially from Anne. However, one need that Greg couldn't deny was that he wanted to have more frequent and more spontaneous sex. "I had this fantasy of coming home and finding Anne in a negligee, eager for sex. But it rarely happened." He finally learned that, if he wanted more sex, he would have to ask for it. "I had to be more direct about my needs. She wasn't going to read my mind."

Anne's problem with the exercise was of a different nature. She had no problem asking for what she wanted. Because of revelations that had come out of her individual therapy, she was well acquainted with her unmet childhood needs, and she didn't hesitate to ask Greg to change his behavior to help meet those needs. What she had a hard time doing was accepting his attentions once he responded to one of her requests. Anne gave the following example. Greg is the owner of an engineering firm and has to leave town frequently on business trips. This separation fuels Anne's fear of abandonment. To ease her anxiety, she asked him to call her up every single day, especially when he was out of town. Greg readily agreed to do this. After a few weeks of receiving these daily calls, however, Anne began to feel anxious. She began to think up reasons why Greg should stop calling her. "It's too expensive," she would say. Or "It takes up too much of your time." Greg was persistent, however, and called every day, despite Anne's unconscious attempts to sabotage his efforts. Eventually she was able to relax and accept the gift.

In the past year, Anne and Greg have gotten better at expressing their needs and asking for what they want. One of the payoffs for Greg is that he spends less time trying to guess what Anne wants. "I used to always be trying to anticipate her needs," says Greg. "I would do all these things that I hoped would make her happy. But she rarely noticed, and I would be exhausted from trying to figure her out. Now I can relax, knowing that, if she wants something, she will ask for it. I like it much better this way. I take care of my own needs. She takes care of hers. We both will go out of our way to meet each other's needs, but we don't do so much mind reading."

One need that Anne has made abundantly clear to Greg is her need for security and affirmation. "I need and want massive doses of reassurance," Anne says. To help meet this need, she informed Greg one day that, whenever she was being overly emotional—whether angry or withdrawn or tearful—what she really wanted was to hear how much he loved her. She wrote down on a card the exact words that she wanted him to say. She handed him the card and said, "Here are your lines." The card read: "I love you. You're the person I want to be with. I want to live with you for the rest of my life." Greg, the man who had once proclaimed that he was not able to console anyone, has been able to deliver his lines with utter sincerity.

Anne and Greg have also learned a new way to fight. Essentially, they do a modified version of the Container Transaction exercise. "We fight in a very healthy manner," says Anne. "We get the anger out, but we don't get into the old garbage. We're real honest and direct." Anne gave me an example. "I looked at Greg's hand the other day and noticed that he wasn't wearing his wedding ring. I felt hurt and betrayed. But instead of stewing about it, I spoke up immediately. I said, 'I'm really hurt that you're not wearing your ring. A ring is a visible sign to other people that we're married, and it's really important to me. I'm really upset. I don't know what it means that you're not wearing it. I don't like it, and I want you to wear it.' Instead of getting defensive or abusive, Greg listened to me and said, 'It makes sense that you feel that way. I understand that you're angry.' Later he explained to me why he wasn't wearing it. It had to do with the fact that I had reverted to using my maiden name, and he was hurt about that. In his mind, not wearing the ring was kind of tit for tat. We didn't resolve the problem immediately, because the issues were complex. But the important thing is that we both got our feelings out. We listened to each other. We defused all the bad energy. And we're not angry anymore. Before, we would have gotten obsessed about it and gone on and on."

Through these efforts, Anne and Greg have been able to meet enough of their needs to attain a new level of acceptance. "I am secure enough in our relationship that I can now accept the fact that Greg is basically a self-contained person," says Anne. "It no longer threatens me. I can wait for him to reveal his feelings. I don't have to press him. When he's upset, my instinct is to make him tell me right now what is bothering him. I just want to get it over with. But that always puts me in the facilitator role. The other thing I found is that, if I wait before I make demands, he usually resolves things himself in his own way. And even when he doesn't, I can live with things the way they are. I've learned that I don't have to fix everything."

Anne and Greg are the first to admit that working to achieve a conscious marriage is not easy. In fact, Anne wants to go on record as saying, "Working things out with Greg is the hardest thing I've ever done." Greg voices a similar opinion. "Marriage is like growing flowers," he says. "You always have to work on it. If you don't, the weeds start to grow and choke out the flowers." He makes another comparison. "When you garden, it's important to have good tools. You can carry water by hand and dig in the dirt with your hands, but it's much much easier to use a hose and a shovel. That's how I feel about living with Annie. We have the right tools and skills to make the kind of marriage we want."

The reason Anne and Greg are willing to put so much effort into their relationship is that they reap daily rewards. Greg thinks that one of the most obvious changes has been in their emotional states. "Early on in our relationship," says Greg, "we were both volatile people, only I kept a lid on my feelings and Anne was too free with hers. Now she's become less crazy, and I'm more emotional. Not that we're trying to become what the other person was—we've just reached a balance. We tend to oscillate around a mean. Sometimes she's more emotional than I am. Sometimes I'm more emotional than she is. But it's like we've established middle ground. Which is very reassuring."

Greg finds that what he's learning in his marriage has helped him become a more effective manager. "I've gotten quite adept at spotting hidden agendas," he says. "I know that the issue that people are talking about is not always the real issue. I look for the underlying problems." He also is better at putting himself in others' shoes. "I say to myself, 'If I were that person, what would I be wanting or needing at this moment?' Being able to empathize with Anne has given me that skill. My marriage has also made me a better communicator and able to withstand more pressure. If someone at work has a problem or becomes angry, I am able to keep from getting defensive. I am able to get things done."

Anne finds that her marriage to Greg has made her a more spiritual being. "The strongest force in the universe is what I would call 'Christ in us' or the Holy Spirit," says Anne. "And to me that's the same thing as the drive to completion. In my mind, our purpose on earth is to be the best that we can be in terms of loving and living and being kind to other people and developing our talents and our skills. I think the best way I can do this is to have full access to who I am. And that means being honest about who I am, the negative part of me as well as the positive. Being free to be complete. That has happened in this relationship. It's a great paradox. Because before I thought I was feeling self-confident, but in reality it was grandiosity. Now I just feel good about myself. All of me. I like being who I am. I can be alone and be happy. I'm more comfortable in my own skin than I have ever been. I'm walking around better on a moment-to-moment basis. My anxiety level is so low. That's a real difference. I feel truly happy and secure for the first time in my life."

I asked Anne if she had any advice for people who would be reading this book and perhaps confronting some of these ideas for the first time. "My advice would be to focus on yourself," she said. "And when I say that, I mean you should realize that what you are doing for your partner is what you're doing for yourself. It's about your own personal growth. I finally learned that, when I was stretching to meet one of Greg's needs, I was reclaiming a part of myself. So, any time your partner asks you to do something, say to yourself, 'Does this make sense? Does it behoove me as an individual to do this?' And if it makes good sense and if it behooves you to do it, then do it, regardless of how you feel about it, because in meeting the needs of your partner you will be recapturing a part of yourself."

KENNETH AND GRACE

KENNETH AND GRACE MET in the 1940s, when they were both in college. Kenneth was a premed student, and Grace was studying art history. They became friends when they happened to sit next to each other on the bus going home for spring vacation. Kenneth has a clue to what attracted him to Grace. "A woman in the seat in front of us had a screaming baby and was having a tough time comforting her. Grace asked the woman if she could hold the baby. Soon after Grace got the baby, it started to settle down. I remember thinking to myself, 'That's the kind of woman that I would like to have as the mother of my children.' Deeper down—although I certainly didn't know it at the time—I was wanting some of that tenderness for myself."

Grace had a positive first impression of Kenneth. "He seemed like such a gentle, kind man." She was also pleased that during the long bus ride he expressed genuine interest in a paper she had written at school. "I liked the fact that he respected my intellect, something that other men hadn't done." She remembers telling her parents as soon as she got home that she had met a young man who was "as good as gold."

Underlying these conscious impressions were more powerful, hidden sources of attraction. What unfinished business did

Grace unwittingly bring to their romance? Grace was the oldest in a family of three children, two girls and a boy. She described her family as "a mixture of love and tumult." They prided themselves on being offbeat and doing unusual things. "We were all artists or musicians," said Grace. "There was a lot of spontaneity. Dad would say, 'Let's take a drive after supper. Leave the dishes!' Mother would say, 'Let me do the dishes first.' And Dad would say, 'If we don't leave now, we'll miss the sunset.' So we would all pile in the car and go off for a drive. We sang in the car, in harmony. We sang in church as a family, so we traditionally ended our family singing with the song 'Blessed Be the Tie.'"

Grace has fond memories of her early childhood. She remembers being her father's "little darling." When she was five years old, her younger sister, Sharon, was born, and she had a rude awakening. "All of a sudden I wasn't the center of attention anymore. I felt cast out. I remember thinking, 'What in the world has happened? Aren't I as cute as I used to be? Why am I not loved?' I just couldn't accept the fact that I was no longer the favorite."

Grace described her mother as a confusing mixture of warmth and petulance. She and Grace rarely got along. "She was so strong that I felt that I had to fight her to maintain my own identity," she recalls. "I think this is why I became a rebel." Her father was warm and caring and a good listener. She remembers having a very close relationship with him. "Some would say too close," says Grace. "I remember coming home from high school and lying down on the couch and having my dad rub my back. It felt perfectly comfortable and normal to me, but I know that it made Mother jealous." In later years she would look back on her relationship with her father with some anxiety. "In a way, it was scary to be that close to him. When I got married, I remember that it was very hard on him. Right before my wedding, he told me, 'I always thought you would stay home and never get married.' He was partly kidding, but I think there was some truth to that." Besides experiencing some discomfort over the closeness of their relationship, Grace wished that her dad had a more forceful personality. "He was not very strong," she said. "He would disappear when things got rough. When Mother and I got into an argument, he would go polish the car or tend to his flowers. He would never defend me."

When Grace was about twelve or thirteen, she experienced a religious awakening. She went to a special youth service and was overwhelmed by the presence of God. She remembers feeling a confusing mixture of elation and guilt. Elation at "having God on my side, but guilt for being a wicked girl, for sassing my mother." Around that time, she remembers a day when her family was scheduled to go on a trip, and Grace stubbornly refused to go with them. "I remember going to my room and praying and crying and carrying on. I have no idea what it was really about, but I remember an awful feeling. Some kind of emotional crisis. I remember feeling 'bad' or 'wicked.'" This negative view of herself was to be a refrain in later years.

Grace often worried about being "dumb." She got this idea from her parents, who would criticize her for doing "stupid" things. "It wasn't that I was really dumb," she says in self-defense. "I would just be thinking about something else and do dumb things." Perhaps another reason Grace developed this idea about herself is that she is by nature a "doer rather than a thinker." As a young girl she had an assertive, take-charge personality and could be counted on to get things done with little wasted effort. After a minimum amount of planning and organizing, she would plunge right in. Sometimes Grace would pride herself on her ability to get the job done, but at other times she would agonize about not being as deliberate and contemplative as others.

One of Grace's strengths is that she is very artistic, something that was important to her as a young adult. When she was in high school, she was an assistant to the art teacher at summer camp and enjoyed helping children express themselves through art. In following years she won prizes for her free-form designs and surrealistic paintings, and art gradually became a primary focus in her life.

Knowing these facts about Grace, let's take a look at Kenneth's early years. Kenneth has had extensive counseling throughout his life. During our initial interview, he told me that he could "tell my life story with one hand tied behind my back." True to his word, in just a few minutes he was able to give a comprehensive synopsis of his upbringing. "My mother was an intense, energetic, passionate woman," he began, "who wanted a lot from life and wanted a lot from my father, who was a passive, quiet, gentle man. My father was a model for me. I learned to be passive and quiet from him. My mother also wanted a lot from me. I experienced her as being hungry with me. Now, as an adult looking back on my childhood, I can see it was because she wasn't being nourished by my father. She had a sharp tongue that could cut, and she was often critical and angry at me. I didn't understand why, and often thought she was being unfair. I can remember as a kid wishing that I had a different mother. We would have some warm times, but I couldn't trust myself to get too close to her; I was afraid she would eat me for breakfast. I didn't even want to share my achievements with her, because I thought she would take them as a feather in her cap. And I wasn't going to let her do that."

There appears to be a basic similarity between Grace's and Kenneth's upbringing. Both had fathers who were passive and withdrawn and mothers who were aggressive and dominant. Kenneth, however, was not close to either parent. Though he greatly admired his father, his father remained at a distance. "We had some nice times together, but he was shy about talking about feelings. I wanted him to like me and be proud of me, but he never told me that he loved me. I learned from other people that he respected me, not from him." His father was especially wary of anger. "If I was ever angry, he would back away. He used the same technique with my mother. When she was angry at him, he would just withdraw. When my mother was angry at me, I tried to copy his evasive maneuver, but I could never back away far enough." Because of this early indoctrination, Kenneth learned to be afraid of his own anger: anger got him in trouble with his mother and alienated him from his father. "I decided at a young age to be nice," he says. But this persona, this "false self," was covering a desperate longing for, in his words, "some tender mothering and some firm and affirming fathering." And underneath this longing was a reservoir of anger at being denied those needs.

Kenneth and Grace exemplify a principle that I talked about earlier, which is that husbands and wives are often injured in the same way but develop opposite defenses. Kenneth and Grace both felt that they had to carve out a separate identity from an overbearing parent. This suggests that their key developmental struggle was in the stage that child psychologists would label "the stage of individuation and autonomy." Kenneth created his psychic space by being passive and "nice," hoping to sidestep his mother's anger; Grace established her identity by being rebellious and angry, trying to counter her mother's invasiveness. Because of their opposite solutions, it makes sense that they would be attracted to each other. Grace admired Kenneth's gentleness and goodness; Kenneth admired Grace's strength and aggressiveness. They saw in each other parts of their own essential nature that were poorly developed. What they didn't realize was that these opposite character traits were an effort to heal the very same wound.

From a vantage point of thirty-five years of marriage, Kenneth and Grace have some astute observations on why they were initially attracted to each other. "I made arrangements to take care of myself," says Kenneth. "I picked up Grace to re-mother me. She was full of warmth and vitality and tenderness." Grace has an equally succinct explanation for marrying Kenneth: "I was a 'bad,' 'dumb' girl looking for a 'good,' 'bright' boy. Kenneth was exactly what I needed." While these undoubtedly were some of their positive reasons for marrying each other, there were some negative ones as well. The most obvious one is that they had each chosen a mate who would perpetuate their struggle with the opposite-sex parent. Grace was dominant and aggressive—like Kenneth's mother—and Kenneth was passive and gentle—like Grace's father. They had chosen partners who had character traits that had caused them a great deal of anguish in childhood.

It was a full year, however, before these negative factors became evident. "The first year was pretty idyllic," says Grace. Problems developed in the second year of their marriage, shortly after the birth of their daughter. Kenneth was a physician at a struggling family-practice clinic. Grace was concerned that he wasn't aggressive enough about attracting new patients. "I kept seeing all of these ways that he could help the clinic," recalls Grace, "but he was content with things the way they were. I kept seeing all these possibilities that he was not seeing."

They had their first real fight when Grace realized that the clinic was losing patients. "For two years Kenneth had ignored all the signs that the clinic was going downhill. Now it was getting too late to do anything about it. Two of his colleagues left to find more lucrative employment. One night I finally blew up." Kenneth remembers the fight and recalls that he appreciated Grace's concern for the clinic but resented her intrusion. "On the one hand, I kind of looked to her for leadership," he says. "But, on the other hand, I was furious with her for being so demanding. She seemed to think that she knew what I should be doing and that she had a right to tell me. I felt like she was my mother, making heavy demands on me."

Looking back on the episode, Grace, too, recalls having mixed emotions. "I was concerned about being too strong, too willful. I wondered whether downplaying my personality would make him more dominant. But I couldn't let things lie." The very factors that had been the key to their mutual attraction— Grace's assertive, outgoing nature and Kenneth's passive, gentle nature—were becoming the basis for a thirty-year power struggle.

Kenneth began to have some additional misgivings about Grace. "I was becoming aware of some things that I wished were different in Grace. For one thing, she didn't have the same intellectual interests that I did. I wanted her to read more and be able to discuss issues." Once again Grace was getting the message that she wasn't "smart" enough. The young man who had once seemed so interested in her academic work was now criticizing her for not being intellectual.

When their daughter was in the first grade, Grace began teaching art part-time at a local high school. In the winter of that year, Kenneth's mother came to visit, and Kenneth and Grace had another significant confrontation. At the time Grace was very involved in the school and was putting out a newsletter at their church as well. She was pleasant with her mother-in-law, but went about her business as usual. "I was too busy to be a good hostess," she recalls. Furthermore, she refused to live up to her mother-in-law's expectation that she be a traditional homemaker and spend all her hours after work "cooking, cleaning, and mending." Kenneth's mother had to entertain herself during most of her visit and was so irate at this treatment that she left two days early, complaining bitterly to Kenneth as he drove her to the train. Being trapped in the car with his angry mother made Kenneth extremely anxious. "There I was, listening to my mother attack Grace and not daring to defend her. I didn't have the nerve to stand up for my own wife."

For Grace this visit was an unpleasant replay of her childhood. Once again she was relying on an ineffective, passive male to defend her against a critical, hostile mother figure. "I wanted Kenneth to stand up for me," she says, "to explain to his mother how busy I was. But he was afraid to ruffle her feathers, and then he had the nerve to be angry at me for failing to placate her!"

As Grace was recounting this episode to me, she remarked on the resemblance between Kenneth and her father. "My dad was a very kind, loving man, but he was not strong. I wanted him to be protective of me, to take leadership—the very same things I wanted from Kenneth." Interestingly, when she was angry with Kenneth, she treated him the same way her mother treated her father. "I would rant and rave, cry and yell, generally terrorize him with my anger. Kenneth would do his best to placate me. But the 'nicer' he got, the angrier I got. It all became quite poisonous." Unknowingly, Grace had introjected her mother's negative traits, the very ones that had plagued her as a child.

On the surface Kenneth and Grace, like many couples, appeared to be polar opposites. Grace as the outgoing, angry one; Kenneth was the passive, pleasant one. However, underneath his superficial "goodness," Kenneth was just as angry as Grace. The way his anger revealed itself was through criticism. This tendency showed up early in their marriage. "From the word 'go,' Kenneth never gave me the feeling that he admired me," says Grace. "Other fellows that I had dated treated me much more kindly. Kenneth was critical of my housekeeping, my parenting, my moods, my lack of intellect. And he was always playing teacher. He would ask me, 'Do you know such and such?'—some obscure fact that had no relevance to me. When I admitted that I did not, he would proceed to lecture me as if I were a high-school student. I was able to put a stop to that particular behavior in the first few years. But he never gave me the feeling that he cherished me. He never loved me the way I wanted to be loved. Gradually I think I lost much of the self-esteem that I had brought into the marriage."

Today Kenneth can be quite candid about the way he used to criticize his wife. "I wanted a lot from her, and I was getting a lot. But I seemed determined to bite the hand that fed me. I needed to keep her unsettled, even though I knew how much this hurt her."

Why was Kenneth so critical of Grace? If you will recall, Kenneth's goal in life was to get tender nurturing from a dominant mother figure, but at the same time he had to stay far enough away so that he would not be absorbed. Unconsciously, he accomplished this delicate maneuver by giving Grace enough love and affection to keep her interested, but maintaining a crucial distance through the use of constant criticism.

Because Grace was getting so little affirmation from Kenneth, she was understandably insecure about the relationship. She felt jealous and suspicious of his outside activities, especially his contacts with women. "There are so many women who fall in love with their doctors," she says, "I was sure he was having an affair." Kenneth admits that for a very long time he had "one foot in the marriage and one foot out. Like maybe somebody better would come along. Like maybe I hadn't picked the best one. It hurts me to say this, but I had only a partial commitment to Grace."

It's no wonder that Grace often felt angry. "The one thing I can't deny," Grace says, "is that there was a constant surge of anger in me." But at the time Grace didn't know where it was coming from. The time that she was most aware of her anger was when she went to bed at night. She would say to herself, "Why am I so angry? Why is this?" But she didn't have any answers. Now, when she looks back on this period of their marriage, it is plain to her that Kenneth was the source of her anger. She remembers that he often had to put in late nights delivering babies or responding to medical emergencies. When she heard the sound of his car coming down the gravel driveway, she would have a rush of what she calls "romantic feelings." She would be eager to see him and she would greet him with an air of expectancy. But within a very few minutes she would be angry. The romance would crumble. "I felt disappointed," says Grace. "Yet I wasn't even sure what it was that I wanted from him."

Kenneth and Grace's marriage went through many changes in those first twenty or so years. They raised four children, lived in three different cities, and had good years and bad years. But the emotional undercurrents were the same. Grace kept wanting more love, strength, and commitment from Kenneth. Kenneth kept wanting more love, softness, and, at the same time, more distance from Grace. The underlying tension was so great that, had they been born in a more permissive era, they probably would have gotten a divorce. "I was always threatening divorce," says Grace. "After the first year of marriage, divorce was a frequently occurring issue. We were very different people, and we weren't willing to accommodate each other." One of Grace's deepest regrets is that she shared her anger at Kenneth with her oldest daughter. "From the time she was old enough to listen, I would complain to her about her father," she says. "To this day, I'm afraid she thinks less of him because of this."

The lowest ebb of their marriage took place when they were in their forties and Kenneth was going through a midlife crisis. Until this point in his life, he had always thought of himself as a "promising young man." Life was an adventure, and there were many avenues open to him. Now he looked around and saw that he was in a lackluster marriage, that he was a "mediocre" doctor, and that he didn't have much enthusiasm for his profession. "I was just delivering babies. I could no longer maintain the fantasy of a promising future," he says. This realization led to a long depression.

Meanwhile, Grace was going through a religious crisis. The church had always been very important to her; suddenly the beliefs that she grew up with no longer made any sense to her. She began to search for new meaning, but the more she searched, the less she found to hold on to. She turned to Kenneth in desperation. "I would say to him, 'Tell me what *you* believe and I'll believe it!' But he would only give me books to read. He gave me Paul Tillich and I would sit and read and cry. I couldn't understand it. I finally decided that I was going crazy. I was going insane. I was too smart to be taken in by the conservative evangelists, and I was too dumb to understand the liberal theologians. I was in a religious vacuum."

Kenneth remembers Grace's tumult. "She wanted me to sort out her moral and religious confusion," he says. "I would try and fail, and there would be a storm of pain and rage from her. She was in anguish for her soul. I felt as if she had her hands around my throat, begging me for answers. I was supposed to provide something for her, and I was failing." He was distressed that he couldn't help Grace, but he was also aware that he was deliberately holding back from her something that she wanted. "She wanted me to be strong, to be decisive. And it wasn't just about religion. It was everything. She wanted to be a little girl and have me be the daddy. But that felt like an unfair position to me. I didn't want to be too strong. Then I would have to give up forever my wish to get what I needed. I wanted to be the child, too."

Gradually the crisis began to diminish. Grace joined a church that was willing to accept her confusion and questioning, and she was deeply relieved to discover that her husband, a very religious man, stuck by her, "even though I was next thing to an atheist." At the same time, Kenneth sought help for his depression by joining a therapy group. In the course of his therapy, he made some important discoveries about himself. One of the most important ones was that he was making Grace carry all the anger in the relationship. "I was projecting all my anger onto her. I was the good, gentle one. She was the bad, angry one. Meanwhile, I had a lot of unexpressed anger of my own, and keeping it inside of me was one of the things that kept me remote and made Grace so angry."

Slowly Kenneth began to test out his capacity for anger. "It was while he was in therapy," recalls Grace, "that Kenneth dared to get mad at me for the first time. I don't even remember what it was about. But I distinctly remember that he actually raised his voice at me. He was dumbstruck that I didn't turn around and kill him. He didn't think he was going to survive his own anger." This was a crucial experience for Kenneth. He had challenged his internal prohibition against anger and lived to tell about it. He began to test his newfound ability. "I got mad at Grace four or five times in one week, just to prove that I could do it. Then I got so that any time she started yelling at me I began to yell back. Only I made sure that I yelled louder." Even though she had always wanted Kenneth to be more assertive, once he started standing up for himself Grace found it hard to get used to. At times she yearned for the old, passive Kenneth.

Despite his wife's apprehensions, Kenneth continued to become more self-confident and aggressive, growth that was supported and encouraged by his therapy group. One of the messages that Kenneth was getting from the members of the group was that he wasn't asking enough for himself. "You act as if you're not entitled to much in life," they told him. Kenneth felt there was some truth to this observation, and he began searching for ways to feel more fulfilled. It was during this time that he had an affair. "I don't blame the group for what I did," he says. "They did nurture in me the notion that I was too self-effacing, but it was my idea to have this affair. I saw it as an opportunity to go for something for me. To spread my wings and fly. It wasn't that Grace and I were at odds with each other. We were actually doing OK at the time—not great, but OK. It's just that I wanted an exciting adventure. This was a way to prove myself."

The affair lasted only a couple of weeks. Grace found out about it when she discovered a motel receipt that had fallen from his pocket. She knew right away what had happened. "I had been suspicious of him for years. Now it had really happened." Grace reacted to the affair in a typical fashion: "I was furious. I yelled and screamed." Two days after her discovery of the receipt, she arranged for an appointment with a marriage counselor. "I wanted help dealing with this," she says. "I felt like I was going to explode. Also, I suppose, I saw therapy as a way to take him to court, make him acknowledge the pain he had caused me."

Through the therapy, Kenneth and Grace were able to come to a resolution. Kenneth agreed to stop seeing the other woman, and Grace agreed to try to rebuild her trust. In the process, Kenneth gained some important insights about Grace. "Her anger over the affair was threatening to me, but it was also very affirming. It showed me how much she cared about our marriage, and that she was willing to pick up the pieces and continue to work on our relationship. We had talked about divorce for so long that I was gratified that she was still willing to see if anything good could come of a bad situation."

Understandably, it took Grace a long time to rebuild her trust. When Kenneth came home at night, she would ask him about his comings and goings in great detail. Kenneth patiently put up with her cross-examination for months, accepting full responsibility for betraying her trust. It was during this critical period of their relationship that the final crisis occurred: Kenneth had to have quadruple-bypass surgery. Even though he responded well to the surgery, Grace was more shaken by his heart condition than by the affair. "One evening," says Kenneth, "we were lying in bed and Grace told me that, if getting out of my life would make my recovery easier for me, she would be willing to leave. She knew that our marriage had not been very satisfying to either of us and thought maybe my heart problem was a sign of my 'disease.' If living apart would be a benefit to me, she would agree to a divorce. She made it clear that she didn't *want* to leave me, but she was afraid that living together was only making matters worse."

Grace's willingness to make this sacrifice was the turning point for Kenneth. "It was then that I decided to put both of my feet into the marriage," he says. "I knew I wasn't going to find a better woman than Grace. She was a remarkable woman. She had been hard to live with at times. But, then, aren't we all? I finally made a full commitment to our marriage."

I suggested to Kenneth that maybe his decision to commit himself to Grace had something to do with her offering him an accepting, nonpossessive love, something that he had always wanted from his mother. He thought about it for a minute. "Yes. Yes. I believe that's exactly what it was. My mother's love always had strings attached. Grace was offering me a selfless love."

Kenneth and Grace didn't have an official ceremony to celebrate their remarriage, although there was one conversation in a restaurant that felt very significant to them. A pianist was playing the song "Someone to Watch over Me" and Kenneth took hold of Grace's hand and said to her, "Let's make a deal. I'll watch over you, and you'll watch over me." It was a simple declaration of love: Let's agree to be each other's protectors, each other's best friends.

Finally, after thirty years of marriage, Grace was getting Kenneth's full attention and commitment. Spontaneously, along with his commitment, Kenneth gained new appreciation for Grace's good qualities. "I think he began to realize that I was intelligent. I wasn't an academic, but I was a gifted artist. I began to feel for the first time that Kenneth truly admired me." The anger that had consumed her for so many years became less intense—because, as Grace put it, "He truly loved me, and I knew it."

It was at this advanced stage of love and acceptance that Kenneth and Grace first came to one of my workshops. On their own they had managed to work through their major impasse, but they still were able to acquire some new insights and skills. For Grace, the most significant part of the couples workshop was watching a demonstration of the Full Container exercise. She was deeply moved to see the couple learn how to handle their anger. It was, she says, the first time that her anger had made any sense to her. "I suddenly realized that I wasn't a 'bad' or crazy person to be angry. Anger had a reason and a purpose. I wouldn't need to deny my explosiveness to be lovable, only channel it and make it a productive part of our relationship. It was a marvelous revelation to me!"

Since the workshop, Kenneth and Grace, like Anne and Greg, have developed their own version of the Full Container exercise. They both feel free to "rant and rave," as they put it, when they have strong feelings. But they are very conscious of what they are doing and are careful not to hurt each other in the process. "We never call each other names," says Kenneth. "We just express our anger and irritation. And the other person knows that this is an important part of keeping our relationship healthy. We don't harbor grudges." Grace feels that this process has dramatically increased Kenneth's acceptance of her emotional nature. "It seems that his attitude toward my anger changed at that workshop. He had already learned to accept his own anger in his therapy group, but he hadn't accepted *mine*. Now he has. I yell and I scream and I'm still loved. We go through it, and we come back together. It's been a very important change in our relationship."

Grace believes that Kenneth's increased acceptance of her has been the determining factor in her own acceptance of herself. "I think the fact that Kenneth accepts my energy and determination and my anger helps me accept what I call 'my mother' in me, the part of me that is like my mother, which I have always tried to deny. Because he likes who I am, I don't have to wage that battle anymore. I don't have to deny who I am."

For Kenneth, the biggest improvement in their relationship has been an increased sense of caring and safety. "We're friends now," he said. "Not antagonists. The key is that I feel safe. She's on my side, committed to my well-being. She is valuing me.

Liking me. And I'm committed to liking her. Supporting her and affirming her. It just feels a lot different. The struggle with my mother is over. A woman is on my side, and it happens to be Grace. I can relax with her and feel safe with her." Grace echoed this last sentiment. "That's important to me, too. I can relax and feel safe with Kenneth." For both of them, the primitive need of the old brain to be in a safe, secure, and nurturing environment has finally been met.

Kenneth and Grace attended two more couples workshops. During these, they noticed that I described the conscious marriage as a journey, not a destination, explaining that even in the best marriages there would always be struggle and the need to adapt and change. To some degree, their experience confirms this observation. "We still have problems," says Grace. "For example, Ken wants me to be more cautious in the things I tell him. To rehearse what I'm going to say, so that I don't risk hurting his feelings. But that's difficult for me to do. I'm an impulsive person. It would feel very strange to filter all my thoughts before I revealed them. And I want the opposite of him. I want him to be more spontaneous, less calculated. But that feels risky for him." They both express ambivalence about the challenge to keep growing. "Perhaps it has something to do with our age," says Kenneth. "Part of me wants life not to be a struggle anymore. Grace and I have arrived at a place that feels very comfortable. It's not that we've stopped growing and changing altogether, but this just feels like a nice place to be." In a way, they were questioning my description of reality love as a journey without end. It may be an endless journey, they are telling me, but it is a journey that becomes more and more effortless as time goes on.

These two love relationships offer an excellent description of what I call "the conscious marriage." Anne and Greg and Kenneth and Grace reveal it to be a state of mind and a way of being based on acceptance, a willingness to grow and change, the courage to encounter one's own fear, and a conscious decision to act in loving ways. It is a marriage built on an entirely different foundation from the infatuation of romantic love, but the feelings are just as joyful and intense.

When we look at marriage in more detail, it is clear that the simple word "love" cannot adequately describe the wide variety of feelings two individuals can have for each other. In the first two stages of marriage, romantic love and the power struggle, love is reactive; it is an unconscious response to the expectation of need fulfillment. Love is best described as eros, life energy seeking union with a gratifying object. When a husband and wife make a decision to create a more satisfying marriage, they enter a stage of transformation, and love becomes infused with consciousness and will; love is best defined as agape, the life energy directed toward the partner in an intentional act of healing. Now, in the final stage of marriage, reality love, love takes on the quality of "spontaneous oscillation," words that come from quantum physics and describe the way energy moves back and forth between particles. When partners learn to see each other without distortion, to value each other as highly as they value themselves, to give without expecting anything in return, to commit themselves fully to each other's welfare, love moves freely between them without apparent effort. The word that best describes this mature kind of love is not "eros," not "agape," but yet another Greek word, "philia,"[2] which means "love between friends." The partner is no longer perceived as a surrogate parent, or as an enemy, but as a passionate friend.

When couples are able to love in this selfless manner, they experience a release of energy. They cease to be consumed by the details of their relationship, or to need to operate within the artificial structure of exercises; they spontaneously treat each other with love and respect. What feels unnatural to them is not their new way of relating but the self-centered, wounding interactions of the past. Love becomes automatic, much as it was in the earliest stage of marriage, but now it is based on the truth of the partner, not on illusion.

One characteristic of couples who have reached this advanced stage of consciousness is that they begin to turn their energy away from each other toward the woundedness of the world. They develop a greater concern for the environment, for people in need, for important causes. The capacity to love and heal that they have created within the marriage is now available for others.

I have found no better description of this rare kind of love than in I Corinthians 13:

Love is patient, love is kind. It does not envy, it does not boast, it is not proud. It is not rude, it is not self-seeking, it is not easily angered, it keeps no record of wrongs. Love does not delight in evil but rejoices with the truth. It always protects. It always trusts, always hopes, always perseveres. Love never fails.

part III

THE EXERCISES

13

TEN STEPS TOWARD
A CONSCIOUS MARRIAGE

THIS PART OF THE BOOK describes a ten-step process that will help you achieve a conscious marriage. It contains sixteen exercises that will assist you in translating the insights you have gained about marriage into effective skills. I have some general comments to make before I describe them.

All of the exercises have been thoroughly tested. With a few minor exceptions, they are the same exercises I have been assigning to couples for the past ten years. The only changes I have made have been to eliminate a few that require direct supervision and to adapt several others so that they work better in a book format. Otherwise they are the same exercises that you would be given if you were to come to a couples workshop or work with me or another therapist trained in Imago Relationship Therapy. These exercises have been shown to be very effective. An independent researcher concluded that couples who attended one of my weekend workshops, which contain approximately the same material as this book, improved their relationships as much as those who had been in private marital counseling for as long as three to six months.[1]

Most of the exercises follow the principle of graduated change, which means that you will begin with an easy task first and move on to progressively more difficult ones. You will be in control of how fast you go and how much you learn. Keep in mind that, the more difficult a particular exercise seems to you, the more potential it contains for growth.

You will discover that doing the exercises requires a significant amount of time and commitment. To complete them all, you will need to set aside an hour or two of uninterrupted time each week for several months. You may even have to hire a baby-sitter or give up some other activity to find the necessary time—just as you would if you were going to a weekly appointment with a therapist. This degree of commitment requires a clear understanding of how important a good marriage is to you, and a continual affirmation of your priorities.

It may be that some of you want to do these exercises but don't have the support of your spouses. Often one person in a relationship is more motivated to work on problems than the other. If you are the only one interested at present in doing the exercises, I urge you to do as many of them as you can by yourself. A relationship is like a balloon filled with air: you can't push on one part of it without affecting the shape of the whole. When you begin to listen with more objectivity, share your feelings with more candor, interfere with your defensive and aggressive reactions, and make an effort to pleasure your partner, significant improvements can occur. Eventually your partner's resistance to change might diminish, and you will be able to go through the rest of the process together.

Some of you may want to do these exercises as a couple, others may want to do them in a group setting, so that you can have the support of other couples with similar goals. A group study guide and a couples' study guide are available to help you structure these sessions. For more information about the study guides and other resource materials, call 800-729-1121 or visit the Web site, www.imagotherapy.com.

As you work your way through the exercises, you will discover that the journey toward a conscious marriage is never a straight line. There will be moments of great joy and intimacy, and there will be detours, long periods of stagnation, and unexpected regressions. During the periods of regression, you may feel despondent or criticize yourself for backsliding. My clients often tell me, "Dr. Hendrix, we've done it again. We've fallen back into the same old patterns. We thought this phase of our lives was over and done with! What is wrong with us?" I respond that there is nothing linear about love and marriage. Relationships tend to move in circles and vortices; there are cycles, periods of calm and periods of turbulence. Even when you feel as if you are going through the very same struggles over and over again, there is always some degree of change. What is happening is that you are deepening your experience or participating in a particular phenomenon in a different way or on a different level. Perhaps you are integrating more unconscious elements into your relationship, or enlarging your consciousness of a change that has already taken place. Perhaps you are reacting more intensely to a familiar situation because you have opened up new feelings. Or, conversely, you may be reacting *less* intensely because you have managed to work through some of your feelings. These changes may seem imperceptible, but there is movement all the same. By continually affirming your decision to grow and change, and by diligently practicing the techniques described in the following pages, you will be able to make sure and steady progress on your journey to a conscious marriage.

DOING THE EXERCISES

As discussed in chapter 7, making a firm commitment at the beginning of the process will help you overcome any potential resistance. Take the time now to examine your priorities. How important to you is creating a more loving, supportive relationship? Are you willing to take part in a sometimes difficult process of self-growth? If you are, take out a separate sheet of paper and write a statement indicating your willingness to participate. You may wish to use words like the following:

> Because our relationship is very important to us, we are making a commitment to increase our awareness of ourselves and each other and to acquire and practice new relationship skills. Toward this end, we agree to do all the exercises in this book in a careful, conscientious manner.

As you work on the exercises, keep in mind these two cardinal rules:

1. The information you gather in the process of doing the exercises is designed to educate you and your partner about each other's needs. Sharing this information does not obligate you to meet those needs.
2. When you share your thoughts and feelings with each other, you become emotionally vulnerable. It is important that you use the information you gain about each other in a loving and helpful manner.

Suggested Ten-Session Time Line

First session: Exercise 1

Second session: Read or recite Relationship Vision (Exercise 1)
New material: Exercises 2–6

Third session: Read or recite Relationship Vision
New material: Exercise 7

Fourth session: Read or recite Relationship Vision
New material: Exercise 8

Fifth session: Read or recite Relationship Vision
Review the need to close additional exits
New material: Exercise 9

Sixth session: Read or recite Relationship Vision
Review the need to close additional exits
Continue with 2–3 caring behaviors a day
New material: Exercises 10–11

Seventh session: Read or recite Relationship Vision
Review the need to close additional exits
Continue with 2–3 caring behaviors a day
Continue to give surprises and engage in high-
    energy pleasurable activities
New material: Exercise 12

Eighth session: Read or recite Relationship Vision
Review the need to close additional exits
Continue with 2–3 caring behaviors a day
Continue to give surprises and engage in high-
    energy pleasurable activities
Continue with 3–4 behavior changes a week
New material: Exercise 13 (14 optional)

Ninth session: Read or recite Relationship Vision
Review the need to close additional exits

Continue with 2–3 caring behaviors a day

Continue to give surprises and engage in high-energy pleasurable activities

Continue with 3–4 behavior changes a week

New material: Exercise 15

Tenth session:

Read or recite Relationship Vision

Review the need to close additional exits

Continue with 2–3 caring behaviors a day

Continue to give surprises and engage in high-energy pleasurable activities

Continue with 3–4 behavior changes a week

New material: Exercise 16

Subsequent
sessions:

Read or recite Relationship Vision

Review the need to close additional exits

Continue with 2–3 caring behaviors a day

Continue to give surprises and engage in high-energy pleasurable activities

Continue with 3–4 behavior changes a week

Read Exercise 16

New material: Add additional caring behaviors and behavior changes as they occur to you.

Note: You will need to save your responses to the exercises so you can refer to them later. I suggest that before you begin work you prepare two loose-leaf notebooks, one for each of you, each containing thirty or forty sheets of lined notebook paper. Do all your work in these notebooks.

EXERCISE 1: YOUR RELATIONSHIP VISION

Time: Approximately 60 minutes.

Purpose: This exercise will help you see the potential in your relationship.

Comments: Do this exercise together.

Directions

1. Take out two sheets of paper, one for each of you. Working separately, write a series of short sentences that describe your personal vision of a deeply satisfying love relationship. Include qualities you already have that you want to keep and qualities you wish you had. Write each sentence in the present tense, as if it were already happening. For example: "We have fun together," "We have great sex," "We are loving parents," "We are affectionate with each other." Make all your items positive statements. Write "We settle our differences peacefully" rather than "We don't fight."

2. Share your sentences. Note the items that you have in common and underline them. (It doesn't matter if you have used different words, as long as the general idea is the same.) If your partner has written sentences that you agree with but did not think of yourself, add them to your list. For the moment, ignore items that are not shared.

3. Now turn to your own expanded list and rank each sentence (including the ones that are *not* shared) with a number from 1 to 5 according to its importance to you, with 1 indicating "very important" and 5 indicating "not so important."

4. Circle the two items that are most important to you.

5. Put a check mark beside those items that you think would be most difficult for the two of you to achieve.

6. Now work *together* to design a mutual relationship vision similar to the following example. Start with the items that you both agree are most important. Put a check mark by those items that you both agree would be difficult to achieve. At the bottom of the list, write items that are relatively unimportant. If you have items that are a source of conflict between you, see if you can come up with a compromise statement that satisfies both of you. If not, leave the item off your combined list.

Our Relationship Vision

Bill		Jenny
1	We have fun together.	1
1	We settle our differences peacefully.	1
1	We have satisfying and beautiful sex.	1
1	We are healthy and physically active.	1
1	We communicate easily and openly.	1✓
1	We worship together.	1
1	We are each other's best friends.	1
1	We have secure and happy children.	1
2	We trust each other.	1
1	We are sexually faithful.	1
2	We both have satisfying careers.	2✓
2	We work well together as parents.	1
2	We share important decisions.	2
2	We meet each other's deepest needs.	2
3	We have daily private time.	4
3	We feel safe with each other.	2
3	We are financially secure.	4✓
4	We live close to our parents.	5✓
5	We have similar political views.	3

7. Post this list where you can see it easily. Once a week, at the beginning of your work sessions, read it aloud to each other.

EXERCISE 2: CHILDHOOD WOUNDS
(review chapter 2)

Time: Approximately 30 minutes.

Purpose: Now that you have a vision of the future, this exercise will take you back into the past. It is designed to refresh your memory of your caretakers and other influential people so that you can construct your imago.

Comments: You may do this exercise together or at separate times. It is important that you be free from distractions for a period of thirty minutes. Read all of these instructions before carrying them out.

Directions
First do some slow stretching exercises to help you relax. Then settle into a comfortable chair. Breathe deeply ten times, becoming more relaxed with each breath. When you are feeling peaceful, close your eyes and imagine your childhood home, the earliest one you can recall. Imagine yourself as a young boy or girl. Try to see the rooms from the perspective of a small child. Now wander around the house and find the people who influenced you most deeply as a child. As you encounter these people, you will be able to see them with new clarity. Stop and visit with each one. Note their positive and negative traits. Tell them what you enjoyed about being with them. Tell them what you didn't like about being with them. Finally, tell them what you wanted from them but never got. Don't hesitate to share your angry, hurt, or sad feelings. In your fantasy, your caretakers will be grateful for your insights.

When you have gathered this information, open your eyes and record it according to the instructions in Exercise 3.

EXERCISE 3: IMAGO WORKUP
(review chapter 3)

Time: Approximately 30–45 minutes.

Purpose: This exercise will help you record and summarize the information you acquired in Exercise 2.

Comments: You can do this exercise individually.

Directions

1. Take out a blank piece of paper and draw a large circle, leaving about three inches below the circle. Divide the circle in half with a horizontal line. Put a capital letter "B" above the line on the left side of the circle, and a capital letter "A" below the line on the left side of the circle. (See illustration below.)

$$\frac{B}{A}$$

2. On the top half, next to the "B," list all of the positive character traits of your mother, father, and any other people who influenced you strongly when you were young. Lump all the positive traits of all these people together. (Don't bother to group them according to individuals.) List these traits as you recall them from childhood. Do not describe your caretakers as they are today. Describe them with simple adjectives or phrases like the following: "kind," "warm," "intelligent," "religious," "patient," "creative," "always there," "enthusiastic," "reliable," etc.

3. On the bottom half, next to the "A," list the negative traits of these key people. Once again, lump all the traits together.

This list of positive and negative traits is your imago.

4. Circle the positive and negative traits that seem to affect you most.

5. In the blank space below your circle, write down a capital letter "C" and complete this sentence: "What I wanted most as a child and didn't get was . . ."

6. Now write down a capital letter "D" and complete this sentence: "As a child, I had these negative feelings over and over again: . . ."

(For the moment, ignore the capital letters. They will be referred to in Exercise 5.)

EXERCISE 4: CHILDHOOD FRUSTRATIONS
(review chapter 2)

Time: Approximately 30–45 minutes.

Purpose: This exercise will help you clarify your major childhood frustrations and describe the way you reacted to them.

Comments: You can do this exercise individually.

Directions
1. On a separate sheet of paper, list the recurring frustrations you had as a child (see example below).

2. Next to the frustrations, briefly describe the way you reacted to the situations. (You may have responded in more than one way. List all your common responses.) Put the capital letter "E" above your reactions as in the example.

Matt's Chart

Frustration	(E) Response
Didn't get enough attention from my older brother.	Was a pest. Kept trying to get his attention.
Father often gone.	Sometimes I was angry. Usually tried to please him.
Felt inferior to older brother.	Resigned myself to my inferiority. Tried not to compete directly.
My father drank too much.	Tried to ignore it. Sometimes I would get stomachaches.
My mother was overly protective.	I kept things to myself. Sometimes I was defiant.

EXERCISE 5: PARTNER PROFILE
(review chapter 3)

Time: Approximately 30–45 minutes.

Purpose: This exercise will help you define the things you like and don't like about your partner and compare partner traits with imago traits.

Comments: Do this exercise individually. *Do not share this information at this time.* The Stretching exercise on pages 272–274 will help you make constructive use of this information.

Directions

1. On a separate sheet of paper, draw a large circle, leaving three inches of blank space below the circle. Divide the circle in half with a horizontal line, as you did in Exercise 3. Put the capital letter "F" above the line on the left side of the circle. Put the capital letter "G" below the line on the left side of the circle.

$$\frac{\text{F}}{\text{G}}$$

2. On the top half of the circle (beside the "F") list your partner's positive traits. Include traits that first attracted you to your partner.

3. List your partner's negative traits beside the "G" on the lower half of the circle.

4. Circle the positive and negative traits that seem to affect you the most.

5. Now turn back to Exercise 2 and compare your imago traits with your partner's traits. Star the traits that are similar.

6. On the bottom of the page, write the letter "H" and complete this sentence: "What I enjoy most about my partner is . . ."

7. Now write the letter "I" and complete this sentence: "What I want from my partner and don't get is . . ."

EXERCISE 6: UNFINISHED BUSINESS
(*review chapter 2*)

Time: Approximately 15–20 minutes.

Purpose: This exercise organizes the information from Exercises 2–5 into a description of your unfinished business, the hidden agenda you brought to your love relationship.

Comments: Do this exercise separately.

Directions
On a separate piece of paper, write down the words below that are written in boldface. Complete the sentences by filling in what you wrote beside the appropriate letters in the exercises cited in brackets.

I have spent my life searching for a person with these character traits [the traits that you underlined in A and B from Exercise 3, pages 256–257]:

When I am with such a person, I am troubled by these traits [the traits that you underlined in A in Exercise 3, step 3, page 256]:

And I wish that person would give me [C from Exercise 3, step 5, page 257]:

When my needs aren't met, I have these feelings: [D from Exercise 3, step 6, page 257]:

And I often respond this way [E from Exercise 4, page 257]:

Exercise 6 completes the first portion of the exercises. You now have a relationship vision; a description of your imago; a record of your early frustrations and coping patterns; a chart listing the things you like and don't like about your partner; and a sheet that describes the hidden agenda you brought to your relationship.

EXERCISE 7: THE COUPLE'S DIALOGUE
(review chapter 9)

Time: Approximately 45–60 minutes.

Purpose: This exercise will train you to listen accurately to what your partner is saying, to understand and validate your partner's point of view, and to express empathy for your partner's feelings. Regular practice of this skill will lead to clear and effective communication, and over time, to a deeper emotional connection. You will learn how to replace reacting with empathic understanding.

Comments: Do this exercise together and often. The Couple's Dialogue is a very effective tool for communication, mutual healing, and deep connection. It is the central therapeutic process in Imago Relationship Therapy. Use it when you share your experience doing all the other exercises.

Directions
1. Choose who will be the sender and the receiver. The one who decides to be the sender should start the dialogue by saying: "I would like to have a Couple's Dialogue. Is now OK?" When using this process in your relationship, after this practice session, it is important that the receiver respond as soon as possible. If now is not possible, then set a time when you will be available so your partner will know when he or she will be heard. You should signal your readiness by saying: "I am available now."

2. The sender now talks for a few minutes, sending the message she or he wants the receiver to hear. The message should

start with "I" and describe what the sender is thinking or feeling. For this exercise, the message should be neutral and simple. Example: "I awakened this morning with a sore throat and don't feel like going to work. I think I will stay home." The receiver then mirrors, using these suggested sentence stems: **"If I got it, you awakened with a sore throat, and since you don't feel well, you are thinking you will stay home from work. Did I get it?"** If the sender indicates he or she was heard accurately, then the receiver says: **"Is there more about that?"** If the sender has more to say, that is added to the message. The receiver continues to mirror and ask "Is there more about that?" until the sender has completed the message. (The question "Is there more about that?" is very important. It helps the sender complete all her or his thoughts and feelings and prevents the receiver from responding to an incomplete message. And, since it is limited to "more about *that*," it helps the sender limit the message to *one* subject at a time.)

3. When the sender has completed the message, the receiver then summarizes all of the sender's message with this lead-in: **"Let me see if I got all of that. . . ."** When the receiver finishes the summary, the sentence should be checked for accuracy with: **"Did I get it all?"** (The summary is important because it helps the receiver understand the sender more deeply and to see the logic in what was said. This helps with validation, which is the next step.) When the sender indicates that all of the message has been heard accurately, you then move to validation.

4. Now the receiver *validates* the sender's message with something like these lead-ins: **"You make sense, because . . ."** or **"It makes sense to me, given that you . . ."** or **"I can see what you are saying . . . ,** (example) given that you have a sore throat and feel bad, it makes sense that you are thinking of not going to work." (This response indicates that the receiver understands the logic of what the sender is saying. It is the sender's "truth." The receiver does not have to agree with the sender, but

it is essential that the receiver "sees" the logic or "truth" of the sender's experience. Since everyone "makes sense," using the phrase "... makes sense..." communicates that the receiver "gets it" and that the sender is not crazy.) The receiver should check to see if the sender feels validated. If so, then the receiver moves to empathy, the final step.

5. Empathy can be expressed with the following sentence stems: **"I can imagine that you might be feeling ...** (example) frustrated that you have to miss a day of work." If the sender's report is about the past, the receiver can say: **"I can imagine that you might have felt....** These lead-ins can be used if the sender has not openly expressed feelings. If the sender has expressed feelings, then the receiver can say: **"I can see that you are feeling ..."** (Feelings are best stated using one word such as angry, sad, upset, happy, etc. If you use more than one word, such as: "you feel you don't want to go to work" you are probably expressing a thought.) Since one never knows for sure what another person is feeling, it is important to check for accuracy by saying: **"Is that what you are feeling?"** or **"Did I get your feeling right?"** If the receiver did not imagine the right feelings or misperceived the expressed feelings, then the sender should say what the feelings are. Also, if the sender shares other feelings that were not picked up by the receiver, the receiver should mirror those feelings and ask: **"Is there more about that feeling?"**

6. When the receiver has gone through all three parts (mirroring, validation, and empathy) then s/he says: **"I would like to respond now."** Then the receiver becomes the sender and the sender the receiver. The sender (former receiver) may respond to the message that is heard or may express the feelings or thoughts about something from his or her experience.

7. This exercise will feel like an unnatural, cumbersome way of relating, but it is a good way to assure accurate communication.

Like learning any new skill, it will be awkward at first, but with practice you will become more artistic and less mechanical. When you have the exercise down pat, you will discover that you do not need to use the structured process all the time. Your communication will become dialogical in spirit. The three steps will be necessary only when you are discussing highly charged subjects or when communication breaks down. Eventually, you will experience a decrease in reactivity, more emotional safety, and deeper connection.

8. Now use the three-step dialogue process to share what you learned about yourself by doing Exercise 2, the fantasy exercise. Take turns. When it's your turn to listen, give your partner your full attention. Mirror what your partner is saying until you get it. Then validate her or his point of view and communicate empathy. You may ask clarifying questions, but do not try to analyze your partner or make interpretations or express frustrations or criticisms. As you listen, try to visualize your partner's childhood wound.

EXERCISE 8: THE NO-EXIT DECISION
(review pages 104–114)

Time: Approximately 60–90 minutes.

Purpose: This exercise serves two purposes: (1) it assures that you will stay together while you are working through these exercises and (2) it gradually increases your level of intimacy.

Comments: Do this exercise together.

Directions
1. Imagine that your relationship is represented by a rectangle with perforated sides. The open spaces are your "exits," all

the inappropriate ways you seek safety and need gratification and drain the energy away from your relationship. Each of the four corners is a catastrophic exit—suicide, divorce, murder, and insanity. Examine your thoughts and feelings to see if you are contemplating leaving the relationship through any of these four corner exits. If so, I urge you to make a decision now to close them for the period of time that you are working together on these exercises.

2. Now take out four sheets of paper, two for each of you. On your first sheet of paper, make a comprehensive list of your ordinary exits. Ordinary exits are such things as overeating, staying late at work, spending too much time with the children—anything that you do primarily to avoid your partner. (See page 108 for a more comprehensive list.)

3. On your second sheet of paper, make a separate list of what you perceive to be your partner's exits.

4. Using the mirroring technique described in Exercise 7, take turns sharing your lists. Invite your partner's comments and additions.

Partner A: I think that one of the reasons you bring work home on the weekends is to avoid spending time with me.

Partner B: You think that I bring home work from the office so that I won't have to spend so much time with you. Did I understand you correctly?

Partner A: Not completely. I said that I think that *one* of the reasons that you bring work home is to avoid spending time with me. I know you have other reasons, too.

Partner B: OK. You are saying that one of the reasons I work over the weekends is to spend less time with you. I may have other reasons, too. Is that right?

Partner A: Yes, you heard me correctly.

5. Complete your list of exits by adding additional ones suggested by your partner.

6. Now, working with your own list, put a check mark by exits that you are willing to eliminate or reduce at the present time. Put an "X" by those that would be difficult for you to change.

7. Write out the following agreement and fill in the blanks: "Starting this week [insert date] I agree to reserve more time and energy for our relationship. Specifically, I agree to: . . ."

Here is a portion of one man's list and his agreement to reduce his exits:

Bill's Exits
Making business calls in the evenings.
Watching sports programs on the weekends.
Staying up late watching TV.
Making plans without consulting my wife.

Getting up later than my wife.
Coming home late for dinner.
Not paying attention when my wife talks.
Going to bed later than my wife.

Bill's Agreement: Starting this week, September 21–28, I agree to keep my evening hours free from business calls. If someone calls me, I will ask that person to call me at work. I also agree to go to bed before 11:00 P.M. and to get up by 6:30 on weekdays.

8. At the beginning of each subsequent work session, set aside some time to talk about how much time you spend together as a couple and decide if it would be desirable for you to close any additional exits. (Use the mirroring technique if you have a difference of opinion.) If you decide that more time together would be beneficial, ask yourself if you are willing to work on eliminating or reducing another activity. Write down an agreement similar to the one above.

EXERCISE 9: REROMANTICIZING
(*review chapter 8*)

Time: Approximately 60 minutes.

Purpose: By sharing specific information about what pleases you and agreeing to pleasure your partner on a regular, consistent basis, you can turn your relationship into a zone of safety.

Comments: You can do steps 1–3 separately if you wish. The remaining steps are to be done together.

Directions
1. The first step in this process is to identify what your partner is already doing that pleases you. Get out separate sheets of

paper and complete this sentence in as many ways as possible, being specific and positive and focusing on items that happen with some regularity: *I feel loved and cared about when you . . .*

Examples: fill my coffee cup when it's empty.
let me read the front page of the paper first.
kiss me before you leave the house.
call me from work just to chat.
tell me important things that happen to you.
massage my back.
tell me you love me.
ask if I want a treat from the store.
bring me surprise presents.
sit close to me when we're watching TV.
listen to me when I'm upset.
check with me first before making plans.
pray with me and for me.
make special Sunday dinners.
want to make love to me.
compliment me on the way I look.

2. Now recall the romantic stage of your relationship. Are there any caring behaviors that you used to do for each other that you are no longer doing? Once again, take out separate sheets of paper and complete this sentence: *I used to feel loved and cared about when you . . .*

Examples: wrote me love letters.
brought me flowers.
held my hand as we walked.
whispered sexy things into my ear.
called me up on the phone to say how much you loved me.
wanted to stay up late talking and making love.
made love more than once a day.

3. Now think about some caring and loving behaviors that you have always wanted but never asked for. These may come from your vision of a perfect mate or from prior experience. (They should not, however, refer to activities that are a present source of conflict.) These may be very private fantasies. Whenever possible, quantify your request. Complete this sentence: *I would like you to* . . .

> Examples: massage me for thirty minutes without stopping.
> take a shower with me.
> buy me some jewelry as a surprise.
> go backpacking with me three times each
>   summer.
> sleep in the nude.
> go out to brunch with me once a month.
> read a novel to me over Christmas vacation.

4. Now combine all three lists and indicate how important each caring behavior is to you by writing a number from 1 to 5 beside each one. A 1 indicates "very important"; a 5 indicates "not so important."

5. Exchange lists. Examine your partner's lists and put an "X" by any items that you are not willing to do at this time. All the remaining behaviors should be conflict-free. Starting tomorrow, do at least two of the nonconflicted behaviors each day for the next two months, starting with the ones that are easiest for you to do. Add more items to your list as they occur to you. When your partner does a caring behavior for you, acknowledge it with an appreciative comment. As you will recall from reading chapter 8, these caring behaviors are gifts, not obligations. Do them regardless of how you feel about your partner, and regardless of the number of caring behaviors your partner gives you.

6. If either you or your partner experiences some resistance with this exercise, keep on doing the caring behaviors until the resistance is overcome. (See pages 126–129 for an explanation of the fear of pleasure.)

EXERCISE 10: THE SURPRISE LIST
(review pages 124–125)

Time: Approximately 15–20 minutes.

Purpose: The purpose of this exercise is to augment the caring behaviors in Exercise 9 with unanticipated pleasures, adding to your feeling of safety and bonding.

Comments: This exercise is to be done separately and must be kept secret from your partner.

Directions
1. Make a list of things you could do for your partner that would be especially pleasing. Don't guess. Draw up your list from your memory of things that have pleased your partner in the past or from hints or comments your partner has made. Become a detective and ferret out your partner's hidden wishes and desires. Keep your list hidden from your partner at all times.

2. Select one item and surprise your partner with it this week. Be sure to do this at least once a week and at random times, so that your partner will have difficulty anticipating the surprise.

3. Record the date when you gave each surprise.

4. On a separate sheet of paper, record and date the surprises you receive from your partner. Thank your partner for surprising you.

EXERCISE 11: THE FUN LIST
(review pages 125–126)

Time: Approximately 20–30 minutes.

Purpose: This exercise is designed to intensify your emotional bond and deepen your feelings of safety and pleasure.

Comments: Do this exercise together.

Directions

1. Make separate lists of fun and exciting activities you would like to do with your partner. These should include face-to-face experiences and any body contact that is physically pleasurable. Examples: tennis, dancing, wrestling, showering together, sex, massage, tickling, jumping rope, bicycling.

2. Now share your lists and compile a third list that combines all of your suggestions.

3. Pick one activity from the list and do it each week.

4. You may experience some resistance to taking part in such exuberant, childlike activities—especially if you have a conflicted relationship. It is important that you do this exercise nonetheless. Go against your natural inclination and experiment with this brief return to childhood.

Exercise 12: Stretching
(*review chapter 10*)

Time: Approximately 60–90 minutes.

Purpose: The purpose of this exercise is to educate you to your partner's deepest needs and to give you the opportunity to change your behavior so that you meet those needs. As you stretch against your resistance, your partner will be healed and you will become a more whole and loving individual.

Comments: This is a very important exercise. I recommend that you give it your highest priority.

Directions

1. The first step in this exercise is to identify the desires that lie behind your frustrations. On a separate sheet of paper, make a comprehensive list of all the things that bother you about your partner. When does your partner make you feel angry, annoyed, afraid, suspicious, resentful, hurt, or bitter? Here's a partial list:

Jenny's List
I don't like it when you . . .
    drive too fast.
    leave the house without telling me where you are going.
    criticize me in front of the children.
    undermine my authority with the children.
    read the newspaper during dinner.
    criticize me in a joking manner in front of friends.
    don't pay attention to what I'm saying.
    turn away from me when I'm upset or crying.
    criticize me for being indecisive.
    criticize me for being a poor housekeeper.
    keep pointing out the fact that you earn more money than
      I do.

2. Now get out a second sheet of paper and write down the desire that lies hidden in each frustration. Skip several lines after each desire. Do not write down the frustration, only the desire. (This is necessary, because you will be showing this second sheet to your partner.)

Example:

Desire (corresponds to the first frustration listed above): I would like to feel safe and relaxed when you are driving.

3. Underneath each desire, write a specific request that would help you satisfy that desire. It is important that your requests be positive and that they describe a specific behavior.

Examples:

Desire: I would like to feel safe and relaxed when you are driving.
Request: When you are driving, I would like you to obey the speed limit. If the road conditions are bad, I would like you to drive even more slowly.

Desire: I would like you to comfort me when I'm upset.
Request: When I tell you that I am upset, I would like you to put your arms around me and give me your full attention.

Notice that these requests are for specific, positive behaviors. The following request is a bad example because it is not specific.

Vague request: I would like you to be more attentive.

It should be rewritten to make it more detailed:

Specific request: I would like you to give me a warm hug as soon as you come home from work.

This next request is a bad example because it is negative:

Negative request: I would like you to stop yelling at me when you're upset.

This should be rewritten so that it describes a positive behavior:

Positive request: When you are mad at me, I would like you to use a normal tone of voice.

4. Share your second list (the one that lists desires and requests but not frustrations) with each other. Use your communication skills to clarify each desire and request so that it is clearly understood. Rewrite the request if necessary so that the partner knows exactly what kind of behavior you want.

5. Now take back your own list and rank each request on the left side of the page with a number from 1 to 5 indicating its relative importance to you, 1 indicating "very important," 5 "not very important."

6. Exchange lists once again so that you now have your partner's requests, and assign a number from 1 to 5 on the right side of the paper indicating how difficult it would be for you to grant each request, with 1 indicating "very difficult," 5 "not at all difficult."

7. Keep your partner's list. Starting today, you have the opportunity to grant your partner three or four of the easiest requests each week. Remember that these behaviors are gifts. Regardless of how you feel and regardless of how many changes your partner is making, keep to a reliable schedule of at least three or four behavior changes a week. (You are encouraged to add more requests to your lists as time goes on.)

EXERCISE 13: CONTAINER TRANSACTION
(review pages 185–187)

Time: Approximately 30 minutes to study the instructions and practice the exercise.

Purpose: This exercise allows you to express your anger and resentment about your partner in a safe and constructive environment.

Comments: This exercise is to become your standard method for dealing with anger. It is very important that both of you use the technique, even though one of you may find it easier to do.

Directions

1. When one of you has an intense frustration, alert your partner by saying, "I have a frustration [or "I am angry"]; are you willing to listen?" Practice saying this now.

2. The containing partner then takes a few deep breaths, tries to visualize the expressive partner as a hurting child, and then indicates a willingness to listen. If the containing partner is busy, he or she should try to arrange to be available as soon as possible, preferably in the next five or ten minutes.

3. Once the containing partner is ready, the expressive partner briefly communicates the frustration. The angry person has to follow these rules: you may describe behaviors that are upsetting to you, but you are not allowed to call your partner abusive names or criticize his or her character (Example: You can say, "I am angry that you forgot to mail the check," but not "You are so irresponsible!"); you may express your anger vocally, but you may not touch your partner in a hostile manner or damage any property.

Practice sending an angry statement at this time. Invent one of your own, or use this one: "I was so angry when you kept interrupting me last night! I felt as if you were totally ignoring what I had to say!"

4. Once the frustration is communicated, the receiving partner paraphrases the frustration without reacting, using the technique described in the Mirroring exercise: "I understand that you were very upset that I was not letting you talk last night. You felt as if I was ignoring you." By going through this process, the containing partner is affirming the expressive partner's right to be angry, but is not necessarily agreeing with the statement.

5. Once the message has been delivered and paraphrased, the angry person can convert the frustration into a behavior-change request and add it to his or her list.

EXERCISE 14: CONTAINER DAYS
(*review chapter 11*)

Time: Approximately 15 minutes to study the instructions.

Purpose: This exercise extends the healing effect of Exercise 13, Container Transaction, over a longer period of time, which allows deeper feelings to emerge and further reduces the fear of anger in both partners.

Comments: This exercise is optional.

Directions

1. The Container Days exercise is an extension of the preceding exercise. On the first day of this exercise, one of you takes the role of the expressive person while the other is the container. If you are the expressive partner, you are free to express your

frustrations at any time, all day long, without fearing a negative response. Your partner listens to you and paraphrases you but is not allowed to react in an aggressive or a defensive manner.

2. On the following day, switch roles. It is very important that you alternate days so that you gain experience on both sides of the encounter.

3. The same rules described in the Container Transaction apply here: no name-calling or abusive remarks, and no damage to people or property.

4. Once again, you can convert your frustrations into behavior-change requests at a later date.

Exercise 15: Self-Integration
(review chapter 2)

Time: Approximately 15–30 minutes.

Purpose: The purpose of this exercise is to integrate aspects of your disowned self, your false self, and your lost self, making you more aware of your essential wholeness.

Comments: Because you have been faithfully performing these exercises for several weeks, you have been enlarging your sense of self by eroding your false self, integrating your denied self, and recovering your lost self. This exercise is designed to help you become more conscious of these changes. You can do the exercise separately or together.

Directions
1. Take out a sheet of paper and draw a vertical line down the middle.

2. Now draw two horizontal lines across the paper so that the sheet is divided horizontally into thirds. Your page should now be divided into six equal boxes, as in the illustration below.

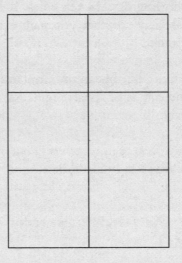

3. Flip through your notebook until you find your response to the Imago Workup (Exercise 3) and the Partner Profile (Exercise 5). In the top left box of the paper you have just divided into six boxes, list the predominant negative traits of your caretakers and your partner. Label these traits "My Disowned Self." Think about the extent to which these negative traits may be true of you. Has anyone, especially your partner, told you that you possess these traits? For the moment assume that these traits are descriptive of you. What would you be like or how would you behave if you *didn't* have these traits? Write a description of the person you would be without these negative traits in the upper right box of your paper. Write them as short, positive statements beginning with the word "I." For example: "I am warm," "I am responsible," "I am nurturing."

4. In the middle box on the left side of your page, list your caretakers' positive traits and your partner's positive traits. It may be that some of these positive traits are a description of your lost self, parts of yourself that you repressed in childhood. Label this box "My Lost Self." Look at this box and ask yourself if you have ever been asked by your partner or other significant people in your life to develop these traits. Assuming that these traits represent repressed aspects of yourself, how would you behave or what would you be like if you had these traits? Write your answers in the middle box on the right side of your page. Once again, use simple, positive statements in the present tense: "I am artistic," "I am spiritual," "I am conscientious," "I am creative."

5. Think about the traits that you had to develop in order to get or keep your parents' love, and think about the kinds of things you do today to try to get people to like you. List those traits in the bottom box on the left side of your page. (Examples: "I try to be perfect," "I am compliant," "I am super-responsible," "I always try to please," "I don't express my anger.") Label this box "My False Self." Now think about the way you would be and behave if you were free of such adaptive characteristics. List these traits and behaviors you would have in the bottom box on the right side of your page. Use simple, positive statements: "I am assertive," "I can express anger," "I can relax and don't have to try to be perfect."

6. On top of the three boxes on the right-hand side of your page, write the words "My True Self." These three right-hand boxes are a description of your true potential. Read this description once a week. As you read it, note areas where the description does not match your current reality. Visualize yourself changing so that the description is a valid one.

EXERCISE 16: VISUALIZATION OF LOVE

Time: One minute three times each day.

Purpose: This exercise amplifies the positive changes you have been making in your relationship through the suggestive powers of visualization.

Comments: This exercise is to become a daily meditation.

Directions

1. Three times each day, do the following: Close your eyes, take several deep breaths, and visualize your partner. Gradually refine the image until you see your partner as a whole, spiritual being who has been wounded in the ways you now know about. Hold this image in your mind and imagine that your love is healing your partner's wounds.

2. Now visualize the energy of love that you are sending to your partner coming back to you and healing *your* wounds. Imagine that this energy flows back and forth between you in a continuous oscillation. When a minute is up, open your eyes and continue whatever you are doing.

Seeking Professional Help

SOME OF YOU MAY WANT to deepen your understanding of marriage and gain additional relationship skills by working with a marital therapist. Fortunately, marriage therapy has lost much of the stigma that it had in earlier years. Years ago only people who were in great pain or who were very courageous signed up for marital therapy. Now more and more couples are deciding to seek help before irrevocable damage is done. They want to enhance the quality of their lives, and they realize that nothing is more important to them than their primary love relationships. They have the healthy attitude that going to a marital therapist is no different from going to any skilled teacher: you learn faster and better if you get expert supervision.

One of the main benefits of seeing a therapist is that you will speed up the integration of material from your unconscious. A therapist can help you maneuver around your blind spots and assimilate material from your unconscious that might take you months or years to assimilate on your own. As a result, you will spend a lot less time spinning your wheels.

Another good reason to enlist the aid of a therapist is to give you an added measure of safety and support. When you are working on new material and begin to experience some anxiety, a therapist will help you understand your fears. Given reassurance and insight, you will probably be able to plunge ahead instead of retreating to safer ground. This will prove especially valuable for couples who are experiencing a great many problems.

A final reason for seeking professional counseling is to provide a structured environment for growth. If you are short on discipline or motivation, having a weekly appointment and paying a therapist a good deal of money can give you added incentive.

If you are interested in working with a marital therapist, I have some general recommendations. My advice is that you look for a therapist whose primary area of expertise is marital therapy, not individual therapy, so that he or she will be well versed in the complexities of love relationships. Furthermore, I recommend that you look for a marital therapist who will work with you jointly, in what is referred to in professional circles as "conjoint" marital therapy. If you see separate therapists or the same therapist at different times, you might inadvertently focus on issues that would help you live more autonomously, not help you live more harmoniously as a couple. Dwelling on matters that are not directly relevant to your relationship may help you as an individual, but there is some evidence that it might not be the best way to strengthen your marriage. When you are seeing a therapist together, you will more clearly see how your personal issues affect the state of your relationship, and both your personal and relationship issues can be resolved together.

How do you go about selecting a marital therapist? A person professing to be a marriage therapist may be a clergyman, a social worker, a psychologist, a psychiatrist, an educator, or, in some states, simply a person with strong views on marriage. A therapist's training may vary from years of postgraduate training to none at all. In some states, all that's required for a license as a marital therapist is a recommendation by someone who already has a license. For this reason, it is wise to choose your therapist on the basis of a referral. Get recommendations from friends or from the minister of a church who has successfully referred a large number of couples. If you are unable to get a referral, look in your phone book under the headings "American

Association of Pastoral Counselors," "American Association for Marriage and Family Therapy," "Association of Clinical Social Workers," "Marriage Counselors," or "Mental Health." If you live in a large city, there may be a special referral service that will match you up with an appropriate therapist.

When you have been given the name of a particular therapist, there are a number of things you should check out. First make sure the therapist is fully accredited by a recognized organization such as the American Association of Marriage and Family Therapists, the American Association of Pastoral Counselors, the American Psychological Association, or the American Psychiatric Association. When you are satisfied that the therapist meets your initial criteria, sign up for a preliminary interview to see if you would feel comfortable working together. (Some therapists will waive the fees for this initial consultation.) Find out the therapist's views on marriage therapy. Most important of all, trust your instincts. You are looking for a therapist who is a caring, warm, sensitive person who gives you a feeling of safety and confidence. Even if you like the therapist, it is wise to interview more than one person, so that you have a basis for comparison.

If you are interested in working with a therapist specifically trained in Imago Relationship Therapy or wish to attend a Getting the Love You Want Couples Workshop, please call 1-800-729-1121 or visit our Web site at www.imagotherapy.com.

Notes

INTRODUCTION

1. A conscious marriage is created by bringing into awareness the unconscious directives and purposes of a romantic or love marriage. A
love marriage is defined as a voluntary union of two individuals
based upon romantic attraction that is stirred by unconscious needs
that have their roots in unresolved childhood issues.

Love marriages have existed throughout history, but they have
not been the dominant cultural form of marriage until the latter part
of the nineteenth century, and then largely in the Western world.
Romantic relationships are recorded in all the world's mythologies
and literature, but they have generally been extramarital and often
adulterous. For a discussion of this phenomenon, see Denis de
Rougemont, *Love in the Western World*, and Morton Hunt, *The
Natural History of Love*.

There are historical indications of the trend toward the fusion of
romance and marriage, creating the love marriage, in the Western
world in the sixteenth century. Following the Renaissance and the
Reformation, which gave birth to the concept of individual rights,
to democratic institutions, and to the changing status of women,
marriage gradually became a source of personal satisfaction and began to shed its function as a stabilizing unit for society. For a detailed historical analysis of this process, see Robert Bellah et al.,
Habits of the Heart, chapters three and four. He presents a brilliant
analysis of the tension between the demands of social roles and social institutions and the emergence of private life, especially in the
arena of love and marriage. He sees this tension, which was rampant
in the nineteenth century, as "endemic" in our culture today.

Prior to the modern period, from the sixteenth century until the present, the dominant form of marriage in the Western world was the arranged marriage, variously based upon economics, politics, or social position, and serving the purpose of maintaining a particular social reality. This form of marriage is still numerically dominant in the non-Western world today. A second form of marriage that has existed throughout history, and still exists in many cultures, is the slave marriage, in which the spouse, usually the woman, is purchased by the man with whatever "coin in trade" is used in that culture—money, pigs, water buffalo, etc. The purchased spouse usually bears and rears the children, does much of the domestic work, owns no property, has no rights, and can be sold if desired or necessary. (I have recently visited the Dani tribe in Irian Jaya, where a wife could be bought for five pigs, and also the Batak people of Sumatra, where the price of a wife was five water buffalo. At the current exchange rate, that was about five thousand dollars.)

Love relationships can and do exist in all cultures, but marriage based on love and mutual selection requires freedom of choice and gender equality. However, freedom is a relative state, and most marriages in the Western world are still arranged and spouses are still selected because of their value. The arena, however, has shifted from the social and objective world to the private and subjective world. Partner selection in a democratic society is arranged by the unconscious, and the value of the partners is determined by unconscious judgment of their ability to provide psychic satisfaction of specific emotional needs. The romantic or love marriage is influenced, perhaps even determined, by the parents, albeit out of the awareness of the actual parents or the marital partners. But in this case the selection is not to do the bidding of the parents but to make up for their deficiencies as caretakers. The romantic marriage is, therefore, an unconscious marriage, with purposes that suit the unconscious. It is the thesis of this book that this subterranean drama must be brought into consciousness, thus creating the conscious marriage, if the psychic purposes are to be realized. Since we view these purposes as positive and constructive, bringing them into consciousness and intentionally cooperating with them results in a type of healing and wholeness that satisfies deep and universal longings.

For the first time in history, marriage can be an arena for personal growth that matches or exceeds the offerings of other forms of personal salvation, such as psychotherapy, religious disciplines, and social revolutions. See Jung, "Marriage as a Psychological Relationship," in *The Portable Jung*, pp. 163ff.

CHAPTER 1: THE MYSTERY OF ATTRACTION

1. This theory, that people tend to select mates who are more or less their equals, also attempts to explain the stability of some couples. In a study of 537 dating men and women reported in the July 22, 1986, edition of *The New York Times* by writer Daniel Goleman, the researchers found that people who perceived their partners to be superior to them felt guilty and insecure. People who perceived their partners to be inferior to them reported feelings of anger. When partners perceived themselves to be equals, their relationships were relatively conflict-free and stable.

2. C. G. Jung, *Two Essays in Analytical Psychology*, pp. 155–56. See also *The Archetypes and the Collective Unconscious*, vol. 9, pp. 122–23.

3. Paul D. McLean, "Man and His Animal Brains." This is one of several ways of looking at the brain distinguished by an evolutionary perspective. I use the terms "old brain" and "new brain" because of their simplicity and illustrative power, as compared with the more familiar terms, the "unconscious" and the "conscious."

4. The question of freedom and determinism divides various disciplines into opposing camps. In philosophy and religion, the question has been debated for centuries with no resolution. Psychological schools are distinguished by their adherence to a mechanistic versus an organismic view of human beings. This question is crucial for marriages, because if we are destined to certain marital fates, then what is the value of therapies that offer hope and change? To my way of thinking, both sides of most polarities are valid. The old-brain/new-brain metaphor offers a resolution to the dialogue—we are both determined and free. The old brain, with its built-in survival programs, determines our basic reactions, and the new brain can become aware of reactions that are not effective and devise new

options. The survival directives of the old brain cannot be overridden, but the new brain can re-educate the old brain with regard to what is dangerous and what is not. We are free within limits, but our limits are not absolute.

5. These primary evolutionary defenses are believed to have evolved in the reverse order of the way I have listed them. Fear, considered the primary affect, is followed much later in evolutionary history by the nurturing response. It is believed that self-preservation as the basic instinct preceded the nurturing response by millions of years.

CHAPTER 2: CHILDHOOD WOUNDS

1. Martin Buber, *I and Thou*, p. 76. The notion that human life includes an awareness of oneness with the universe is endemic in most religions in most cultures and is often referred to by the term "mystical." This experience was reduced by Freud to an "oceanic feeling" reminiscent of prenatal union with the mother, thus polarizing with Buber. Silverman et al., in *The Search for Oneness*, subject Freud's thesis to empirical research and conclude that "unconscious fantasies of oneness can enhance adaptation if a sense of self can be preserved" (pp. 1ff).

I take the position that the search for oneness is multidimensional. It expresses our awareness of our separation from essential aspects of ourselves, a split in the psyche caused by the repressive aspect of socialization, which disturbs our awareness of our union with the universe, which Buber so poetically says "we forgot at birth." The desire for union with the mother, an empirical reality, expresses this deeper desire for union with split-off parts of the self, a search for personal wholeness, which when achieved restores our awareness of our essential union with the universe out of which both the self and the maternal matrix arise. From this I hypothesize that in marriage the impulse to unite with the partner is unconsciously an attempt to reunite with the split-off parts of the self, which are projected onto the partner. Since there is a fusion of the partner and the parent in the unconscious, a positive emotional bond with the partner (achieved by loving in the partner that which is split off from the self and projected) restores a sense of personal wholeness and an awareness of our essential union with the universe. This gives marriage an essentially spiritual potential.

2. The brief summary of the developmental stages of childhood is based upon the work of Margaret Mahler, *On Human Symbiosis and the Vicissitudes of Individuation.* I take full responsibility for the liberties I have taken with identifying developmental issues that reappear in marriage, since this was not her intention. Developmental theories are distinguished by the interests of the theoretician. Current theories include childhood viewed from the perspective of sexual, social, cognitive, moral, and faith development. All these dimensions are involved in the developmental processes of every child, and their fate is reflected in every marriage. The elaboration of this thesis would be book-length itself, and that is not my present intention. I wish only to identify the issues of childhood that appear in marriage as a basis of understanding and grounding the thesis that marriage, at the unconscious level, is an attempt to resolve those issues, and, indeed, must resolve them if the marriage is to be a growth experience.

3. The English language has only one word for the phenomenon of love, and that word is used in so many contexts to describe so many emotions that it has no distinct meaning. We use it to say "I love New York," "I love the movies," "I love sex," "I love you," and everything else about which we may have positive feelings. Consequently, its meaning is determined largely by its context.

Until recently, psychology made little reference to love, and it is noticeably absent in most studies of marriage. Perhaps that is because the association of love and marriage is, as discussed earlier, a recent historical phenomenon. Theories of marriage and marital therapy have focused on contract making, conflict resolution, systems analysis, and restructuring rather than love. Freud and Jung used the Latin word "libido," but in different ways. Freud spoke of a libidinal love and a narcissistic love; the first is a generalized sexual energy directed to others, notably the infant to the mother as a first love object, and later redirected to others. The second, narcissistic love, was a consequence of psychic injury that resulted in focusing libido on the self. He called this "primary narcissism." The resolution of this self-invested love led to the redirection of libido to another, or secondary narcissism. (See Sigmund Freud, "On Narcissism: An Introduction.") Jung used "libido" to refer to a generalized life energy. (For a discussion of love by psychoanalytically oriented psychologists and psychiatrists, see Rollo May, *Love and Will*; Erich Fromm, *The Art of Loving*; Reubin Fine, *The Meaning of Love in Human Experience*; Willard Gaylin, *Rediscovering Love*; and Nathaniel Brandon, *The Psychology of Romantic Love*.)

To avoid the vagueness of the word "love," I have elected to use three Greek words: "eros," "agape," and "philia." These words have precise meanings and refer to various phases of one phenomenon. They also make possible a description of a developmental view of love as a possibility in marriage. "Eros" is the root word of the word "erotic," which in our culture has a sexual, even pornographic connotation, but in Greek means "passionate love of the world." (See Bauer, *A Greek-English Lesson*, p. 311.)

The broader meaning of "eros" is "life force," which is directed outward in passionate appreciation of the world. This includes but is not limited to sexuality. It also denotes the sense in which the self and its demands and needs are emphasized. In my view, when eros is frustrated or blunted by deficient nurturing or excessive socialization, it turns back upon itself in self-absorption and becomes preoccupied with organismic survival. This condition remains until the experience of romantic love, when eros is redirected to another, the romantic partner, in an attempt to restore the original condition of wholeness. The failure to achieve the original situation results in the power struggle, which is ultimately a defense against death. In this I take issue with Freud, who posits a "death instinct," or "thanatos," as a polarity to eros. (Freud, "The Instincts and Their Vicissitudes.") I see eros as a singular life energy expressing itself in the face of the fear of death, not the "pull" of death. See Chapter 10, note 1, for a further discussion of eros.

4. Plato, *The Symposium*, pp. 143ff.

CHAPTER 3: YOUR IMAGO

1. The reconstruction of the past by selecting a partner who resembles one's parents was originally given the name "repetition compul-

sion" by Freud. This idea was expanded by Fritz Perls, founder of Gestalt Therapy, and given the name "unfinished business." For Perls, this consists of feelings and memories that are unconscious and avoided but are expressed in behavior. Some view this repetition as an attempt to restore the familiar, thus as a static and nonpurposive process. I side with Freud's view of the purposive character of repetition as an attempt at resolution.

2. In Webster's dictionary, "imago" means the "representation of a person or a thing," "a copy," "likeness," "a mental picture." The term was used in psychology by Freud. In fact, it was the title of a now defunct journal edited by him. Jung also uses the term in his *Collected Works*, vol. 9, pp. 6off., to mean the "inner representation of the opposite sex." In this book I depend in principle upon Jung rather than the "object-relations" school, who would define it as the "significant other." In either case, the image is formed out of the internalization of all childhood caretakers, and its projection generates the feelings of romantic love.

   In Jungian psychology, the anima image is projected by the man and the animus image is projected by the woman. In this book, the imago is a fusion of the traits of all significant caretakers and may have dominant same-sex or opposite-sex qualities and can be projected by either sex. In other words, from clinical experience it is obvious that a man may choose a woman who is like his father and a woman may choose a man who is like her mother. In all cases the imago selection is a combination of same- and opposite-sex traits.

3. See Wilder Penfield, *The Mystery of Mind*, p. 20.

CHAPTER 4: ROMANTIC LOVE

1. The experience of romantic love, an intensely passionate and often sexual relationship between a man and a woman, is among the oldest recorded experiences of mankind. It inflames the relationship between the ancient gods and goddesses (Zeus and Hera), sometimes between gods and humans (Cupid and Psyche), often between famous persons (Dante and Beatrice, Isaac and Rebekah, Franklin D. Roosevelt and Lucy Mercer), and surely among many ordinary mortals, although history shows little interest in lesser persons. Some

of these relationships inspired by the fires of eros have changed the course of history (Antony and Cleopatra, Paris and Helen of Troy); others have inspired great literature (Dante and Beatrice, Tristan and Isolde); all constitute the most endearing and enduring stories of humankind, most of which end in tragedy and death (Romeo and Juliet, Samson and Delilah, Lancelot and Guinevere). (See *Love Through the Ages*, by Robert Lynd.) Explanations of the source of this energy have ranged from the "infusion of the gods" or a "demon" to the result of a disease. People fell in love because they were struck by Cupid's arrow, were tricked into drinking a magic potion, or happened to be born under favorable stars. In every case, something external, even extraterrestrial was involved. Today, with the decline in the belief in the supernatural, explanations tend to be more psychological and subjective, with the energy believed to be arising from within the persons.

The forms of romantic love seem to have undergone three changes in history, each reflecting changes in the male/female relationship, and its fate has been determined by social structure and cultural practices. Prior to the eleventh century, the dominant form of romantic love was called "heroic love." The major theme in heroic love is the pursuit and capture of the woman by the man. The societies in which this form of love existed were feudal aristocracies in which romantic love was sought and mainly existed either in passionate extramarital love or in romanticized nonsexual relationships. Contributing factors to this situation were the existence of slavery, the bias of free-born men against labor, the association of slavery with the functions of the home, and the consequent difficulty of associating love with home. Thus the fulfillment of love was sought outside the home and outside marriage.

A radical reversal in male-female relationships occurred in the eleventh century with the appearance of the troubadours and their love ballads in southern France. In a short time, heroic love was replaced with what is known as "courtly love," in which the theme of pursuit and capture gave way to the image of male supplication and entreaty of the female. Images of force and rape were replaced with the refinements of courtship. This led to the formation of "courts of love," where the merits of love were debated and where judgments were usually rendered that true love was attainable only outside of marriage and often only if there was no sexual communion. The form of modern love relationships was influenced and developed against this background.

Romantic love as the door to marriage had to await the evolving freedom and rights of individuals to choose their fate and to determine their own forms of government. That and the emerging freedom and equality of women were the forces that led to modern marriage, with its attendant psychological baggage. (See Morton Hunt, *The Natural History of Love*, and Isidor Schneider, ed., *The World of Love*, vol. I.)

2. Quoted in Jane Lahr and Lena Tabori, *Love*, p. 189.

3. Michael R. Liebowitz, M.D., *The Chemistry of Love*, pp. 37ff.

4. In contrast to classical views of romantic love, which attribute its source to external forces, modern psychologies of love locate its origin to the human mind. In this book, love is viewed as a single energy that is directed to outside persons or to the self, depending upon need and motivation. Although it is a singular phenomenon, its distinctive forms are represented as stages. However, since the experience of romantic love seems to us to be stimulated by an outside source, namely the loved one, the ancients' belief in the external origins of love can be understood as the objectification of our inner sensations. Now, however, we understand that the external person has no power to activate such passions, but instead is endowed by the unconscious with attributes that appear to give him or her that power. The passions are self-activated by the association of an internal need-gratifying image with the character makeup of the loved other.

5. Lucius Apuleius, *The Golden Ass*, in Robert Lynd, *Love Through the Ages*, pp. 1165ff.

CHAPTER 5: THE POWER STRUGGLE

1. My first encounter with a full discussion of the unconscious expectations couples bring to marriage was in *Marriage Contracts* by Clifford Sager. Sager has worked out a very detailed analysis of conscious, preconscious, and unconscious contracts.

2. Early-childhood experience also seems to be the source of other beliefs that characterize the power struggle. The intuitive response of parents to childhood stress, especially in the preverbal stage, leads to the belief in the omniscience of spouses: they know what we need without having to ask. We resent our needs not being responded to automatically. Having to ask breaks the illusion that our partners know what we need. Another belief is that they have what we need and can satisfy us if they would. This is called the "illusion of partner omnipotence." Finally, we believe they should always be available to meet our needs and have no needs of their own. This is the belief in partner omnipresence. Their failure to meet our needs creates emotional pain and leads eventually to the belief in the partner as evil and therefore the enemy.

3. Robert L. Barker, *Treating Couples in Crisis*, p. 20.

4. The stages of grief in a dying person were worked out by Elisabeth Kübler-Ross and described in her book *On Death and Dying*.

5. The bargaining stage in the power struggle, an expression of the quid pro quo that most couples naturally evolve in their attempt to negotiate their needs, is the stage most couples present to the therapist when they enter therapy. In my opinion, this is the source of earlier methods in marital counseling that attempted to help couples develop contracts and negotiate their conflicts. Therapists responded to what couples were trying to do and sought to help them do it better. They did not recognize it as a stage in the power struggle and unwittingly helped couples stay in it, rather than help them move to the next stage, despair, and to the surrender of their illusions. The surrender of illusions is a precondition for the conscious marriage and precedes the final step of acceptance.

6. This estimate is attributed to Virginia Satir, a well-known family therapist.

CHAPTER 6: BECOMING CONSCIOUS

1. The idea of "becoming conscious" refers to processes common to psychology and the spiritual traditions. Long before Freud's development of his theory of the unconscious, which states that our lives are directed largely by forces not in our consciousness nor under its

control, the ancient mystical traditions of the East and the West perceived our ordinary, everyday consciousness as an illusion, a state of "waking sleep." While there are important technical distinctions between the "unconscious" and "waking sleep," both views are in agreement in perceiving that things are not the way they appear and that a fundamental change in mental life is necessary if we are to know the "truth." These changes consist of "insight" and "awakening," respectively.

Insight brings unconscious contents into consciousness, and awakening gives us direct experience of "reality" that has been hidden behind our symbolic constructions. I use the phrase "becoming conscious" to combine these two processes as they apply to marriage.

2. The Bible, Exodus 12:37ff.

CHAPTER 7: CLOSING YOUR EXITS

1. The no-exit decision is an adaptation of the "escape-hatch" concept developed by Frank Ernst, a transactional analyst, who conceived the idea of the OK Corral (see bibliography). The purpose of the exercise is to engage the rational mind, the new brain, which can make cognitive decisions not to act on impulses and emotions that would be destructive to therapy, to the self, or to a relationship. My experience that couples will make this decision and still not improve led to the discovery that they use many noncatastrophic exits to avoid positive involvement with each other.

2. I first learned about the concept of graduated change from Kurt Lewin, an analytically oriented social psychologist who pioneered in the area of the social psychology of group process and group change. Graduated change is also commonly used in behavioral psychology and social-learning theory.

CHAPTER 8: CREATING A ZONE OF SAFETY

1. Richard Stuart, *Helping Couples Change*, p. 17.

2. I am greatly indebted to Stuart and to behaviorism in general for the idea of a structured therapeutic change process. I was also influenced

by Transactional Analysis (which talks about giving people permission to want) and by John Whitaker, a Dallas psychiatrist and transactional analyst, who developed the idea of the "want" list.

One key difference between the Reromanticizing exercise and Stuart's Caring Days exercise is that I ask couples to generate their list of caring behaviors by writing down three different kinds of pleasurable transactions: ones they experienced during the romantic stage of their relationship, ones they are currently experiencing in their relationship, and ones that they would like to experience but have never asked for, because of fear of being criticized or rejected. All three kinds of pleasurable transactions tap into unmet childhood needs. The enactment of these behaviors touches childhood issues in the unconscious and creates an environment in which the deeper conflicted issues can later be addressed.

CHAPTER 10: DEFINING YOUR CURRICULUM

1. Agape is the second word in the Greek language for "love." It is used to express human love, the love of humans for God, and the love of God for humans. It also refers to a love feast that expresses brotherly love. In every case it seems to mean a love for another without regard for conditions—unconditional love. It is not dependent upon the worth or value of the other, and when it is expressed it carries no obligation. It is an unconditional gift. (See Bauer, *A Greek-English Lexicon*, p. 6.)

In Greek philosophy, agape is one of the forms of love on a continuum with eros and philia. Therefore, it is not another kind of love, but a special way in which love is expressed. In this book, I view agape as the act of directing eros, the life energy, away from oneself and toward the welfare of the other. In that sense it is sacrificial, but what is sacrificed is not the self but preoccupation with the self. Although it is used as a noun, and thus denotes an attitude, it is also used as a verb, and thus denotes the way one acts toward another. The merger of these two senses means that agape can be understood as an attitude that is expressed in behaviors. On this basis, I call it the "power of transformation" that directs eros to the other, thus creating a new quality in relationships, called "philia."

CHAPTER 12: PORTRAIT OF TWO MARRIAGES

1. The focus of this book has been on the power of love for psychological and spiritual healing. Evidence is now being accumulated by research psychologists and physicians on the positive effects of altruistic love on the immune system (McClelland) and on the healing process in general (Siegel). This means that love influences body functions as well as psychological processes such as depression (Weissman). Evidence that marital stress results in psychosomatic symptoms by depressing the immune system (Kiecolt-Glaser) and influences psychological stress such as adolescent suicide, high blood pressure, depression (Folkenberg), and possibly cancer (Levenson) is correlated with evidence that an altruistic lifestyle, a life of loving energy directed to others, improves physical and emotional health (McClelland). The implications emerging from this research indicate the significance of a positive marriage, or the idea of marriage as a passionate friendship, for a general sense of well-being and health. Safety is posited as the invariant and essential component behind mental, physical, emotional, and spiritual health.

2. "Philia" is the root of the English word "filial." Its basic meaning has to do with brotherly love. But in Greek "brotherly" is not limited to and does not necessarily refer to kinship. It also refers to an attitude and a quality of relating in which the feelings of care that are experienced between people who are connected by blood are experienced between people who are not blood-related. Such bonding is a desirable human condition, because it would remove the reality of the other as strange and therewith all attendant threats from the outside or the other. Philia is thus the basis of friendship and refers to love among equals. (See Bauer, p. 866.)

   To distinguish friend from foe is essential for personal and group survival. This polarity is the basis of personal and group conflict, violence, and war. True peace—that is, peace without fear—exists only among friends. Peace with fear can exist between foes, but it is always unstable. Again, this appears to be an old-brain function—to respond to this perceived distinction in the service of organismic survival. The admonition by Jesus in the New Testament to "love your enemies" collides with this old-brain directive, but it is the highest concept humans have been able to develop to deal with the animal residues of evolution.

It is interesting that, in a research project of "happy" couples, the item ranked first by all couples was "we are each other's best friend" (Lauer and Lauer, "Marriages Made to Last"). This form of love between friends is a love among equals that is created through agape, a new quality of relating.

CHAPTER 13: TEN STEPS TOWARD A CONSCIOUS MARRIAGE

1. Craft, Harriet, "A Descriptive Study of the Love or Illusion Workshop," 1984, unpublished manuscript, East Texas University.

Bibliography

Apuleius, Lucius. *The Golden Ass,* in *Love Through the Ages* by Robert Lynd, Coward-McCann, Inc., New York, 1932.

Barker, Robert L. *Treating Couples in Crisis,* The Free Press, New York, 1984.

Bauer, W. A. *Greek-English Lexicon of the New Testament and Other Early Christian Literature,* trans. W. F. Arndt and F. W. Gingrich, The University of Chicago Press, Chicago, Illinois, 1957.

Bellah, Robert, Richard Madson, William M. Sullivan, Ann Swidler, and Steven M. Tipton. *Habits of the Heart,* The Perennial Library, New York, 1985.

Brandon, Nathaniel. *The Psychology of Romantic Love,* J. P. Tarcher, Inc., Los Angeles, California, 1980.

Buber, Martin. *I and Thou,* Charles Scribner's Sons, New York, 1958.

Craft, Harriet. "A Descriptive Study of the Love or Illusion Workshop," 1984, unpublished manuscript.

Ernst, Frank. "The OK Corral: The Grid for Get-on-With," *Transactional Analysis Journal* 1:4 (October 1971).

Folkenberg, Judy. "Multi-Site Study of Therapies for Depression," *Archives of General Psychiatry* 42 (March 1985).

Freud, Sigmund. "On Narcissism: An Introduction (1914)," in *General Psychological Theory: Papers on Metapsychology,* Collier Books, New York, 1963.

————. "The Instincts and Their Vicissitudes (1915)" in *Collected Papers,* vol. 4, Basic Books, New York, 1959.

Fromm, Erich. *The Art of Loving,* Bantam Books, New York, 1956.

Gaylin, Willard. *Rediscovering Love,* Viking Penguin, Inc., New York, 1986.

Hunt, Morton. *The Natural History of Love*, Alfred A. Knopf, New York, 1959.

Jung, C. G. *The Archetypes and the Collective Unconscious*, trans. R. F. C. Hull, Bollingen Series XX, Princeton University Press, Princeton, New Jersey, 1969.

———. "Marriage as a Psychological Relationship," in *The Portable Jung*, ed. Joseph Campbell, The Viking Press, New York, 1971.

———. *Two Essays in Analytical Psychology*, in *Collected Works*, vol. 7. Translated by R. F. C. Hull, Bollingen Series XX, Princeton University Press, Princeton, New Jersey, 1969.

Kiecolt-Glaser, Janice K. "Marital Quality, Marital Disruption, and Immune Function," *Psychosomatic Medicine*, in press.

Kübler-Ross, Elisabeth. *On Death and Dying*, The Macmillan Company, New York, 1969.

Lahr, Jane, and Lena Tabori. *Love: A Celebration in Art and Literature*, Stewart, Tabori and Change, Publishers, New York, 1982.

Lauer, Jeanette, and Robert Lauer. "Marriages Made to Last," in *Psychology Today* 19:6 (June 1985).

Levenson, Frederick F. *The Anti-Cancer Marriage: Living Longer Through Loving*, Stein and Day, Publishers, New York.

Liebowitz, Michael, M.D. *The Chemistry of Love*, Little, Brown and Company, Boston, 1983.

Lynd, Robert. *Love Through the Ages: Love Stories of All Nations*, Coward-McCann, Inc., New York, 1932.

Mahler, Margaret. *On Human Symbiosis and the Vicissitudes of Individuation: Infantile Psychosis*, International Universities Press, New York, 1968.

May, Rollo. *Love and Will*, W. W. Norton and Company, Inc., New York, 1969.

McClelland, David C. "Some Reflections on the Two Psychologies of Love," *Journal of Personality* 54:2 (June 1986).

McLean, Paul. "Man and His Animal Brains," *Modern Medicine*, February 3, 1964.

Penfield, Wilder. *The Mystery of Mind: A Critical Study of Consciousness and the Human Brain*, Princeton University Press, Princeton, New Jersey, 1975.

Perls, Frederick S., with Abraham Levitsky. "The Rules and Games of

Gestalt Therapy," in *Gestalt Therapy Now*, ed. Joan Fagen and Irma Lee Shepherd, Science and Behavior Books, Palo Alto, California, 1970.

Plato. *The Symposium*, in *The Portable Plato*, ed. Scott Buchanan, The Viking Press, New York, 1948.

de Rougemont, Denis. *Love in the Western World*, trans. Montgomery Belgion, Doubleday Anchor Books, Doubleday and Company, Garden City, New York, 1957.

Sager, Clifford J. *Marriage Contracts and Couples Therapy: Hidden Forces in Intimate Relationships*, Brunner/Mazel, Publishers, New York, 1976.

Schneider, Isidor, ed. *The World of Love*, vols. I and II, George Braziller, New York, 1948.

Siegel, Bernard. *Love, Medicine and Miracles: Lessons Learned About Self-Healing from a Surgeon's Experience with Exceptional Patients*, Harper and Row, Publishers, New York, 1986.

Silverman, Lloyd H., Frank M. Lachmann, and Robert L. Milich. *The Search for Oneness*, International Universities Press, New York, 1982.

Stuart, Richard. *Helping Couples Change: A Social Learning Approach to Marital Therapy*, The Guilford Press, New York, 1980.

Weissman, Myrna M. "Advances in Psychiatric Epidemiology: Rates and Risks of Major Depression," *American Journal of Health*, in press.

About Imago Relationship Therapy

Imago Relationship Therapy, originating in the partnership of Harville Hendrix, Ph.D., and Helen LaKelly Hunt, M.A., M.L.A., integrates and expands the seminal interpersonal insights of major Western psychological systems, behavioral sciences, and spiritual disciplines into a uniquely comprehensive theory of primary love relationships. Developed from the exclusive study of couples, and the integration of the relational implications of various psychological and spiritual systems and personal experience, it presents an approach that builds on previous efforts to understand intimate partnerships and extends those efforts to create a relational theory and therapy that mirrors the view that the basic characteristic of the universe is inter-relational and interdependent.

Imago Relationship Therapy (IRT) is an expression of the new paradigm of relationality that includes and transcends the traditional paradigm of the individual. In the relationship paradigm, all things in the universe, from particles to galaxies, constitute an unbroken wholeness. This means that couples are essentially connected, although they may experience themselves as separate, especially when in conflict. IRT utilizes a variety of clinical procedures to help all couples—and singles desiring an intimate union—understand that the unconscious forces that influence partner selection, and the inevitable power struggle that follows, is an unconscious attempt to restore connections that were ruptured in childhood. The goal of therapy is to help couples achieve a "conscious marriage." This includes assisting them in identifying and interpreting their defenses against intimacy, which precipitates the power struggle, as a paradoxical yearning for connection, and helping couples restore connections within themselves, between themselves, and with the universe. The process of the therapy includes: identifying frustrations rooted in primitive and illusory ideation of one's love partner; recognizing the failure of archaic behavior to gratify needs and achieve self-completion; and perceiving one's partner realistically without the encumbrance of one's own unconscious projections. Other aspects of the Imago process involve learning new skills and changing hurtful behavior, in the course of which partners consciously aim to meet one another's needs and thereby restore the lost, disowned, and denied parts of themselves. A core skill is a three-part dialogue process that helps couples make contact by breaking out of defensive and symbiotic relating and by promoting differentiation from each other, compassion and empathy for each other, and connection and communion with each other. Therapy is ultimately made obsolete as each partner becomes a skilled advocate and "container" for the other's growth process. The Imago process, when consistently applied in any relationship, has the potential to be a transformational journey toward mutual healing, emotional maturation, and spiritual evolution.

Imago Products and Services

Imago resources include national and international workshops for couples and singles, as well as training programs for qualified therapists in the theory and practice of Imago Relationship Therapy. Over thirteen hundred Certified Imago Therapists, over one hundred Workshop Presenters and an Institute Faculty of twenty Clinical Instructors offer therapy, workshops, products, training, and conduct ongoing research of significant relationships for the purpose of enhancing the systematic theory of Imago Relationship Therapy. For more information please visit our website at www.imagotherapy.com.

POCKET
BOOKS

KEEPING THE LOVE YOU FIND

A Single Person's Guide to Achieving Lasting Love

Harville Hendrix

Your dream of finding a partner is a natural and normal human instinct and your dream is perfectly achievable. Whatever your history, whatever your heartbreak, as a single person you are in an ideal position to learn what you need to know and what you can do to greatly improve your chances for finding, and keeping, love.

Filled with wisdom and compassion, *Keeping the Love You Find* will help get your next relationship off to the best start and keep your love strong for a lifetime.

ISBN 0 7434 9593 4

PRICE £7.99

SIMON &
SCHUSTER

RECEIVING LOVE

Letting Yourself Be Loved Will
Transform Your Relationship

Harville Hendrix and
Helen LaKelly Hunt

It's easy to give love, but how do we receive love,
absorb it and let it change us? Rather than learning *how*
to love, perhaps the gretest test of an intimate relationship is learning to receive love. Such is the argument of
the bestselling author/relationship therapist team,
Harville Hendrix and Helen LaKelly Hunt in their
groundbreaking new book.

In *Receiving Love*, the focus is on how this phenomenon
operates in intimate relationships, shaping conflicts and
disappointments, and on the steps needed to dissolve
the barriers to enable us to open our hearts to love.

ISBN 0 7432 6364 2

PRICE £10.99